◆ BECOMING ASIAN AMERIC

Becoming Asian American

SECOND-GENERATION CHINESE AND
KOREAN AMERICAN IDENTITIES

Nazli Kibria

The Johns Hopkins University Press

BALTIMORE AND LONDON

The Johns Hopkins University Press
2715 North Charles Street
Baltimore, Maryland 21218-4363
www.press.jhu.edu

Library of Congress Cataloging-in-Publication Data

Kibria, Nazli.
Becoming Asian American : second-generation Chinese and Korean
American identities / Nazli Kibria.
     p.   cm.
Includes bibliographical references and index.
ISBN 0-8018-6879-3 (hardcover : alk. paper)
1. Chinese Americans—Ethnic identity.   2. Korean Americans—Ethnic
identity.   3. Chinese Americans—Social conditions.   4. Korean
Americans—Social conditions.   5. Chinese Americans—Cultural
assimilation.   6. Korean Americans—Cultural assimilation.
7. Children of immigrants—United States—Social conditions.   I. Title.
E184.C5 K45   2002
305.8951073—dc21   2001002795

A catalog record for this book is available from the British Library.

■ *For Allen*

CONTENTS

AS THE TWENTY-FIRST CENTURY OPENS, the United States appears to be on the brink of a momentous transformation. According to the estimates of demographers, nonwhite racial minorities already constitute an increasingly significant proportion of the U.S. population, and their numbers will continue to grow. Furthermore, the composition of this minority population is itself changing, with rising numbers of Latinos and Asians. Exactly what these changes will mean for the racial system of the United States is clearly a central question of our time.

In this book I offer a glimpse into the emerging American racial landscape. I do so through an analysis of the accounts of second-generation Chinese and Korean Americans, as told to me during in-depth interviews, about race and identity in their lives. I look at how second-generation Chinese and Korean Americans negotiate race and come to make sense of who they are within the broader racial and ethnic landscape of the United States. With a focus on these issues, the chapters that follow explore the experiences of second-generation Chinese and Korean Americans in a variety of life contexts and situations, ranging from childhood neighborhoods to encounters with pan-Asian or Asian American organizations in college. As we will see, these experiences are frequently marked by the dilemma of how to make sense of the significance of race for Asian Americans in relation to a popular discourse that has focused mainly on "black" and "white" experiences. A growing sense of identification with a pan-Asian or Asian American community—a topic that I explore in some detail—has been one of the responses to this dilemma.

■

Questions of ethnic identity have long been of deep interest to me. I grew up the daughter of a diplomat, moving every two or three years from one country to another. Even as they encouraged me to learn from the varied cultures to which I was exposed, my parents, fierce Bangladeshi nationalists, were emphatic in their efforts to instill in me a deep sense of Bengali identity. I quickly learned that "home" and "belonging" are complicated and fluid matters that cannot be taken for granted.

During the years while I have been working on this book, I have often found myself confronting what I now take to be an inevitable query: "Why are you, a person of Bangladeshi origin, studying Chinese and Korean Americans?" My response to this question has evolved over time. My initial impulse was to offer an academic rationale: looking at these two groups made sense because of the specific sociological issues of interest to me, and so forth. I have, however, increasingly—and for the most part fruitfully—made use of the question as an opportunity for dialogue on the relative meaning and significance for a researcher of an "insider" versus an "outsider" identity.

Analyses of ethnographic research have brought attention to the fluidity and multiplicity of "insider" and "outsider" identities. As Vo (2000) notes, when the insider-versus-outsider distinction is seen in static and one-dimensional terms, it "reinforces essentialized conceptions of racial and cultural groups" (19). Speaking of her own fieldwork in a pan-Asian organization, she further writes: "As a researcher of Asian ancestry studying the Asian American community, I could be considered an insider, which is beneficial in attaining rapport with individuals. Yet there were noticeable differences—including ethnic, cultural, political, generational, class, education, and gender—that were acute reminders of the differences between Asian individuals who were my informants and myself" (19).

If the disparity in ethnic origins (Bangladeshi vs. Chinese or Korean) between myself and the study-participants is what has most often caught the attention of those who have heard about the project, my own concerns have been a little different. In the course of conducting interviews, I became more and more intrigued with the significance of another dimension of identity: that of *Asian American*. The relationship of persons like myself, of South Asian origin, to the category of *Asian American* is, on the whole, a rather ambiguous one. South Asian Americans are today part of the official rubric of *Asian American,* but because they do not conform to popular American notions of Asian phenotype, they are not routinely labeled, in nonbureaucratic encounters, as *Asian.* As a result, even Asian Americans themselves may not clearly see them as part of the Asian American community.

I found the ambiguities of my identity as an Asian American to be embedded in the ways in which second-generation Chinese and Korean Americans related to me. Some informants, especially those with a history of involvement in pan-Asian organizations, made pointed self-conscious references to the fact that I, like them, was Asian American. More commonly, informants would use my experiences as an informal point of comparison for their own, in varied and shifting ways. They often made comments such as, "You're Asian, you know what that's like." But they also made many references, both oblique and direct, to the idea that I was not Asian, or at least not in the same way that they were. Over time I came to see my fluctuating place on the insider-outsider continuum of "Asianness" not as a liability but rather as a possible source of insight into constructions of Asian American identity.

■

This project began when I was living in Los Angeles and working at the University of Southern California. Jeff Murakami, of the Asian Pacific American Student Services Center at the University of Southern California, helped to get the study off the ground by sharing with me his contacts and knowledge of the local Asian American community. In the Boston area, Linell Yugawa of Tufts University did the same, generously taking the time to talk and help me formulate research strategies. A grant from the Zumberge Faculty Research and Innovation Fund of the University of Southern California provided the initial resources with which to launch the study. Henry Tom of the Johns Hopkins University Press expressed interest and enthusiasm for the project early on in its development and waited patiently for the final product. Many thanks to Meeae Chae, Sarah Macri, Katie McNamara, Janis Prince, and Louise Rollins for transcribing interview tapes and helping me to get the manuscript ready for publication. Thanks to Janet Biehl for her careful copyediting of the manuscript.

For reasons of anonymity, I cannot personally thank here the sixty-four persons whose willingness to spend time talking with me made this book possible. The interviews were long, and I offered no financial compensation for participation. But even so, and on top of often busy schedules, they took the time to be interviewed. For many, it was a gesture that they hoped would contribute to the building of a meaningful body of scholarship on Asian Americans. I hope that I have not betrayed their trust and confidence.

I am grateful for the tremendous support that I have received, while writing this book, from colleagues, friends, and family. For helping me to think through my research questions and strategies in the very early days of the project, I thank a number of my former colleagues at the University of Southern California: Barry Glassner, Pierrette Hondagneu-Sotelo, Eun Mee Kim, Michael Messner, Jon Miller, and Ed Ransford.

For their readings of and feedback on various parts of the manuscript, I thank

Jean Bacon, Nancy Foner, Anita Garey, Steve Gold, Karen Pyke, and Barrie Thorne. Dan Monti not only gave me extensive comments on several chapters but also provided moral support. I particularly remember one hot frustrating summer afternoon when I despaired of ever producing anything worthwhile. Dan assured me that I could and would do so and shared valuable strategies for coping with the ups and downs of the writing process. For stimulating conversations, collegiality and friendship, I thank Brigitte Berger, Greg Brooks, Sue Chow, Yen Espiritu, Marilyn Halter, Karen Hansen, Rosanna Hertz, Kathleen Jordan, Taeku Lee, Monika Mitra, Melinda Pitts, Bandana Purkayastha, Cathy Riessman, Miri Song, Annemette Sorensen, Rajini Srikanth, Mary Waters, Corky White, Diane Wolf, and Alan Wolfe. Many thanks to Glenn Loury, who by generously including me at the Institute on Race and Social Division at Boston University, gave me the physical and psychological space I needed to complete the manuscript.

My family, in more ways than I can express, has made my work possible. My mother and father have given me encouragement and also inspiration, challenging me through their own life works to make a positive difference in the world. My brother, Reza Kibria, has been there for me at every turn, helping me to deal with the life challenges that have come my way. Shubhash, Shovon, and Madhuri have been close to my heart and spirit throughout the writing of this book.

It is hard for me to imagine writing this book without the presence and support of James Allen Littlefield in my life. His urgings to "go work on the book and get it done" have made a huge difference. With the birth of our beautiful son, Shomik Kibria Littlefield, he has constantly worked to make sure that I have enough time to devote to my writing. I thank him for this and for many other things, big and small, that make my work both possible and meaningful.

■ BECOMING ASIAN AMERICAN

CHAPTER ONE

Asian Americans and the Puzzle of New Immigrant Integration

THE MID- TO LATE 1960S marked the beginning of a new phase of immigration to the United States. The social changes of this time, including immigration law reforms and the enactment of civil rights legislation, launched the country into a period of what is often referred to as the "new immigration."[1] Like their predecessors in previous times, the new immigrants of the post-1960s years have been the focus of considerable anxiety and often of anti-immigrant fervor and activity on the part of the dominant society. Undergirding these concerns have been questions about the course of the integration of these newcomers into American society, particularly in comparison with the European immigrant experience. Will the new immigrants follow the tried-and-true trajectory established by their European predecessors? That is, will they and their descendants, gradually over time, become so well-integrated or assimilated as to be largely indistinguishable from the prototypical mainstream American? Will their ethnic affiliation eventually become a vestigial and peripheral matter? Or will their integration be quite different, owing to both their own characteristics and the environment into which they have stepped?

These questions constitute what I am calling the "puzzle" of the new immigration into the United States. This book is an effort to explore one part of the puzzle: that of race. The new immigrants, reflecting their mostly Asian, Caribbean, and Latin American origins, are largely non-European and nonwhite in their racial makeup. This fact alone, many contend, means that their path of

---

1. The idea of the "new immigration" has received criticism, particularly when it is defined as a product of the 1965 immigration law reforms. Immigration from Latin America, it is argued, rose before the 1960s, challenging the 1965-centered view of immigration history. While recognizing these limitations, I see the concept of the new immigration as useful in calling our attention to important shifts, starting from the late 1960s or so, in the social and political context of immigration and immigrant adaptation. The legacy of the civil rights movement—the reforms and other changes that it initiated—are a particularly important aspect of this context.

integration will be quite different from that of the earlier, European waves of immigration. According to this view, race works to shape the possibilities and realities of integration for the new immigrants in fundamental ways. In this book I explore the question of race and integration with reference to the experience of some Asian Americans. My analysis focuses specifically on the dynamics of race, adaptation, and identity among second-generation Chinese and Korean Americans—the U.S.-born or -raised adult children of Chinese and Korean immigrants. Based on 64 in-depth interviews conducted in the Los Angeles and Boston areas during 1993–97, I offer a detailed, in-depth account of their racial experiences and how these experiences shaped the ways in which they have come to define and situate themselves within the American social landscape.

The question of how Asian Americans will, over time, integrate or become part of American society has been approached and assessed in several quite different ways. Some observers consider Asian Americans to be the bearers of the European immigrant tradition of assimilation into the mainstream. This model of integration may be termed the *ethnic American* model, involving an ultimately harmonious reconciliation between *ethnic* and *American*. But others see the Asian American experience through a very different lens: a *racial minority* model. This model emphasizes the significance of race and the identity of Asian Americans as racial minority persons. According to the latter perspective, it is not the European ethnic experience but that of African Americans and other "colonized minorities" that most resembles the ways in which Asian Americans will become part of American society.[2] The spirit of this perspective is captured by Okihiro's (1994) passionate exclamation: "Insofar as Asians occupy the racial margins of 'nonwhite' with blacks, yellow is a shade of black, and black, of yellow" (xii).

My analysis of second-generation Chinese and Korean American lives makes clear the difficulties that lie in using either the ethnic American or racial minority model alone as a way of making sense of Asian American integration. This

---

2. My use of the term *colonized minorities* draws on the work of Blauner (1972) and Ogbu and Gibson (1991), who emphasize the significance of the circumstances of settlement to understanding the development and character of minority communities. Ogbu and Gibson thus draw a distinction between immigrant or voluntary minorities, who more or less chose to migrate, and castelike or involuntary minorities, who were brought to the United States through slavery, conquest, or colonization and incorporated against their will. Examples of castelike or involuntary minorities include American Indians, black Americans, Mexican Americans, and native Hawaiians.

is not to say that these perspectives do not offer useful insights and ideas. But the Asian American case particularly challenges the presumed opposition or dichotomy of the two models. As suggested by the term *racialized ethnics,* used by Tuan in her work on third- and fourth-generation Chinese and Japanese Americans (1998),[3] Asian Americans are both racial minorities *and* ethnic Americans. In short, their experiences merge features of the experiences of European ethnics as well as those of racial minorities. It is, I would argue, precisely this transgressive aspect of the Asian American experience that makes it particularly valuable as a source of clues to the puzzle of new immigrant integration.

Despite this lack of fit with the established paradigms, let me nonetheless begin by arguing that one of them—the ethnic American model—sets the basic stage for Asian American integration. As mentioned earlier, the ethnic American model sketches a mode of integration in which *ethnic* and *American,* as aspects of affiliation and identity, coexist in relative harmony. To be more specific, one's ethnicity does not threaten or impinge on one's ability to be American; indeed, it may actually contribute to or enhance it. The *symbolic ethnicity* that some studies of third- and fourth-generation European ethnics have described is a particularly graphic example of a type of ethnic affiliation that contains these qualities (Alba 1990; Gans 1979; Waters 1990). Symbolic ethnicity is voluntary, centered on ethnic symbols; is highly subjective and intermittent in character; and entails few if any sustained commitments. This way of "being ethnic" provides one with a way to feel distinctive and part of a community without in any way detracting from one's status and legitimacy as a mainstream American.

While symbolic ethnicity highlights some of the general qualities of the American ethnic model in a particularly vivid way, it represents just one form of ethnicity that is possible under that model. For the ethnic American, ethnic affiliation may be much more than a symbolic matter. It may be a central basis for the organization of family and community and perhaps a means of collective organization and assertion in American political life. But across these varied forms, what is important is that ethnic affiliation does not make it especially difficult for individuals to be accepted and to participate in the institutions and

---

3. Tuan (1998) defines *racialized ethnics* as those for whom "racial and ethnic identities cross-cut and compete with each other for dominance, with race almost always overriding ethnicity" (22). I use the term in a somewhat different manner, to refer to those who are engaged in racializing the ethnic American model, in reworking and reinterpreting established ideas about how to "be ethnic" in light of their racial experiences.

groups of the dominant society, in particular its white, middle-class sectors. Relatedly, while important compulsions may be at work in maintaining ethnic affiliation, these compulsions are not imposed by the dominant society. In other words, the pressures that one feels to "be ethnic" come from within oneself and from the ethnic community rather than from the dominant society.

But for Asian Americans, the stage that is set by the ethnic American model does not ultimately remain standing, at least in its original form. My materials suggest that the Asian American experience of the ethnic American model is centrally marked by a confrontation with its largely hidden and unstated racial character. This confrontation reveals that the model presumes an ethnic group's "whiteness"; it is difficult for those who are nonwhite to be ethnic Americans. The challenges posed by racial minority status to the notions and expectations of the model are in many ways a defining feature of the Asian American experience. This was perhaps particularly true for the informants of my study, given that they were second-generation immigrants and of largely middle-class status. In many ways they felt a strong sense of proximity to the ethnic American model and simultaneously a strong sense of frustration and marginality in relation to it. In short, in their negotiations of adaptation and identity, the challenges of race to the ethnic American model were a central point of tension and focus.

What these negotiations ultimately suggest is not so much a complete abandonment of the ethnic American model as its racialized reworking, or transformation, to reflect a racial minority experience. It is with this transformation in mind that I see second-generation Chinese and Korean Americans as *new ethnic Americans,* carving out new paths or ways of being ethnic Americans. The core of this book is about the activity and experience of this carving—its underlying dynamics, character, contradictions, and consequences.

Three interrelated questions weave through and organize my analysis: What are the social conditions and processes that sustain and give meaning to the ethnic American model for second-generation Chinese and Korean Americans, enabling and encouraging them to identify with it? How do the dynamics of race challenge their identification as ethnic Americans? And finally, What strategies do they use to cope with the challenges of race and, more generally, to make sense of their identity as racialized ethnic Americans?

In my analysis of these questions, I pay particular attention to the *ethnicization* of Asian Americans, or the emerging meaning and significance, for second-generation Chinese and Korean Americans, of an Asian American identity. The idea of ethnicization brings our attention to the complex conceptual distinctions between race and ethnicity. The word *race* generally refers to a system of power, one in which the dominant group draws on physical differences to construct and give meaning to racial hierarchies and boundaries. When racial boundaries become ethnicized, however, an ethnic group emerges, one that is marked by "perceived common ancestry, the perception of a shared history of some sort, and shared symbols of peoplehood" (Cornell and Hartmann 1998, 32). Critical, then, to the formation of an ethnic group is the emergence among its members of a self-conscious (rather than imposed) and shared sense of belonging to a distinct group.

■ *Assimilation, Race, and the New Immigration*

While focused on the Asian American experience, this book is informed by what I have described as the puzzle of new immigrant integration and specifically the question of how the dynamics of race will shape adaptation and identity among the immigrants of today. The framework of assimilation is a critical piece of this puzzle. Developed in relation to the experience of late-nineteenth- and early-twentieth-century European immigrants and their descendants, the concept of assimilation has marked both popular and scholarly understandings of the American immigrant experience. While the character and extent of ethnic retention among later-generation European ethnics is a matter of some debate, there is little disagreement about the essential thrust of their experience over time: a successful integration into the dominant society. In other words, over time, the descendants of European immigrants have successfully integrated into the mainstream. They have become a part of what is quintessentially American rather than separate from it (Alba 1990; Lieberson 1980; Waters 1990).

In recent years, studies such as Ignatiev's (1995) *How the Irish Became White* have alerted us to the racial developments involved in European assimilation (also see Perlmann and Waldinger 1997; Roediger 1991). Backed by an ideology of scientific racism, the dominant society initially defined Irish Catholics, Italians, and Eastern Europeans as different from and inferior to the Anglo-Saxon core of the country in an essential, biological sense. The successful integration of these groups involved, then, a waning of that ideology and, concurrently, its redefinition in racial terms. These groups were able to gradually incorporate themselves into a developing notion of "whiteness," an idea that came to fundamentally define the dominant society in twentieth-century America.

What then can we expect when it comes to the largely non-European-origin immigrants of today? Are the racial shifts that are a part of the European American past likely or even possible for them? How will their ability or inability to achieve "whiteness" shape their processes of integration? Some argue that the descendants of the new immigrants may very well, over time, become "white." The assimilation of European Americans did not, after all, occur overnight but took place over the course of several generations; it is, at the very least, too early to dismiss this trajectory as a possibility for the new immigrants as well (Alba and Nee 1997).

In contrast to these assessments, however, most analysts take the view that the European trajectory is not likely to be repeated with today's immigrants and their descendants. The explanation most commonly invoked here is the greater physical distinctiveness of the new immigrants. While immigrants from South, Central, and Eastern Europe were perhaps initially seen as physically different from the dominant group, their white skin gave them the potential eventually to become invisible, to meld into the mainstream. By contrast, it is argued, the immigrants of today have skin color that does not allow for such invisibility, whatever the circumstances: "Their [European immigrants'] skin color reduced a major barrier to entry into the American mainstream. For this reason, the process of assimilation depended largely on individual decisions to leave the immigrant culture behind and embrace American ways. Such an advantage obviously does not exist for the black, Asian and mestizo children of today's immigrants" (Portes and Zhou 1993, 76).

Such explanations, pointing to a group's degree of physical distinction from the dominant group, appeal to our common sense, reflecting and reinforcing as they do popular notions of race in the United States. According to these notions, racial definitions are fixed and discrete matters that are rooted, not in the tenuity of social conditions, but in the presumed stability of biology and given physical characteristics. But in fact, as even a cursory glance at the historical and comparative picture makes clear, racial definitions, along with the perceptions and meanings that surround the physical distinctions on which they are based, are fluid and evolving social constructs. Thus, for example, the "dark," "swarthy" characteristics that in the past the dominant society understood to physically and racially distinguish Italians have today ceased for the most part to be issues of much note and distinction.

The point is that the physical distinctions upon which racial definitions are based are a matter of changing perception; they can be seen and understood in many different ways. Cornell and Hartmann (1998) make this point well, in their discussion of the concept of race: "A race is a group of human beings socially defined on the basis of physical characteristics. Determining which characteristics constitute the race—the selection of markers and therefore the construction of the racial category itself—is a choice human beings make. *Neither markers or categories are predetermined by any biological factors*" (24, emphasis added).

Besides physical differences per se, other conditions also make it difficult to envision the new immigrants' transformation into "whites." Among them is the central oppositional place that persons of African, Asian, and Latin American descent have historically held to the concept of whiteness. They have, in short, signified what "whiteness" is not—embodying the opposite of "white." If the construction and consolidation of the idea of whiteness arose simultaneously with the integration and definition of Irish Catholics, Italians, and Eastern Europeans as "white," then the exclusion of non-European-origin persons— of Mexicans, Africans, and Orientals—from "whiteness" was also critical to its development (Almaguer 1994; Omi and Winant 1986). To put it simply, the very ways in which "whiteness" has been defined—in opposition to non-European-origin peoples—make it difficult to imagine the collective incorporation of the new immigrants into its boundaries. Clearly, such incorporation would require a very radical shift in our understandings of "whiteness"—so radical as to perhaps threaten the dissolution of the concept itself.

But it is not simply an enduring identity of "nonwhiteness" that distinguishes the new immigrants from the older European settlers. Important changes have also taken place in the larger environment—the conditions that surround and give meaning to "nonwhiteness." Scholars of the new immigration often observe that the traditional pattern of assimilation is unlikely to be replicated not just because of race but because of other factors as well. Among these factors is the economic restructuring of American society that has resulted in a declining in the number of manufacturing jobs that in previous immigrant eras were a stepping-stone into the mainstream (Gans 1992; Portes and Zhou 1993). Furthermore, while immigrants have always, to some extent, been ambivalent about the prospect of becoming American, today's social conditions may especially foster this attitude among the new immigrants, improving their ability to challenge and resist integration into the dominant society.

The post–civil rights United States, with its (albeit contested) support for multiculturalism and diversity, has in general been far more supportive of pluralism and the retention of ethnic attachments than in the past. Moreover, today's immigrant communities also experience a heightened transnationalism, involving active and ongoing linkages between their societies of origin and their society of settlement (Glick-Schiller, Basch, and Blanc-Szanton 1992).

The actual extent of transnationalism among the new immigrant communities and whether it is significantly different from what existed in the past are matters of some debate (see Foner 1997). But the developments that have supported transnationalism, such as improvements in communication and travel technology, are clearly part of a setting that in some important ways allows the new immigrants to maintain and cultivate ties with their societies of origin. In these ways, the contemporary situation poses a particular challenge to the imagery of the assimilation framework: of immigrants and their descendants thrust into an engine of amalgamation into the dominant society, in a process over which they ultimately have little control.

So if the new immigrants do not assimilate in the sense of movement into the mainstream, then what can we expect of them? As suggested by the influential work of Portes and Zhou (1993) on segmented assimilation,[4] one possible path is that they will maintain a continued orientation toward their immigrant community. That is, rather than allowing their ethnic ties to wane, the children of today's immigrants will remain part of the community of their immigrant

---

4. Focusing on the children of today's immigrants — the "new second generation" — Portes and Zhou (1993) identify three possible types of adaptation for them. The first path is the traditional course of assimilation into the white middle class, which Portes and Zhou see as unlikely for much of the second generation, because of both their color and the declining opportunities of the postindustrial economy. In fact, because many new immigrants settle in central-city areas, second-generation youth are at risk for absorption into the urban underclass. In the inner-city neighborhoods in which they grow up, they are exposed to the "adversarial outlook" of native minority youth. Developed in response to racism, this outlook actively rejects and rebels against mainstream norms and values, including that of achievement in school. Acculturation into this outlook, along with the social and economic consequences that flow from it, is the second path of assimilation that Portes and Zhou believe the second generation may take.

The third possible path is for the second to avoid this trajectory of downward mobility by continuing to identify and be involved with the immigrant community of their parents. The immigrant community provides an alternative to the adversarial youth culture that surrounds them. Through its networks, it may also provide benefits of other sorts, such as economic opportunities and resources: jobs, loans, and so forth.

ancestors, drawing on the particular opportunities and resources that it offers them. Alternatively, they may experience racial ethnogenesis: that is, they may become part of an established racial minority grouping in the United States, such as black or Latino, developing ties and identification with it.

There is today much uncertainty about which, if any, of the above trajectories will predominate over time for the descendants of the new immigrants, not least for Asian Americans. For a variety of reasons, the question of Asian American integration has been a difficult one, a particularly thorny piece of the puzzle of new immigrant integration.

■ *Asian Americans and New Immigrant Integration*

The first phase of Asian immigration into the United States took place from about the mid-nineteenth to the early twentieth century. This "old Asian immigration," as it is often called, consisted largely of unskilled laborers, actively recruited by American companies to fill jobs in construction and agriculture. Chinese and Japanese dominated the ranks of this early immigration stream, followed by much smaller numbers of Filipinos, Koreans, and Asian Indians. These early Asian immigrants encountered sharp racial hostility and harassment. Perceived by white workers as an economic threat, they were forced out of jobs and neighborhoods and into segregated niches and areas. Their racial status barred them from attaining citizenship through naturalization and thus, with the 1913 Alien Land Law, from obtaining the right to own land in the United States. But perhaps nowhere did anti-Asian hostility express itself with more vengeance than in the realm of immigration law. In an atmosphere charged with concerns about the yellow peril—the specter of "unassimilable" and threatening "yellow hordes" taking over the country—Congress enacted a series of measures designed to end Asian immigration, most notably the 1882 Chinese Exclusion Act.

It was not until the late 1960s, following passage of the 1965 Immigration Act, which lifted discrimination based on national origin, that the flow of Asian immigration resumed significantly. Since then, Asians have been an important component of the new immigration. For example, between 1980 and 1988, Asians composed 40 to 47 percent of all entering immigrants (Min 1995a). Reflecting these high rates of immigration, the Asian-origin population has grown in size and is expected to continue to grow in the coming decades. According to census figures, Asian Pacific Americans had moved from 0.7 percent of the total population in 1970 to 2.9 percent in 1990 (Min 1995a). Current projections are that by 2050 this figure will rise to about 8 percent, with Asian Pacific American numbers reaching more than 40 million (Yip 1996).

This second, contemporary phase of immigration has transformed the Asian-origin presence in the United States not only in terms of size but in other ways as well. Perhaps the most important of these changes is the wider ethnic range of the groups—the increased ethnonational diversity—that fall under the *Asian American* rubric. In contrast to the largely Japanese and Chinese origins of Asian Americans in the first half of the century, today's Asian Americans are highly diverse in their national origins. Asian Indians, Koreans, and Filipinos, for example, are among the fastest-growing segments of the Asian American population.

Also of note is the socioeconomic diversity of today's Asian Americans, marking a general shift away from the overwhelmingly working-class origins of the old Asian immigrants. Many post-1965 Asian immigrants have come from professional, white-collar, and highly educated backgrounds (Min 1995a). But especially in recent years, Asian immigrants have also included a significant component of persons with low levels of education and occupational skills. As a result, the Asian American population today has been described as polarized, consisting of two sharply disparate socioeconomic segments (Mar and Kim 1994; Ong and Hee 1994).

The current diversity of Asian Americans, in terms of class and ethnonational origin, is important to solving the puzzle of race and new immigrant integration. In what follows I elaborate on this diversity, focusing on two particular sets of questions that it raises.

■ *"A Part Yet Apart": Where Do Asian Americans Fit In?*

As I have mentioned, analyses of the new immigration often emphasize patterns of identity and adaptation that are oriented away from assimilation into the dominant white society, defined by their separation from that society rather than their engagement with it. But in some ways these analyses do not do justice to the complexity of emerging relationships with the mainstream for an important segment of the new immigrants. In essence, Asian Americans today challenge modes of integration that involve *either separation from or inclusion in* the dominant group. To borrow a phrase, Asian Americans seem to be "a part yet apart"[5] from the dominant society.

Reflecting this position of both inclusion and exclusion, Asian Americans seem to defy established ways of thinking about racial inequality. Among the standard indexes that are commonly used to measure racial inequality are those of average income, education, and occupation; these measures are used to gauge the extent to which a minority group is disadvantaged, relative to the dominant group, in its access to socioeconomic resources. In general, Asian Americans fare well on these measures.

This pattern, in conjunction with the growth and success of East and Southeast Asian economies in the latter part of the twentieth century, has lent support and credence to the popular image of Asians as a "model minority"—a group that is culturally programmed for economic success. In 1990 median household income for Asian Americans was $38,449 compared with $31,231 for whites. While Asian Americans are employed in a range of occupations, a greater percentage are employed in managerial and professional specialty occupations—31.2 percent compared with 26.4 percent in the total population. Reflecting the middle-class background of many post-1965 immigrants, rates of educational attainment for Asian Americans exceed those of the general population. Thus, for example, 46 percent of Asian and Pacific Islander men had a bachelor's degree or more compared with 31 percent of non-Hispanic white men. The comparable figures for women were 39 percent and 25 percent, respectively (Humes and McKinnon 2000).

Many analysts have been critical of the above measures of Asian American socioeconomic achievement, arguing that they paint a deceptive and incomplete picture (see Cabezas and Kawaguchi 1988; Fong 1998; Hurh and Kim 1989; Nee and Sanders 1985; Ong and Hee 1994). For one thing, as pooled measures they mask the sharp polarities in the socioeconomic circumstances of Asian Americans. Despite a higher median household income, for example, Asian Americans also have a higher poverty rate: 13 percent, as reported by the U.S. Census Bureau in 1999, compared with 8 percent in the non-Hispanic white population. Moreover, as some have pointed out, the high figures for median household income

5. I borrow this phrase from the title of a 1998 book, edited by Shankar and Srikanth, on South Asian Americans. They use this phrase to refer to the relationship of South Asian Americans to the Asian American concept and movement.

are misleading, covering up as they do the fact that Asian Americans tend to have a greater number of workers per family in comparison with other groups.[6] Asian Americans also tend to live in states where wages and the cost of living are higher, a situation that inflates nationwide figures for their income. But most importantly perhaps, Asian Americans appear to be disadvantaged in the labor market in several respects. They receive fewer economic returns (in income and job status) for their education than do white workers. Asian Americans are also held back in promotions by a "glass ceiling," as evidenced by their absence from top executive positions, despite their large numbers in professional occupations.

Taken together, this information suggests a complex mixture of advantage and disadvantage. The picture becomes even cloudier when we try to assess structural assimilation at the primary level—another measure of integration into the dominant society (see Gordon 1964). That is, to what extent are Asian Americans part of the relatively small and intimate groups of the dominant society, in particular family and friendship cliques? Like measures of average income, education, and occupation, those of neighborhood of residence and intermarriage offer a generally optimistic picture. Recent Asian immigrants, especially those from China and Korea, often reside in segregated enclaves with co-ethnics, but many Asian Americans reside in largely white suburban areas (Alba and Logan 1993; Massey and Denton 1987; Min 1995a). Asian Americans also show high rates of intermarriage, especially among the U.S.-born. While intra-Asian marriage (i.e. marriage among Asian Americans) seems to be growing, especially in California,[7] many of these outmarriages are to whites. In an analysis based on 1990 census data, Lee and Fernandez (1998) report a 40.1 percent rate of exogamy or outmarriage among U.S.-born Asian Americans.

In general, what this information shows is that many Asian Americans do participate in the institutions and groups of the dominant society; they are not segregated or removed from these arenas. But, as suggested by the phenomenon of the glass ceiling, they also lack acceptance in the dominant society, *in conjunction with and despite their involvement and participation in it.* In contrast to the generally favorable picture that is frequently drawn by aggregate measures of

6. The 1990 census shows that 20 percent of Asian families have 3 or more workers, compared with 13 percent in the total population (U.S. Department of Commerce 1993).

7. According to Shinagawa and Pang (1996), intra-Asian marriages in California increased for Asian Pacific men from 21 percent in 1980 to 64 percent in 1990. For women they rose from 10.8 to 45.5 percent.

institutional integration into the dominant society, cultural analyses of imagery and meaning—the stereotypes and connotations that surround and mark the experience of Asian Americans—provide a more negative view. Thus Tuan's (1998) study of third- and fourth-generation middle-class Japanese and Chinese Americans brings our attention to the ways in which Asian Americans, regardless of their nativity and socioeconomic achievements, feel themselves to be marginalized—not fully accepted members of the dominant society. A powerful aspect of this marginality is the notion, deeply ingrained in American society, that Asians are "forever foreigners"—unassimilable aliens who are fundamentally and unalterably outside of if not diametrically opposite to what is American (Hsu 1996; Lowe 1996).

The accusation of "foreignness" has historically been an important weapon in the expression of hostility toward Asian Americans. For example, an environment charged with concerns about the primordially alien and "unassimilable" nature of Asians contributed to the passage of the 1882 Chinese Exclusion Act, which banned Chinese immigration into the United States. But as highlighted by a series of events in the 1990s, ranging from the so-called Asian campaign finance scandal of the late 1990s to the media depiction of Michelle Kwan, a U.S. ice-skating champion, as "foreign," Asian Americans continue, in contemporary times, to face challenges to the legitimacy of their membership and belonging in the dominant society.

In sum, among the particular conditions that Asian Americans bring to the puzzle of race and new immigrant integration is a position of being "a part yet apart" from the dominant society. As I have described it, a complex confluence of inclusion and exclusion characterizes their relationships with the dominant society. A central question that emerges, then, is, What patterns of adaptation and identity flow from this confluence, this position of being "a part yet apart"?

■ *What Does "Asian American" Mean to Asian Americans?*

Collective identity shifts, which are often referred to as *ethnogenesis,* have long been recognized as a critical feature of the immigrant experience in the United States. As part of a larger process of integration into the host society, immigrants and their descendants gradually merge into established and more inclusive groups, based upon newly realized affiliations such as those of nationality and religion (Glazer and Moynihan 1963; Greeley 1974; Herberg 1960). Thus, for example, immigrants who previously understood themselves in local, regional terms (members of their home village or province) begin to see themselves in broader, national terms, such as *Italian* or *Chinese*.

In recent years, *racial ethnogenesis* has been suggested as a possible mode of integration for the new immigrants. The basic idea here is that immigrants and their descendants will merge into established racial groupings in the United States. They will be driven to do so by the forces of racial labeling and exclusion, as well as by their own declining involvement over time with the ethnic affiliations of their immigrant past. As they merge, imposed racial identities will take on new meaning and significance for members of the groupings themselves, becoming more than labels imposed from outside. In short, racial boundaries become ethnicized, coming to signify membership in a collectivity of shared ancestry, history, and culture.

But with the possible exception of immigrants from the Caribbean and Africa who find themselves labeled *black,* the actual significance of racial ethnogenesis for the new immigrants is not at all clear. Among Asian Americans, for example, ethnogenesis appears to be quite limited; racial boundaries have not in fact been transformed into ethnic boundaries. The ethnonational boundaries *within* what has come to be known as "Asian America" remain prominent[8] — despite the fact that the contemporary social and political context has encouraged pan-Asian ethnogenesis in some important respects.

Asian American history is marked by ongoing flux between the dominant society's treatment of Asian Americans as homogeneous, on the one hand, and as ethnically differentiated, on the other. The Asian settlers of the late nineteenth and early twentieth centuries often found themselves categorized or lumped together as "Asiatics" and "Orientals" and subjected to the same discriminatory treatment. But at other times the dominant U.S. society did make distinctions. During the World War II period, for example, Japanese Americans were vilified and sent off to internment camps. Chinese Americans, in contrast, experienced an opening up of employment opportunities. Fong (1998) notes that in an ap-

---

8. I use the terms *ethnonational* and *ethnic* interchangeably in this book. The term *ethnonational* brings our attention to the ways in which national identities can converge and reinforce ethnic ones. This becomes particularly useful when talking of the various ethnic distinctions internal to Asian Americans, in part because it draws a clear distinction between *Asian American* and these other identities. In other words, *Asian American* is clearly not a reference to a nationality, in contrast to many of the established ethnic divisions within Asian America, such as *Korean American, Japanese American,* and so forth.

parent reversal of previous Japanese and Chinese stereotypes, "a 1942 Gallup Poll characterized the Chinese as hardworking, honest and brave, while Japanese were seen as treacherous, sly and cruel" (18).

It was not until the 1960s that Asian Americans themselves self-consciously embraced the idea of their shared predicament. As Espiritu (1992) details in *Asian American Panethnicity,* in the 1960s young U.S.-born Asian American activists on college campuses, inspired by the civil rights struggles of the time, organized the Asian American movement. Among the legacies of the movement is the very term *Asian American.* The founders of the movement intended *Asian American* to mark not just a semantic shift away from *Oriental* but a fundamental transformation in the relationship of Asian-origin persons to their shared racial construction. That is, instead of the denigrating and imposed label of *Oriental, Asian American* signaled a means of political empowerment, a self-conscious and positive assertion of identity.

Like the other panethnic collectivities promoted by the movements of the time (e.g. Native American, Latino/Hispanic), the *Asian American* concept has become an institutionalized dimension of the contemporary American racial system. Like the others, it has been a basis for monitoring antidiscrimination efforts and for organizing access to government resources. Further reinforcing its significance has been the multiculturalist movement, which often draws on panethnic categories to organize the promotion of cultural diversity (Hollinger 1995).

Since the early days of the movement, Asian American groups and organizations that aim to mobilize and advance pan-Asian interests have proliferated. There is today an extensive network of pan-Asian associations (such as the Asian American Resource Workshop, the Pacific Asian Women's Network), as well as pan-Asian publications (such as *AsianWeek, A. Magazine, Amerasia Journal*), whose stated goal is to serve a pan-Asian audience. Recent years have also seen the growth of Asian American studies classes and programs on college campuses.[9] Among the specific consequences of these various institutional developments is the emergence of forums and opportunities for persons of Asian origin to meet and develop friendships and networks that stretch across Asian ethnic lines.

---

9. A 1999 *New York Times* article notes that "today, there are at least 43 Asian American studies undergraduate programs—twice as many as a decade ago" (Sengupta 1999).

Clearly the *Asian American* concept has gained institutional and political prominence in recent times, yet the meaning and significance of *Asian American* for those who are encompassed by it remains an uncertain matter. Most observers would agree that, for the majority of Asian Americans, their Asian American identity is powerfully overshadowed in importance by their ethnonational identity—as Chinese, Filipino, and so forth. In the post-1965 era, ongoing immigration has given visibility to many Asian-origin communities, rejuvenating their membership and allowing ethnic institutions to flourish. The development of transnational networks, mentioned earlier, and a general emphasis on ethnic pluralism and multiculturalism in public discourse also fortify ethnic allegiances. In short, contemporary conditions have been generally favorable to the retention of ethnonational allegiances for Asian Americans.

The importance of ethnonational identity to Asian Americans is often noted in analyses of the development and future of the Asian American movement (Dirlik 1996; Espiritu 1992; Kibria 1998). The notion of *Asian American* advanced by the movement has essentially been that of a community of shared racial location and political interests. The impact of this notion is evident in pan-Asian organizations, which tend to encourage solidarity among their diverse constituents by stressing shared racial interests (Espiritu and Ong 1994, 302). As suggested by the introductory section to a 1996 directory of Asian American studies programs, this official ideology of pan-Asianism, with its emphasis on racial and political solidarity, has been an organizing framework for Asian American studies: "Its [Asian American studies'] subject matter is the diverse (but united by *'racial' construction, historical experience, political ends)* peoples from Asia—from West to East Asia, South to Southeast Asia—who liv(ed) and work(ed) in the U.S." (emphases added).[10]

Still, post-1965 developments in Asian America have raised important questions about this vision of pan-Asianism and its ability to inspire and bring together Asian Americans. The post-1965 period has been a time of increased ethnic and class diversity within Asian America itself. That is, reflecting both immigration patterns and processes of definitional expansion, the concept of *Asian American* today includes groups and persons from a wider array of back-

---

10. The directory is published by the Asian American Studies Program, Cornell University, Ithaca, New York.

grounds than was the case in the 1960s, when the concept was first developed.[11] This diversity poses challenges to the notion, integral to the *Asian American* concept, that Asian Americans share racial and political interests. There are, for example, important differences among Asian-origin groups in their socioeconomic profiles. As mentioned earlier, rosy statistics on Asian American socioeconomic status often mask sharp disparities among Asian Americans, disparities that often coincide with ethnonational boundaries. For example, the income levels and poverty rates for Vietnamese Americans contrast sharply and negatively with those of Japanese and Filipino Americans. Ethnonational groups also have important differences in occupation. For example, Korean immigrants are distinguished by a particularly high rate of self-employment; small convenience stores in low-income urban black neighborhoods have been an important business niche for them, more so than for other Asian-origin groups.

The point of all of this is that economic and political interests may be seen and experienced differently across Asian-origin groups. Under these conditions, a group's ethnonational affiliation may appear to be a more viable and meaningful way of defining its political interest than *Asian American*. To be sure, the original reasons that spurred the formation of the *Asian American* concept and movement still exist. Asian Americans are often still lumped together and still experience indiscriminate racial attack, without regard to their national origin. And Asian Americans may still derive important strategic advantages from coming together to form a numerically significant political coalition. It is not, then, that the *Asian American* concept has lost its political value; rather, ethnonational identities have gained in visibility and strength as a competing basis for political mobilization among Asian Americans.

It seems to me that the pressing question is not whether the *Asian American* concept is still significant (it clearly is) but rather exactly *how* it is significant. While the political and institutional development of the concept has been quite extensively studied, most notably by Espiritu (1992), far less attention has been paid to the ways in which individual Asian Americans experience, understand, and respond to this designation. Today, persons of Asian descent are quite likely

---

11. Since the 1970s, the use of the label *Asian American* has been expanded to apply to groups such as South Asians that were previously marginalized or not considered to be Asian American at all (see Kibria 1998).

to have some experience of being identified as Asian American. They will, for example, encounter the label *Asian American* when they fill out forms that ask for their racial identification. But beyond such institutional encounters, how else is the notion of *Asian American* significant? Does it provide a basis for friendships and membership in groups and organizations, guiding patterns of social association? How is it a part of subjective understandings of self and belonging?

Most observers would agree that among foreign-born Asians, who constitute a major segment of the Asian American population today, the significance of the *Asian American* concept is likely to be relatively limited. Indeed, the foreign-born may even feel a certain animosity toward the idea of pan-Asianism because of their identification with the intra-Asian tensions that are part of the history and geopolitics of the Asia Pacific region. By contrast, a pattern of pan-Asian amalgamation has been seen as more likely for the descendants of Asian immigrants, who are more removed from these historical divisions and other homeland currents. Yet the scope and character of this pattern remain largely unexplored. That is, we do not know much about whether *Asian American* has come to be more than an institutional label, a meaningful basis of ethnic identity for second- and later-generation Asian Americans. What we do know highlights ethnonational identity as an important element of the general context within which the identification of *Asian American* develops and takes shape.

■ *Studying Second-Generation Chinese and Korean Americans*

My analysis draws on 64 in-depth interviews with second-generation Chinese and Korean Americans, conducted over a span of about five years, from 1992 to 1997. More than half of these interviews took place in and around Los Angeles and the remainder in the Boston area. These two parts of the country are clearly very different in terms of the Asian American presence. When the fifty states are compared with respect to numbers of Asian and Pacific Islanders, California is ranked as the first and Massachusetts as tenth. Specifically, in 1990 Asian Pacific Islanders were 9.6 percent of the state population in California, which had 39 percent of the total Asian Pacific Islander population living in the United States. The comparable figures for Massachusetts were 2.4 percent and 2 percent, respectively (Fong 1998, 45). Furthermore, within California, Los Angeles County has had a large concentration of Asian Pacific Islanders—nearly 1 million, or 11 percent of the total county population (Min 1995a, 20). For Korean

Americans, Los Angeles—informally dubbed "the Korean capital of the United States"—has been particularly important. The number of Chinese in Los Angeles is also high, although New York and San Francisco have somewhat larger Chinese American communities.

Although both Los Angeles and Boston are important metropolitan regions, many of those whom I interviewed were not originally from either city but had grown up in other parts of the United States. Roughly half had moved to these areas for school- or work-related purposes, suggesting an experience of upward socioeconomic mobility. If Los Angeles and Boston are relatively similar in their ability to attract persons from other parts of the country, they are also of course quite different in many important ways. I began the study with the idea that the clear-cut differences in population concentration—of Asians, Chinese, and Koreans—between the two areas would make a difference to patterns of adaptation and identity. These effects ultimately turned out to be far less pronounced than I had expected.

I limited my interviews to the adult children of Chinese or Korean immigrants, between the ages of 21 and 40, who had been born or raised in the United States since the age of 12 or younger.[12] By prompting them with open-ended questions, I asked them to talk about their racial and ethnic experiences over the life course in such spheres as work, family, and neighborhood. The interviews lasted from one and a half to four hours, and most were tape-recorded and later transcribed.

I recruited persons to interview through the membership lists and referrals of local Asian American, Chinese American, or Korean American groups of various sorts, including churches, professional and social clubs, and college and university alumni associations. I expanded my sample through "snowballing," or the referrals of interviewees to other potential participants. In doing so I made an effort to avoid oversampling from particular social networks by limiting the number of referrals from any one "snowball chain" and continuing my efforts to

---

12. In recent years scholars have debated the parameters of *second generation* with respect to a person's age at the time of immigration to the United States. While there is no question that the U.S.-born children of immigrants are part of the second generation, there has been less consensus about whether all those raised in the United States from the age of 12 or younger (the heuristic definition adopted in this book) qualify as "second generation." Arguing that *the first and second generations* as a classification leaves out the experiences of an important in-between group, some have proposed the use of the term *1.5 generation* to refer to those who arrived in the United States during late childhood or adolescence (see Zhou 1999).

TABLE I.I
Chinese American Women

Name	Age	Occupation	Education (Highest Degree/ Number of Years)	Marital Status	Age at Immigration
Brenda	mid 30s	career counselor	M.S.W.	married	4
Connie	mid 30s	college counselor	B.A.	married	U.S. born
Cynthia	late 20s	accountant	B.A.	married	U.S. born
Jane	early 30s	corporate manager	B.A.	single-partnered	U.S. born
Jenny	mid 30s	clerical worker	B.A.	single	U.S. born
Joan	late 20s	lawyer	J.D.	single	U.S. born
Karen	mid 20s	electrical engineer	B.S.	single	U.S. born
Katie	late 30s	dentist	D.D.S.	single-partnered	U.S. born
Lillian	early 40s	librarian	14 years	married	4
Lily	early 30s	corporate manager	B.A.	single	U.S. born
Margaret	early 40s	community organizer	B.A.	married	U.S. born
Meg	early 20s	clerical worker	B.A.	single-partnered	U.S. born
Mei Han	late 30s	lawyer	J.D.	married	U.S. born
Renee	mid 30s	accountant	B.A.	divorced	U.S. born
Terry	early 30s	real estate salesperson	B.A.	married	8
Wai Han	early 30s	mechanical engineer	B.S.	single-partnered	7

TABLE I.2
Chinese American Men

Name	Age	Occupation	Education (Highest Degree/ Number of Years)	Marital Status	Age at Immigration
Bill	mid 30s	self-employed computer salesperson	B.A.	single	6
Chi Wai	late 20s	chemical engineer	B.S.	single-partnered	U.S. born
Dave	early 30s	graphic arts designer	B.A.	single	6
Duncan	late 30s	physician (internal medicine)	M.D.	married	7
Glenn	late 20s	financial analyst	B.A.	married	U.S. born
Gordon	mid 30s	physician	M.D.	single	U.S. born
Greg	early 30s	computer programmer	15 years	single	U.S. born
James	late 30s	electrical engineer	B.S.	married	U.S. born
Lanhee	early 20s	food retailer	12 years	single-partnered	2
Paul	late 20s	marketing executive	B.A.	single-partnered	U.S. born
Robert	mid 20s	unemployed	B.S.	single	2
Simon	late 30s	architect	M.S.	married	1
Soo Kee	late 30s	financial investment adviser	B.A.	married	12
Steve	late 20s	accountant	B.A.	married	U.S. born
Wayne	early 30s	writer/clerical worker	B.A.	single-partnered	U.S. born

recruit participants from other sources. I particularly sought referrals to persons who would expand the range of my sample, especially in terms of occupation and education, as well as membership and involvement in Asian American, Chinese American, or Korean American associations.

The group of informants who ultimately constituted my study sample was largely middle-class. Tables 1.1 through 1.4 provide a summary list and description of the informants, including their assigned names, ages, and occupations, as well as other basic information about them. A quick glance through the list reveals a wide range of occupations, jobs, and work situations. There are, to name just a few, clerical workers, homemakers, lawyers, screenwriters, and persons who were unemployed at the time of the interview. Nonetheless, what is notable is that a high proportion of them worked in professional occupations, while those involved in small business and unskilled service jobs were relatively absent. The generally middle-class profile of the sample is confirmed by the fact that the majority of the study participants were college-educated. Fifty-five of the 64 informants had bachelor's degrees from a four-year college or university, and some had graduate or professional degrees as well. Of these 55 persons, 23 had attended a public institution (i.e. a state/city college or university), while 32 had been to a private one. Two of the others interviewed had obtained a two-year associate's degree from a community college. Of the remaining informants, 2 had never attended college and 5 had attended but left before completing their undergraduate degree.

While the occupational and educational characteristics of my informants are generally suggestive of middle-class status, it is important to also note the heterogeneity of their socioeconomic *backgrounds*. They had grown up in families that were quite varied in socioeconomic terms. Some came from professional, upper-middle-class homes, while others had grown up in working-class or small business families. Reflecting the general patterns of occupational adaptation among Korean Americans, small business was an especially common family background among my Korean American interviewees.

Of the 64 persons who came to participate in the study, 31 were Chinese American and 33 were Korean American. The sample included 31 women and 33 men. While they ranged in age from their early twenties to late thirties, a large cluster consisted of persons in their late twenties and early thirties. Twenty-seven of the informants had been born in the United States; of the remainder,

TABLE I.3
Korean American Women

Name	Age	Occupation	Education (Highest Degree/ Number of Years)	Marital Status	Age at Immigration
Cori	late 20s	public relations/film producer	B.A.	single	3
Hea Ran	late 30s	social worker	M.S.W.	married	7
Hyesook	mid 30s	corporate manager	B.A.	married	10
Jamie	mid 30s	nurse	B.S.	single-partnered	12
Katherine	late 20s	actress/clerical worker	B.A.	single	U.S. born
Kyung Sook	early 20s	community activist (nonprofit organization)	B.A.	single-partnered	U.S. born
Mi Ra	mid 30s	fashion retail sales	13 years	married	U.S. born
Michelle	late 30s	homemaker	B.A.	married	12
Min	early 20s	fashion designer	B.A.	single-partnered	U.S. born
Sandra	late 20s	building manager	B.A.	single	U.S. born
Sonia	late 20s	unemployed	B.A.	married	5
Soo Jin	mid 20s	lawyer	J.D.	single-partnered	1
Sung Joo	mid 30s	homemaker	B.A.	married	6
Susan	mid 30s	lawyer	J.D.	married	11
Tammy	mid 20s	community worker (nonprofit organization)	B.A.	single	8

TABLE I.4
Korean American Men

Name	Age	Occupation	Education (Degree/ Number of Years)	Marital Status	Age at Immigration
Ben	early 20s	administrative assistant	13 years	single	3
Cliff	late 30s	unemployed	associate's degree	divorced	10
Curt	mid 30s	landscape architect	M.S.	married	12
David	mid 20s	store manager	associate's degree	single	8
Eugene	mid 20s	financial investor	B.A.	single	5
George	late 30s	physician (ENT)	M.D.	married	10
Jae Wook	late 30s	lawyer	J.D.	single	4
Jeff	early 20s	marketing researcher	B.A.	single-partnered	6
John	late 20s	lawyer/accountant	J.D.	married	7
Ken	late 30s	minister	M.A., Divinity	married	U.S. born
Ki Hong	early 20s	food retailer	12 years	single	8
Matthew	early 20s	community worker, nonprofit organization	14 years	single	U.S. born
Philip	late 20s	unemployed	B.A.	single-partnered	7
Sam	mid 30s	lawyer	J.D.	married	7
Sung	mid 20s	financial market analyst	B.A.	single	U.S. born
Tae Bong	mid 20s	coordinator, public health organization	14 years	single	8
Tom	mid 30s	screenwriter	B.A.	single	3
Young Min	early 30s	bank manager	B.A.	single	4

the majority had entered by the age of 8 or earlier. As for marital status, 25 were married and 2 had been divorced. Of the remaining 37 single informants, about half described themselves as in a "serious, long-term" romantic relationship.

■ *The Ethnic Contexts of Chinese and Korean America*

The inclusion of two different Asian-origin groups in this study provides an opportunity to explore the ways in which different ethnic contexts shape the dynamics of race, adaptation, and identity. Persons of Chinese and Korean origin in the United States undoubtedly do share the racial label *Asian,* but how this shared racial construction plays out against the backdrop of ethnic contexts that are both similar and different is among the questions that inform this book. In what follows I briefly explore and compare the ethnic contexts of Chinese and Korean America. I pay particular attention to the contemporary picture, and to the broad structural developments and characteristics that have marked the Chinese and Korean American populations since the mid-1960s.

With the exception of about 7,200 Koreans who came to work in the sugar plantations of Hawaii in the early part of the twentieth century, Korean immigration to the United States has historically been low (Min 1995b, 200). The Chinese, in contrast, constitute a major element of the "old Asian immigration." By 1880, more than 105,000 Chinese were living in the United States, primarily in the western regions of the country (Wong 1995, 61). The Chinese Exclusion Act of 1882, which both banned Chinese settlement and explicitly denied naturalization rights to Chinese, stymied the growth of the Chinese American population for several decades. The environment of hostility that surrounded the act forced the Chinese to insulate themselves in Chinatowns. Chinese employment patterns also shifted in the aftermath of the act, from urban labor to self-employment in service occupations such as laundries, restaurants, and grocery stores. Reflecting the ban on immigration as well as other obstacles to family formation, the Chinese American population was at this time composed largely of men.

For both the Chinese and the Korean American communities, the 1965 Immigration Act has been a critical turning point. The Chinese American population grew from a total of 436,062 in 1970 to 806,040 in 1980 and 1,645,472 in 1990. The increase has been even sharper for Korean Americans, who numbered 69,1550 in 1970, 354,593 in 1980, and 798,849 in 1990 (Min 1995a, 16).

Both groups contain a large proportion of immigrants: in 1990 the U.S.-born were only 30.7 percent of the Chinese American population and only 27.3 percent of the Korean American population (Min 1995a, 29). In summary, both Chinese and Korean Americans are today part of dynamic and growing ethnic communities that have been vitalized by post-1965 immigration. Both populations are numerically dominated by immigrants rather than U.S.-born persons. But reflecting a longer historical presence in the United States, there is more generational diversity (not just second generation but also third and fourth) among U.S.-born Chinese Americans than there is among Korean Americans.

Comparatively speaking, the ethnic context for Chinese Americans appears less homogeneous and solidary than that for Korean Americans. Besides having a greater range of generations, the Chinese American population is heterogeneous in other ways as well. While the early Chinese immigration originated largely from two southern provinces in China, today's Chinese immigrants come from Hong Kong, Taiwan, and mainland China, as well as Southeast Asian countries such as Vietnam and Singapore. These different points of origin have given rise to important distinctions in language, identity, political ideology, and socioeconomic background. In contrast, Korean immigrants all arrive from South Korea, and all share a common language and national identification. Once they are in the United States, most Koreans affiliate with Korean immigrant churches and join at least one ethnic association, thus further enhancing the solidarity that is suggested by premigration commonalities (Min 1995b, 215). Among Chinese Americans, ethnic institutions and associations tend to be organized around linguistic, national, and regional divisions. Citing a 1988 study by Mangiafico, Min (1995b, 214) argues that Korean Americans are much more likely than Chinese Americans to join ethnic associations.

Reflecting the occupational provisions of the 1965 act, immigrants from middle-class backgrounds have been an important component of both the Chinese and the Korean influxes. But for both groups, increasingly significant numbers of settlers come from less prosperous backgrounds as well, with lower levels of education and skill.[13] Overall, the socioeconomic profile of Chinese Americans is more favorable than that of Korean Americans. According to the 1990 census, Chinese Americans had a median family income of $41,316, while Korean

13. Abelman and Lie (1995, 75) note the decline, in the mid-1970s, of the number of highly skilled professional Koreans settling in the United States. Of Koreans entering in 1973, 55 percent were professionals.

Americans had $33,909. Korean Americans also have a higher percentage of families in poverty—14.7 percent compared with 11.1 percent for Chinese Americans (Min 1995a, 28). Thirty-six percent of Chinese Americans but only 26 percent of Korean Americans are engaged in professional and managerial occupations (Fong 1998, 60).

Unable to find jobs in the United States that were commensurate with their premigration backgrounds, many Korean immigrants have turned to small business. The rate of self-employment among Korean Americans is extremely high—16.9 percent. For Chinese Americans it is 6.7 percent, comparable to the general U.S. population figure of 6.9 percent (Fong 1998, 50). While they are engaged in a range of self-employment activities, an important business niche for Korean Americans has also been small retail grocery, deli, and liquor stores that serve non-Korean and particularly low-income inner-city black customers. As a result, Korean Americans have been affected in especially prominent ways by contemporary urban conflicts and unrest. The 1992 Los Angeles riots, for example, represent an important chapter in the contemporary Korean American experience. During the riots, Korean businesses were attacked and looted, resulting in enormous losses for the Los Angeles Korean American community. Some observers consider the Los Angeles riots to be an important watershed in the development of racial consciousness and political activity among Korean Americans (see Park 1999). Elaine Kim (1993) argues that the riots have been to Korean Americans what the internment of World War II was for Japanese Americans, part of an "Asian American legacy of violent baptism." That is, the riots have forced Korean Americans to confront the question of their place and role in the racial and social landscape of the United States.

In their provocative book, *Blue Dreams,* Abelman and Lie (1995) discuss how the media contributed to the popular view of the riots as a black-Korean conflict, ignoring the larger racial structures and inequities that underlay the unrest. The media emphasis on the "black-Korean division" was partly achieved by counterposing images of "model minority" Korean Americans against those of an African American "urban underclass." As I show in Chapter 5, the stereotype of the "model minority"—a minority group successful because of its cultural orien-

---

The percentages declined to 35 percent in 1977 and 22 percent in 1990. The occupational structure of Chinese Americans, especially the foreign-born, has been described as bipolar, with a clustering of workers both in high-paying professional and managerial occupations and in low-paying service jobs (Wong 1995, 77).

tation—has been prominent in contemporary understandings of Asian Americans. But reflecting the constant interplay of racial and ethnonational identities in the Asian American experience, the model minority stereotype has also been a marker of distinction *among* Asian Americans. At times, some Asian American groups have been more closely associated with the stereotype than others. While Koreans have been associated with it more recently, both Chinese and Korean Americans are today more rather than less likely to be seen as a model minority. The global context, I believe, has been critical to this perception. Since the 1980s, South Korea, Hong Kong, Taiwan, and mainland China have been applauded for their economic success—so much so that they have been labeled as "Asian tiger economies," driven by Confucian values. The Asian economic crisis of the late 1990s has undoubtedly challenged and complicated this perception in important ways, but I would nonetheless argue that the general perception of East Asian countries as powerful players in the global economy, in the future if not at present, has remained an important one. This is particularly so for the People's Republic of China, which, given its size and resources, is widely viewed as a potentially formidable economic force.

This global context holds other implications for Chinese and Korean American adaptation as well. For immigrants, homelands that are economically successful and that are perceived to be favorably situated within the currents of economic globalization may encourage the development of transnational networks and activities. In this sense, both of the ethnic contexts being discussed here have generally favored the development of transnational connections. In other words, for Chinese and Korean Americans, the economic realities and perceptions that surround their homelands have supported them in maintaining ongoing ties with those homelands from their positions in the United States.

To summarize then, the ethnic contexts of Chinese and Korean America are clearly different from each other in important ways, most notably in the more solidary and homogeneous nature of Korean America. But for both Chinese and Korean Americans, the dynamics of race, identity, and adaptation take shape in a general context in which their ethnic communities are strong and vital, with a large and ongoing immigrant presence.

CHAPTER TWO

Growing Up Chinese and American, Korean and American

The children of the immigrants, those born here or brought very young
. . . They were Irish and Poles and Italians, yet not Irish or Poles or
Italians; they were Americans and not Americans. They were double
alienated, marginal men."   (Herberg 1960, 24–25)

THERE IS in the United States an established immigrant narrative —
a classic, prototypical story of the immigrant experience. Centered on the assimilation framework and the general history of the European American experience as it has come to be popularly understood, this immigrant story is part
of the cultural baggage — the myths, beliefs, and symbols — that surrounds and
informs the ethnic American model. Reflecting its assimilationist premises, the
story is essentially one of immigrants and their descendants becoming American, moving toward integration and acceptance in the dominant society. The
basic organizing theme of the story is the march toward Americanization, toward
absorption into American culture, and relatedly, a movement away from immigrant traditions.

In this drama of cultural change, it is members of the second generation who
are at the center of the internal and familial conflicts that the process generates.
As the children of immigrants, they are enmeshed in the immigrant community
but are also, by virtue of having grown up in the United States, more attuned
to American culture than their parents may be (see Child 1943). The second
generation represents, then, a high point of tension in the march of Americanization. They are in between two different worlds, the immigrant world and the
American, and they are not fully comfortable in either one. As suggested by
the quotation above, from Herberg's classic work on European American ethnicity, the result is a powerful sense of marginality, a marginality that is a de-

fining feature of the second-generation experience as portrayed in the immigrant story.

Marginality, cultural clashes, living in two worlds—these and other themes of the classic second-generation experience as defined by the classic immigrant story also laced through the growing-up accounts of the second-generation Chinese and Korean Americans whom I interviewed. This chapter explores their stories, and the experiences and understandings of race, adaptation, and identity that were a part of them. In relating their childhood histories, my informants often spoke of "growing up Chinese and American" or "growing up Korean and American." As suggested by this turn of phrase, their childhood recollections often centered on the idea of growing up in two realms that were not only different but opposed to each other: the ethnic and the American.

For these second-generation individuals, then, growing up was, at least in part, about confronting and negotiating their own position in relation to this opposition and, more generally, addressing the question of its meaning and significance—identifying the character of the two worlds and their relationship to each other. What did it mean to be both Chinese and American, Korean and American? If, in the classic immigrant story, second-generation conflicts stem from differences of culture, for my informants the second-generation collisions were also about race. Their childhood memories were marked by a gnawing sense of racialized marginality from the identity of *American*.

■ *Growing-Up Stories and Neighborhood Social Landscapes*

The childhood memories of my informants revealed that neighborhood, in particular neighborhood social landscape, was significant to their experiences and understandings of race, adaptation, and identity. I use the term *neighborhood social landscape* to refer to the social character and composition—in particular by race, ethnicity, and class—of a particular area, in this case one where informants lived and went to school. In contrast to the era of old Asian immigration, in which most Asian Americans lived in segregated enclaves with their fellow ethnics, for the new Asian American immigrants a single dominant pattern of residence and settlement is far more difficult to identify. This is not to say that there are no general trends. Asian Americans are concentrated in California and New York, and they tend to live in urban rather than rural areas. But within urban areas, they live in a variety of locations, ranging from inner-city ethnic enclaves (Chinatown, Koreatown) to middle-class suburban neighborhoods.

This diversity of residential patterns was reflected in the variety of neighborhood social landscapes that my informants related to me. They grew up, as they told it, in a range of settings—from small working-class towns in the Midwest to the exclusive suburbs of Los Angeles. As a way of exploring the implications of these differences, I present here a series of case studies—four of their accounts of growing up in different kinds of neighborhood social landscapes. In these accounts, the theme of "Chinese versus American worlds" or "Korean versus American worlds" appears to have been for them a broad organizing idea, a way of making sense of childhood, if only in the sense of providing a way of asserting how their childhoods were different from what was expected. As we will see, in the settings of different neighborhood social landscapes, the story of growing up "Korean and American" or "Chinese and American" may take a variety of twists, turns, and shapes.

James: An All-American Childhood and the Specter of Normalcy

A Chinese American in his mid-thirties, James was born and raised in Pittsburgh, the younger of two sons. At the time of our interview, he was working as an engineer and living in the Los Angeles area with his wife, a white American, and their young daughter. James's father had come to the United States from mainland China in the 1940s as a student, to pursue a doctorate in physics. He remained in the United States after the Chinese Communist Revolution and was joined by his wife a few years later. Throughout his career he had worked in scientific research, in both university and corporate settings. James's mother had been a homemaker.

James's family lived in two different neighborhoods in Pittsburgh, he told me, both of them suburban and white but different in class composition. When he was five, the family moved from an "average middle-class" neighborhood to a "fancy, very wealthy" one. He attended the public schools in these areas until the tenth grade, when he went to a local private school.

James described himself as "very American" in his cultural practices, worldview, and sense of self. Much of this outlook had to do, he felt, with his parents, who had not emphasized Chinese culture and identity to their sons at all. His parents had never, for example, asked or encouraged them to learn the Chinese language, or spoken to them of Chinese traditions and history. But despite having, as he put it, "grown up American," James's childhood memories were marked by powerful feelings of not wanting to be different: "I wasn't really Chinese, bottom line. I just played with the other kids. I don't think I ever really consciously dealt with it. I realized I was physically different, Asian. But I think that subconsciously I was just like any other kid in that I didn't want to be different. I do remember that I didn't want to be weird, or different, or stand out."

As this remark suggests, James as a child experienced a certain frustration—a sense that even though he was not actually different, others saw him as such because of his physical Asian features. For the most part, he said, the fact of his difference was conveyed to him in subtle rather than explicit ways; blatant acts and expressions of racism were not part of the "polite and respectable" middle- and upper-middle-class milieus in which he grew up. Like virtually all of my informants, however, he was sometimes teased and taunted with racial slurs (*chinky, nipface*) as a young child. He ruefully admitted to me that as a child he had secretly wished he was white; the fact that he was not was, after all, the only thing that made him stand out, barring him from what was "normal."

Like a number of other informants, James also spoke of having a heightened consciousness of his physical difference from whites as he entered into adolescence and began to negotiate the body-conscious, angst-filled American world of teenage dating and sexuality. But it was not only his racial identity—"looking Asian"—that marked him as different, he felt. As a teenager his reputation as a studious "nerd," and the fact that his family was not as wealthy as the neighbors, also meant that he did not quite fit in:

> As a teenager, I was still like any other kid and didn't want to stand out. I think the only thing that changed was that I became more aware that I was physically different—I looked different, I was a minority. When I was at the high school level we were in a very wealthy area, a very preppy area. I did sort of feel like an outsider. But I don't know how much of it had to do with the fact that I was Chinese. I look back on it now, and probably a good portion of it did. But I was also studious and my parents were not wealthy, so I wore cheap clothing, less stylish clothing. I mean, I was a classic nerd.

James's childhood memories were marked by a powerful remembrance of his difference from his peers. The neighborhood social landscapes in which he grew up were an integral part of his experience and helped form his understanding of this difference. As a child, he understood "looking Asian" to be a barrier to normalcy. In the homogeneous, all-white social world of his childhood, to be "normal" was to be white. The absence of racial minorities in this world meant that this conception of normalcy and its racial assumptions were so firmly established and unchallenged as to have an invisible, taken-for-granted quality, and to require little overt or active affirmation from whites. In general, James spoke of growing up in a racially benign atmosphere, with no blatant expressions of racial ill-will that could easily fit conventional definitions of "racism." While he was reflecting on these conditions in our interview, he conveyed a general sense of confusion, of uncertainty about the significance of the sense of difference that he felt from his peers.

James's feeling of puzzlement was compounded in certain ways by his lack of connection to and identification with his Chinese background. Raised in a family that did not emphasize the cultivation of Chinese community, traditions, and identity, he perceived himself to be culturally American, as "American as apple pie," as he once put it. Under these conditions, it was particularly difficult for him to accept the idea that he did not fit in because he was "culturally Chinese." He was forced to conclude that it was the physical aspects of his Chinese identity, the fact that he looked different, that set him apart from what was considered American.

Cynthia: From "The American Kid on the Block" to "The Foreigner"

A Chinese American in her late twenties, Cynthia was born and raised in the Chinatown section of Los Angeles, living there for much of her childhood. At the time of the interview, she was working as an accountant and living in the Los Angeles area with her husband, a Chinese American. Her father had immigrated to the United States in the 1950s and her mother in the 1960s, from southern China and Hong Kong, respectively. Trained as an engineer, Cynthia's father eventually left the field of engineering because of what he felt to be discriminatory treatment from company managers. With his wife as a partner, he entered into a long string of entrepreneurial ventures, eventually settling into the restaurant business. Cynthia had one brother and one sister.

Until the age of 15, Cynthia lived and went to school in Chinatown, which during the course of her childhood became increasingly populated by new immigrants from Hong Kong, Vietnam, and Mexico. According to Cynthia, by the time the family moved out and into a nearby suburban area (when she was 15), there were few remaining families in Chinatown that, like her own, had been in the United States for several decades. Some of their Chinatown neighbors had, like her own parents, been owners and operators of small businesses. The majority, however, had worked in unskilled manufacturing and service jobs — in garment production, sales, cleaning, and so forth.

Cynthia's childhood friends had been both Chinese and Mexican Americans, but she had little to do with the new Asian immigrant children in the neighborhood; in fact, her relations with this population were poor. She described the immigrant children from Hong Kong and Vietnam who hung out in her neighborhood and school as "cliquey," unfriendly, and exclusionary in their behavior toward her. So she turned instead to friendships with Mexican American children as well as other "ABCs" — American-born Chinese — like herself:

> I didn't get along with the Asian kids. I remember they were really unfriendly, hanging out together and not letting anyone else in who wasn't like them. I found that very narrow-minded. I remember them making fun of me because I couldn't speak the language. I can speak a little of my mother's dialect, which is different from what they spoke. I actually found the Hispanic kids to be more open. I had some Mexican friends and that was fine. [How about Chinese Americans?] Oh yes, I had friends who were like me, Americans basically, ABCs. But there were fewer and fewer of us. I think that's one of the reasons why my parents decided to move out of Chinatown. There was more crime, more drugs.

When Cynthia was 15, she began, as part of a school busing program, to attend a high school outside of the city, in a wealthy white suburban area. She continued there after her parents moved the family out of Chinatown and into Monterey Park, a middle-class area suburban area that had a growing community of Chinese American families. For Cynthia, the new high school was a startling and eye-opening experience. It was, she remarked, her "first real contact with white kids." Given Chinatown's location near downtown Los Angeles, she hastened to add, growing up there had not been as insulated an experience as one might imagine. But it was certainly true that in Chinatown, she had not grown up with white age peers. Entering the new high school thus marked an important turning point, a watershed in her identity development:

> I was bused to a school in the Valley. That was the first time I realized I was not American, as far as other people [were concerned]. I had grown up thinking of

myself as the American kid on the block. Suddenly, I was the foreigner. At the school [in the Valley] there were some other minority kids, mainly black and Hispanic, who were bused too. The school was VERY white, very wealthy. [Pause.] These kids owned sports cars and went to Rio for the weekend.

[What was that like?] It was weird, a little difficult. I mainly kept to myself, did my work, that was it. I did hang out some with the black and Hispanic kids. I sort of dated a Mexican guy for a while. But I mainly kept to myself. I had to work very hard because the schoolwork was more challenging than before. My social life didn't change that much. You know, every night I would come home, and on the weekends I hung out with Chinese friends.

[Were the students at the school unfriendly?] No, well—yes. Like I said, they were very rich and spoiled and snobby. I felt like I was in another galaxy, something out of TV. I couldn't relate to their lives. I guess I felt a little intimidated too. They looked better than me. I remember these long tall leggy blondes wearing designer clothes. They were very confident, self-assured. Like, if a teacher ever told me that something was wrong, I wouldn't even think about arguing with them. But for these kids—they would think nothing of bringing in a lawyer and suing the teacher. My father used to tell us, "Whites think they own the world and the rest of us are just here for them."

In the suburban high school, Cynthia turned for friendship to other minorities, with whom she felt a sense of commonality. Besides, she had always had Mexican American friends, even when she was living and going to school in Chinatown. Cynthia also found herself compartmentalizing her social life away from school, so that she could focus exclusively on academic work when she was at school. Her social life continued to center on her home and neighborhood, and to involve mainly Chinese Americans. In fact, her transition to the suburban high school had coincided with a renewed sense of consciousness and commitment to her Chinese identity. As a child, she said, she had not given much conscious thought to what it meant to be Chinese. But in the setting of the new high school, she became increasingly aware of her Chinese identity and committed to cultivating this aspect of herself.

For Cynthia, notions of race and identity were profoundly affected and complicated by the transition to the suburban high school. In the neighborhood social landscape of Chinatown, she had grown up with a consciousness, among her peers, of the differences and divisions between immigrant and U.S.-born

Chinese. In Chinatown, then, by virtue of her American upbringing, she had both defined herself and been defined by others as "Americanized," in contrast to the "Chinese Chinese," as she at one point put it. This self-definition was challenged by the move to the largely white suburban high school, where she developed an awareness that in the eyes of others she was not American but a foreigner. She thus emerged from her suburban high school experience with a sharp consciousness of the significance of race in American society, and specifically of the privileges of "whiteness." Her awareness of the wide gulfs in social class between herself and many of her white school peers was clearly an important part of this consciousness.

Another important force in the development of Cynthia's racial consciousness was her father, who often spoke of his experiences with racial discrimination in the labor market. In response to these conditions, and a growing sense of racial exclusion, Cynthia had in her high school years become consciously engaged with and committed to the cultivation of her Chinese identity.

Ben: "Accommodating Successfully, to a Point"

A Korean American in his mid-twenties, Ben had come to the United States in the early 1970s at the age of 3, with his parents, two older brothers, and a sister. At the time of our interview, he was working as an administrative assistant in the personnel department of a health care facility in Boston. Ben had grown up in Merrimack, a town in New Hampshire. The family had been sponsored for immigration by Ben's aunt, who had married an American soldier during the Korean War and then settled in New Hampshire. While Ben was growing up, his parents had worked at a variety of factory jobs, in meat-packing, electronics, and shoe production.

The area where Ben grew up, he recalled, was exclusively white; he and his family members were the only members of a racial minority around. The neighborhood was a working-class one: like his parents, many of its residents were or had been employed in blue-collar jobs in the area's factories. Incidents of racial harassment and hostility were prominent in Ben's earliest memories. Once while he was very young (in elementary school), he remembered, the windows of their house were broken, and the family sometimes received harassing phone calls in which they were told to "go back home." He also recalled racial taunting and harassment at school. His older brothers, who were not shy about defending themselves from such attacks, got into many physical fights with hostile class-mates during these years.

Ben spoke of these difficult early years, of which he had vivid memories, as an "adjustment phase." By the time he entered junior high school, he said, things had changed. In contrast to the hostility of the past, he and his siblings had become popular and well-regarded members of their schools. His sister and brothers excelled in academics and sports and were leaders and active partici-pants in a variety of school organizations and clubs. As their little brother, Ben said, he had benefited from his elder siblings' reputations. But his own social route of adjustment was somewhat different. He became the rebellious one in the family, gaining a reputation not in the respectable activities of schoolwork and organized athletics but for partying. He became known as the class clown, and his popularity with girls earned him the voted title of "class flirt" in his senior year:

> I was one of those bratty kids in high school. I was kind of a punk, breaking cur-few at home and staying out late to party. We were really well accepted to a point. [What do you mean, to a point?] You know, the fact that you look different, you're never quite one of them. Little things, I guess. Stares you get. And once a girl I was dating in high school, her father didn't want his daughter to date an Oriental. He was ugly about it, I mean, not subtle at all, chasing me out of their house with a shotgun!
>
> But like I said, we were pretty well accepted. All of us had adjusted well. We were willing to go with the flow, we didn't impose ourselves on other people, we didn't pose a threat to anyone. Even my mother and father. They were very Korean, didn't speak much English, and preferred to hang out with Korean people. But we all kind of assimilated. They made friends with the neighbors and tried to participate in community events. We went to a Catholic church, not a Korean one but an American one in Merrimack.

When the hostility of the earliest years eased, Ben understood it to be a result of the family's successful adjustment to their surroundings. They had worked hard to establish themselves as respectable and achieving. They had also accom-modated to the community, making sure not to appear threatening or challeng-ing it any manner. Rather than flaunt or display ethnic difference, they had tried to make themselves inconspicuous, to blend in. Ben saw the strategy of accommodation to be a largely successful one, but he also recognized that it did not completely obliterate the significance of racial difference.

According to Ben, his parents had encouraged and participated in this strategy of accommodation, but they had also cultivated and valued relationships with other Korean Americans. Although the contacts were not very frequent because of the distances involved, his parents maintained active friendships with other Korean immigrant families living in nearby towns and cities. Ben found encounters with these families to be uncomfortable, he recalled. It was at these times, when he was with Koreans rather than with Americans, as he put it, that he had felt different, out of place. He did not have much interest in his Korean background, an attitude that had been the source of some conflict with his father:

> Growing up, my main contact with Koreans was with my parents' friends and their children. We, my brothers and sister, we were much more Americanized than these other kids. So I felt uncomfortable when I was in a crowd of Korean people, not when I was with Americans. My parents were not as demanding as a lot of the other Korean parents [were] about their kids staying very Korean in America. But we did have fights. Like if I met an older Korean, I would just shake his hand instead of bowing and saying the proper greeting. That made my father furious. And I changed my name, I dropped my Korean name and started calling myself Ben. It was a name I saw in a book about a hamster. My father gets upset about that.

Dominating Ben's account was the theme of accommodating, of working to adjust to the local surroundings by blending in, by assimilating. He spoke confidently both of the effectiveness of accommodation and of its limits. That is, if one was willing to make the effort, it was possible to be accepted, to a point. The exclusions of race could be greatly but not completely overcome.

While growing up with a strategy of accommodation that was both successful and limited, Ben felt distant from fellow Korean ethnics and, more generally, from his Korean heritage. He grew up with a sense of himself as American in his cultural orientation and behavior, especially in interactions with other young Korean Americans. In ways that echo the scripted intergenerational clashes of the classic immigrant story, his lack of knowledge of and interest in his Korean heritage was a prominent source of conflict with his father. But if Ben felt himself to be positioned as "the American" in the cultural clash of Korean and American, he was also conscious of how he was ultimately always somewhat of an outsider.

Hyesook: Wondering about "the 'Brady Bunch' World"

A Korean American in her mid-thirties, Hyesook at the time of our interview was working as a manager in a large communications company in downtown Boston. She and her husband, a white American, had recently had their first child. Hyesook had arrived in the United States at the age of 10, in the mid-1970s. She, her mother, and five brothers and sisters had followed her stepfather, who had come a few years earlier to join his brother. They settled in Queens, New York, an area with a growing Korean American population and where several of Hyesook's aunts were living. Over the years, Hyesook's mother and stepfather had owned and operated a variety of small businesses in New York, including an import-export company and a dry cleaning store.

Hyesook grew up, she said, in a neighborhood that was "very diverse," with many new immigrants from different parts of the world. While it did have some middle-class families, it also had a significant number of families who were struggling to get by. The student bodies of the public schools that she attended were racially diverse, including Asians, blacks, Hispanics, and whites. This diversity, Hyesook said, initially overwhelmed her, in her first years in New York. But at school she made friends with other new immigrants like herself, who were also struggling to learn English and adapt to the United States.

It did not take long for Hyesook to overcome her language difficulties. By the time she reached high school, she had established herself as a serious and high-achieving student. It was, she felt, this academic orientation and reputation that distinguished her in the social milieu of the high school. She described the high school as a "rough place," with gangs, drugs, and various divisions and feuds among students. She hung out with a crowd that was distinguished by its commitment to academic achievement. While not exclusively so, this circle was largely Asian American:

> My best friend was a Russian Jewish girl. We hung out with some other kids who
> were the high achievers. The school was big, and people found their special niches.
> For me it was schoolwork, getting the best grades possible. So I found others like
> me. We were the high achievers, taking AP classes, prepping for tests. We were

interested in getting out into the world, getting into good colleges, good professional jobs. We stayed away from a lot of the shit happening around us.

[What was the ethnicity of the people you hung out with?] Oh, it was diverse. Mostly not American, though. I mean, there were some Jewish kids who were part of the "A" crowd, but it was mainly immigrants, minorities: Russian, Chinese, Indian, Korean. [A lot of Asian Americans?] Yeah, that's where the whole model minority phenomenon comes in. For whatever reason, it's true that a lot of Asian kids do well. And that makes for a lot of resentment. [Did you feel resentment?] Sure, yeah, from other students. Koreans are not real popular with blacks and Hispanics, especially blacks. Because Koreans open businesses in these poor neighborhoods, they're accused of racism, of exploiting blacks.

When Hyesook was not busy with schoolwork, she spent her time helping out with the family business or with the care of her three younger siblings. She and her family were also active members of a local Korean Protestant church. She was a member of the church choir and had once even traveled to Korea on a church-sponsored singing tour. Outside of school, her closest friends had been fellow church members who were "1.5 Korean Americans" like herself.

All of this led Hyesook to conclude that she had grown up in a "very Korean atmosphere." She had not seen or experienced her Korean identity to be a difficult issue, or a source of conflict within herself or in her relations with family members. In this way, she explained self-consciously, her childhood experiences contradicted the general expectation that immigrant children would grow up with identity conflict: "I grew up very Korean. So I didn't have the identity conflicts you're supposed to have. We ate Korean food, spoke mainly Korean, and followed a lot of the Korean rituals. A lot of my friends were Korean. But until I got to college, it was not something I consciously thought about. I never agonized: 'Am I Korean?' I knew I was Korean, I didn't have to think about it."

The neighborhood social landscape of Hyesook's childhood was marked by the presence of new immigrants and a significant and vital Korean American community. In this environment, Hyesook had not felt her Korean background to be a source of cultural or identity crisis. This did not mean that her Korean identity did not at times place her in a position of potential conflict with others. Especially given her family's involvement in small business activities, she had been aware, while growing up, of hostility and resentment toward Korean Americans, especially from other minorities. Also marking her recollections was a deep consciousness of the separation between her local world, populated largely by racial minorities, and the worlds that were "out there," of prosperous whites. She remembered feeling a sense of curiosity about how whites, especially prosperous suburban whites, lived: "I always wanted to live in a place like *The Brady Bunch,* to see what it was like. I mean, you know, big suburban house and lawn and white picket fence, and everything all nice and clean and orderly. Where I lived was like another America. Everyone lived in apartments, and there were lots of people who didn't speak English, and there were hardly any whites. I was really curious about the *Brady Bunch* world."

Achievement was the theme that dominated Hyesook's childhood recollections. Her academic efforts and accomplishments were key to her personal history and her sense of self. Among other things, they colored her experience and understanding of what it meant to grow up "Korean and American." For Hyesook, her Korean identity did not in any way contradict a positive orientation toward academic achievement; in fact, it was very much part of it. The perceived relationship between achievement and American identity was, however, more complicated.

In general, Hyesook's account highlights the differentiated character of immigrants' perceptions and definitions of American society—the multiple and situational meanings that they attach to the word *American.* There were times when Hyesook used *American society* to refer to the neighborhood, the local community in which she grew up. As far as achievement was concerned, in this context, *American* had negative meanings for her, connoting academic failure and absorption into the oppositional culture of minority underclass youth. At these times, the idea of *American* seemed to function for Hyesook as a negative counterpoint, a means by which she could assert what she was not.

But in ways that make prominent the intersecting meanings of class and *American,* Hyesook also spoke of *American* in consonance with achievement, in fact as an outcome of it. That is, she associated academic achievement with socioeconomic mobility and hence with a path of integration into the professional, middle-class sectors of American society. At several times during the interview, she remarked that her school achievements had allowed her to "make it," to move out of the social worlds of her childhood, into more professional and "American" ones. In this transition, she had moved from a world populated largely by minorities to one marked by the overwhelming presence of whites.

■

The four accounts that I have presented hint at the tremendous range and variety of childhood experiences that my second-generation Chinese and Korean American informants related to me. Simply put, their stories show that there is no monolithic second-generation Chinese American or Korean American experience of childhood. For example, against the backdrop of varied neighborhood social landscapes, the dilemmas of race, adaptation, and identity take different shapes. While both Ben and James grew up in all-white environments, they experienced and understood racism differently, in ways that reflected the different class composition and dynamics of their neighborhoods. Other informants described different levels of engagement and involvement, while growing up, in Chinese and Korean communities and culture. As children, they thus experienced important differences in how ethnic affiliation mediated the dilemmas of race and identity for them.

In the midst of this diversity, however, one common theme ran through these childhood memories. For all my informants, part of the experience of growing up involved developing an awareness that a nonwhite racial identity functioned as a marker of exclusion in American society. To be sure, this awareness did not appear in the same form or to the same degree. But all my informants remembered their childhood as a time of emerging consciousness of their racialized exclusion from a mainstream American identity. As the accounts that I have presented make quite clear, at some times members of the second generation identified themselves as "American" instead of as "Chinese" or "Korean." But at other times they felt a pervasive sense of distance from what was American, at least in the eyes of others, by virtue of how they looked: their racial identity.

■ *Messages of Race: Lessons from Parents on Coping with Racism*

I turn now from the role of the neighborhood to that of the family in my informants' childhood experiences of race, adaptation, and identity. In both popular and scholarly thinking, intergenerational relations in immigrant families are, it is assumed, shaped by powerful cultural conflicts. In this narrative tensions are caused when homeland-oriented and tradition-bound immigrant elders attempt to impose their ideas and values on their increasingly Americanized children. The theme of culture clashes with parents was quite clearly an important one in the childhood memories of my informants.

But as an orienting theme, this theme was deeply intertwined with and often subsumed by another theme: lessons about race. As my informants recalled their childhood family environments and relationships, they explained that their parents had tried to teach them about the nature of racism in the United States, and the best strategies by which to deal with it. These familial teachings offered them particular ways of understanding and responding to their sense of marginality, of not being accepted as American by others, because of their race.

For racial minority groups, the family is expected to be an important site of *race socialization,* or the teaching of children about race and racism in the dominant society. Studies of African American families have given particular attention to the topic of race socialization, noting that black parents and other elders teach the young a sense of pride and identification with black history and traditions in the face of denigrating messages and treatment from the dominant society (Billingsley 1992; Hill 1999; Taylor et al. 1990). In contrast, race socialization has not received much attention in studies of Asian American families. This is indicative, I believe, of a widespread tendency to see Asian American families in narrowly cultural terms, as entities driven by an internal logic of cultural tradition, rather than as influenced by the structural features and arrangements of the society of which they are a part.

In this section I look at the experiences of race socialization that my informants described in their childhood accounts. More specifically, I look at the *messages*—the lessons, ideas, and strategies of race—that were a part of their relationships with their family elders, in particular their parents. In contrast to *socialization,*[1] with its connotations of rigidity and consensus, the notion of *messages* is, I believe, more suggestive of the fluid, interactive, and contested character of race education processes in the family. As we will see, the lessons of race that family elders convey to their children are neither fixed nor given, and the young are far from passive recipients of those messages.

---

1. As Thorne (1993) notes in *Gender Play,* "the concept of 'socialization' moves mostly in one direction. Adults are said to socialize children, teachers socialize students, the more powerful socialize and the less powerful get socialized" (3).

Ethnic Consciousness, Pride, Blood, and Authenticity

Running through the childhood accounts of my informants were recollections of being counseled by parents and other family elders to be conscious and proud of their Chinese or Korean origins. References to the racial exclusions of the dominant society were an integral part of this counsel. That is, elders advised the second generation to maintain ethnic consciousness and pride as a response to racism, as a strategy for coping with it. My informants often recalled that their parents gave them these messages of ethnic consciousness and pride often in the aftermath of incidents of racial taunting and harassment.

Meg, a Chinese American, grew up in Las Vegas, in a working-class neighborhood that was largely white but was also experiencing an influx of minorities. Like many other informants, she recalled that childhood incidents of racial teasing were occasions for exceptionally focused discussions with her parents about strategies for dealing with racism. One of Meg's most vivid early memories, from when she was about 8 years old, was that of a group of neighborhood children, primarily white, following and harassing her as she walked home from school. They pulled their eyelids up to make fun and chanted racial slurs. When Meg got home, her parents comforted her. Besides advising her to ignore the attacks, they also emphasized that she should take pride in her Chinese ancestry: "They told me to not pay any attention, that the kids were just ignorant and mean. They also told me that I was Chinese, I should never forget that, always be proud of it. I would always be Chinese, it was in my blood, it wasn't something to be ashamed of. It was one of the few times they actually talked about it, but I think it was really important to them that we be proud of being Chinese."

Philip, a Korean American, also remembered that his parents advised him to maintain a sense of pride in his ethnonational origins. As was the case for my Korean American informants in particular, references to a nationalistic history of struggle and triumph over adversity were a significant part of how his family elders affirmed to him the importance of Korean identity and pride. Philip grew up in largely white neighborhoods in suburban Boston. When he was in his early teens, he punched out a student at school who had been bothering him with racial insults:

My dad had to come and talk to the school officials, the principal. He was not happy about that. I think they let me off the hook with some quite minor punishment like after-school detention. [How did your father react?] Like I said, he wasn't too happy. But my father's a very proud person. If someone insulted him, especially the fact that he was Korean, I don't think he would hesitate to defend himself. He told me, "Whatever people tell you here, you are Korean. Don't forget it, be proud of it. Koreans have faced a lot of difficulties in their history, but we've always come through."

Some informants recalled that the message of Chinese or Korean identity and pride was unspoken rather than an explicit, self-conscious parental directive. This was the case for Gordon, a Chinese American who was raised in a suburban area of Chicago. Gordon professed to have grown up in a home where "being Chinese" was not greatly emphasized, at least not through the self-conscious transmission of Chinese traditions and language. Appreciative of the fact that these activities had not been forced on him, he nonetheless felt that he had been raised in a family that was proud of its Chinese origins. He saw this sense of pride to be an appropriate and dignified response to the racism of American society:

> My family never tried to push Chinese culture on us, and I respect that. But I know they were proud of being Chinese and they taught us that. They taught us that even if Americans look down on you because of the color of your skin, it's important to be proud of being Chinese. [How did they teach you that? What were some of the specific ways?] Well, it was not specific. It was just like how I saw my mother deal with the salesgirl who was rude to her because of her English. It was just the way they were. They were just very dignified people. They knew who they were, they were proud of it, they weren't going to apologize for it. And they were interested in teaching us that, not so much the specifics of Chinese culture.

Like Gordon, Sam remembered that his parents conveyed to him a sense of ethnic pride by example rather than by self-conscious verbal pronouncements or active efforts. A Korean American, Sam grew up in Los Angeles, in close proximity to the Koreatown area, surrounded by a large extended family of aunts, uncles and cousins:

> We grew up very Korean, but it was not something artificial or forced on us. We could tell that it was important to our parents that we understand that we were Korean and that we be proud of it. My father was really aware of the racism around him, and he wanted to make sure that we weren't ashamed of who we were. It

wasn't so much that they placed any kind of importance in the sense that we had to go to school or attend language class and so on. But it was more in the way they would tell us about their upbringing, what they did in Korea. They didn't have to tell us that they were proud of being Korean. You could sense that in their stories, and their history and their understanding of the culture. [Laughing] Whether or not all of it was accurate is secondary.

By contrast, Kyung Sook, a Korean American woman, recalled that the message of ethnic identity and pride that she was taught had a more embattled quality to it. Kyung Sook grew up in a home where her father strenuously emphasized the practice and cultivation of Korean traditions and ties, so much so that it was a source of family conflict. For Kyung Sook, the message of Korean identity and pride was intertwined with these conflicts and the traditional, authoritarian Korean family dynamics from which she understood them to stem. At the same time, the racial underpinnings of the message were not lost on her; she recognized her father's emphasis on "being Korean" to be, at least in part, a response to the racial exclusions of American society:

> I did not like being Korean when I was growing up. What I mean is that it felt to me like a restriction: "Go to church, learn Korean dance, always be respectful, do this, do that." My father's very Korean, very nationalistic; he talks about retiring in Korea, although I don't think he actually will do it. He used to give us long lectures at the dinner table where, you know, he had a captive audience. For him, you were either Korean or American, and if you were Korean by blood, you had no choice, even if you were born here. He would tell us stories about Korea, Korean history, all the suffering, et cetera.
>
> My sisters and I would get tired of it, which made him even angrier. It's not that I don't sort of get where he's coming from. Part of it is that he's very traditional. But it's also that Koreans are very proud people, [and] the way they deal with not being accepted by Americans is to become even more Korean: "You're going to reject us, but we don't care."

Taken together, these accounts highlight the diversity of family experiences and contexts within which the message of Chinese or Korean identity and pride was transmitted. For some of my informants, the message was shrouded in family conflict, while for others, it evoked memories of family unity and consensus. More generally, the message was a part of family settings that varied as much as ethnic contexts. That is to say, some informants grew up in families that were deeply embedded in Korean or Chinese ethnic communities, and the networks and groups that were a part of them. In these cases, the social life of the family was dominated by relationships with fellow ethnics. Others, in contrast, described growing up in relative isolation from fellow Chinese or Korean Americans.

Families also varied in the extent to which they actively transmitted ethnic cultural practices. For some, like Kyung Sook, the parents expected and even demanded that their children learn and follow Chinese or Korean cultural practices, such as language, etiquette, and so forth. In contrast, others, such as Gordon and Sam, did not remember their parents making an explicit and active effort to educate them in the ways of Korean or Chinese culture.

Among the factors that lay behind these differences in family ethnic context was that of geographic location and, more specifically, the neighborhood social landscapes that were a part of this location. We would expect, for example, a Chinese American family living in New York's Chinatown to be in a different position, with respect to opportunities and resources for ethnic involvement and cultivation, from a family in a midwestern town with a small Chinese American population.

At the same time, my informants' accounts made clear to me that the factor of geographic location was complex and could be mediated by the orientation and attitudes of parents, and the strength of their resolve to raise children in a culturally Chinese or Korean environment. For example, some of my informants grew up in mostly white regions and neighborhoods with few Koreans or Chinese. Yet they had nonetheless, through the efforts and insistence of their parents, learned the language and other aspects of Korean or Chinese culture, and socialized with other Chinese or Korean Americans, perhaps through travel.

Reflecting the high level of church membership that has been reported for Korean Americans, my Korean American informants were especially likely to have participated in a Korean church community when they were children, often in activities specifically designed for second- and 1.5-generation persons like themselves. Let me emphasize here that my Korean American informants were far from monolithic in their experiences of Korean ethnicity while growing up. Nonetheless, I did find the family ethnic contexts of Korean Americans to be, in general, more self-consciously and actively "ethnic" than those of their Chinese American counterparts.

These variations in family ethnic context were clearly influential in how the second generation experienced and understood the message of ethnic identity and pride. As one might expect, for those who grew up in homes embedded in Chinese or Korean communities, where elders actively worked to transmit and educate the young in the ways of the homeland culture, the message resonated in particularly powerful ways. For such persons, the admonition to "remember and be proud that you are Chinese or Korean" gained meaning through these conditions, as did the sense of identification with Chinese or Korean culture and community that they promoted. In other words, their families' community embeddedness and active efforts to educate the young into Chinese or Korean culture supported the message of ethnic consciousness and pride, affirming to them that they were indeed Korean or Chinese. But while these conditions clearly strengthened the message in certain ways, it did not ultimately seem to be dependent on them. I found the message to be a powerful and meaningful part of the recollections of informants who had grown up in a range of ethnic contexts.

Embedded in the message of ethnic consciousness and pride was a particular conception of Chinese or Korean membership. This conception was a critical part of the general potency of the message, its ability to withstand a variety of ethnic contexts, to have meaning across them. In this conception, being Chinese or Korean is "given" or primordial, a matter of blood or shared descent from a common ancestor. It is, as Pan (1994) writes in her work on the Chinese diaspora, "not so much language, or religion, or any other markers of ethnicity, but some primordial core or essence of Chineseness which one has by virtue of one's Chinese genes" (267).

Among Chinese and Korean immigrants, these notions, which have been a part of nationalist conceptions and sentiments in both China and Korea, constitute an important framework for the formation of Chinese or Korean identity (Dikötter 1992; Kim Jae-Un 1991). Seen in this light, being Chinese or Korean is an essential, unalterable matter, rooted in the deep-seated, biological forces of blood. Ties among group members can take on a fundamental, elemental quality, as captured by the idea of *chong,* a word used by Koreans to describe their relations with each other. *Chong* refers to a complex mixture of relational qualities that work together and have a primordial cast to them: love, affinity, empathy, obligation, entanglement, bondage, and blood (Abelman and Lie 1995, 39).

Reflecting the influence of these notions, my informants often spoke, without conscious thought, of belonging to the "Chinese race" or the "Korean race."

More specifically, they described learning of this primordial understanding of Chinese or Korean membership from Chinese or Korean immigrants and nationals. Often in this connection they mentioned language and study programs in China or Korea, especially the Korean American informants, in whose accounts the notion of being "Korean by blood" appeared in especially self-conscious and well-defined ways, as part of a general conception of Korean national history and character. But for both Chinese and Korean Americans, the idea of primordial Chinese or Korean membership was also an integral part of the message of ethnic consciousness and pride. In other words, along with counseling children to remember and be proud of being Korean or Chinese, their parents also affirmed to them that they were Chinese or Korean by blood.

The close intertwining of these ideas—ethnic pride, remembering, and blood—is suggested by the account of Sandra, a Korean American. Like several other informants (as I will explore in more detail in Chapter 6), Sandra remembered family discussions about intermarriage as times of particularly intense reflection and exchange with parents about questions of Chinese or Korean identity. Her father's insistence that Sandra marry Korean was closely related to his message to her of ethnic pride and consciousness. "Marrying Korean" was for him an affirmation of Korean identity, itself a strategy for coping with the racial exclusions of American society. It was also a matter of blood, and of respecting the sanctity of blood:

> Koreans are very very proud and stubborn people, and my father is even more so than most Koreans. He tried very hard to give us pride in being Korean. A lot of his friends, the old-timers—their children can't speak Korean, have married non-Koreans, and in general are not really Korean-identified. It really bothers him; he says, "I don't even want to talk about it." He talks about Korean blood. Koreans are very nationalistic, they want to keep the Korean blood pure. He's told me that it was unacceptable for me to marry a non-Korean. When he came here, you know, he really felt the prejudice; it was the 1960s, and there weren't too many Koreans around.
>
> He remembers that, and he tells me, "You think you're American, and you think that you're widely accepted, but remember that people still see your physical features. If you spend time with them, they realize that you were raised here and you speak English fluently. But you don't have the time to sit with every person, to educate every person on the bus or the subway."

My informants' reactions to this conception of Chinese or Korean membership as primordial were complex. On the one hand, they expressed an aversion to it, since it clashed with ideas of freedom of choice with respect to identity. They also understood that these primordial notions, with their emphasis on bloodlines and purity, smacked of racism. But they nonetheless often tempered or complicated these evaluations with an understanding of the important ways in which American racial exclusions were a part of the message, informing and undergirding it. For example, Sandra understood her father's concern with the maintenance of Korean identity to be related to his experiences of racial exclusion in the United States. His message to his daughter about the importance of maintaining Korean blood purity was accompanied by observations about the inability of persons of Korean descent to achieve full acceptance in the United States.

Like Sandra, Bill, a Chinese American, also understood his parents' concern with Chinese blood and purity as, in part, a reaction to their exclusionary experiences in the United States. But he was also quite openly critical of this concern, seeing it as evidence of racist thinking. His account highlights the deeply contested character of these primordial notions of membership, which could be a major bone of contention in relationships with family elders:

> Chinese are really xenophobic, kind of racist. It's a fact. I see it with my parents and uncles. For them, being Chinese is about blood. They think Chinese blood has to stay pure; marrying a non-Chinese is like a sin. I argue with them, I've said to them, "You people are racist." I do kind of understand where they're coming from. My parents have struggled so much, they've had to face all kinds of hurdles and problems. There have been times when they've been treated poorly just because they're Chinese.

Notwithstanding these uncertainties and tensions, the notion of being "Chinese by blood" or "Korean by blood" was critical to the widespread imprint of the message of ethnic consciousness and pride, its ability, as described earlier, to have meaning across a range of ethnic contexts. In terms of behavior, however, these primordial conceptions of membership had a certain flexibility. On the one hand, the notion of Chinese or Korean ties as inexorable, rooted in blood, suggests that cultivating these ties is important: the identities are, after all, "given" and so cannot be ignored. Their primordial quality also means that their cultivation can bring social and emotional rewards of a particularly intense and special nature. Jane, a Chinese American in her early thirties, for example, recalled that her parents reacted in these terms to her declaration that she no longer wanted to go to Chinese language school: "We were forced to go to Chinese school for a few years. It was after school, three or four days a week. I hated it because it was so strict and boring. My parents weren't too happy when I told them I wanted to quit. They said I would always be Chinese on some level, no matter how Americanized I was. They said it was really important to know something about the Chinese culture because it was a deep part of me, it was something special."

Conversely, however, the conception of Chinese or Korean identity as "given" also suggests that its cultivation is not so urgent and can be postponed. That is, given the essential nature of this identity, its existence is not fundamentally threatened by an absence of active cultivation. Under these conditions, the identity assumes perhaps a dormant form, waiting for an opportune moment to rise to the surface and be activated.

These themes of blood and self-discovery have been important ones in popular Asian American literature. For example, in Amy Tan's best-selling novel *The Joy Luck Club* (1989), Jing-Mei Woo, an immigrant mother, tells her incredulous second-generation daughter that "once you are born Chinese, you cannot help but feel and think Chinese. . . . Someday you will see, . . . it is in your blood, waiting to be let go" (306). Similarly, one of my informants—Renee, a Chinese American—spoke of the primordial pull of her Chinese identity, which had, until recently, not been of much interest to her: "Growing up, I didn't care about being Chinese, and I didn't know much about it. But my mother always said, 'It's in your blood, if you want it, it's there.' And I feel that's true. Some basic deep part of me is Chinese, and one way or another I'm going to come back to that."

Primordial notions of membership, then, were an important means for my informants to lay claims to and to feel themselves to be Chinese or Korean. It was particularly important for them, considering the powerful currents of uncertainty that otherwise surrounded these claims for them. As second-generation persons, they could not, for the most part, invoke birth or upbringing in the homeland in making claims to Chinese or Korean identity. In fact, the challenges of others as well as their own doubts about the genuineness of their ethnic identity were a critical part of how they experienced the message of ethnic consciousness and pride. For my informants, their parents' advice to "remember and be proud that you are Chinese or Korean" was, to put it simply, surrounded by questions about the very authenticity of their own Chinese or Korean identity. While "blood" acted as an important counterpoint to these uncertainties, it certainly did not dispel them.

In the settings of the dominant society (as I will discuss in Chapter 3), second-generation Chinese and Korean Americans tended to face few challenges to the authenticity of their identity as true Chinese or Koreans. In contrast, encounters with Chinese or Korean immigrants were a particularly ripe forum for such challenges. My informants identified these challenges as an aspect of intergenerational ethnic community tension—of fissure between immigrant and second-generation community members. As my Chinese American informants often told me, among the appellations used by Chinese immigrants to refer to second-generation Chinese Americans is the Cantonese term *jook sing*. Literally meaning "hollow bamboo," it is generally used to convey that American-born Chinese are Americanized and distant from their Chinese heritage. It also implies that they lack real substance: the second generation has, by virtue of being U.S. born or raised, lost its true, core Chinese self.

During trips to Chinese or Korean societies in the homeland, my informants could become painfully aware of how suspect they were as true Chinese or Koreans. The majority of my informants had been on homeland trips—visits to societies of their ancestral origin. Some of these were family trips, while others were of a more institutional nature, such as study tour programs that offer local travel and classes in Chinese or Korean language, culture, and history, usually geared quite specifically toward the descendants of expatriates. Reflecting their interest in cultivating ties with their overseas populations, many of these programs have enjoyed the support and sponsorship of Korean and Chinese governments. While there are many different such programs, two are particularly well known among second-generation Chinese and Korean Americans. For Korean Americans, Yonsei University in Seoul has been a favored destination. For Chinese Americans, there has been the Overseas Chinese Youth Language and Study Abroad Tour to Taiwan, more popularly known as "The Love Boat" due to its reputation as an opportunity for fun, parties, and romantic encounters (Chen 1995).

My informants recalled vividly that during these homeland trips, members of the local population saw them as different. The issue of language was especially important. Jeff, a Korean American, went to Korea on a study tour program after his senior year in high school. While in some ways the trip affirmed his sense of connection to Korea, it had also made him aware that he was quite different from the native Koreans:

> The natives looked down on us because a lot of us couldn't speak Korean—although I could understand what they were saying. They were basically saying, "You're so stupid. You're Korean, but you can't speak Korean." There were some isolated incidents when we were yelled at, harassed. I guess I felt a little weird with my relatives too because I couldn't really communicate that well, and sometimes I felt they were talking about me behind my back: "Oh, he's American, that's why he's like that."

During these trips, my informants did not experience challenges to their identity as "true Chinese" or "true Koreans" in uniform ways. Some were more easily able to deflect the challenges by displaying their cultural proficiency. Not surprisingly, a particularly important marker here was the ability to speak the Chinese or Korean language fluently. Many of my interviewees indicated that their language proficiency was low, a trend that is consistent with the general shift toward English that has been part of the American immigrant and ethnic experience (Portes and Schauffler 1994). There were 23 fluent speakers in my sample; these included a number of persons who had come to the United States at a relatively late age (8 to 12) as well as those who had acquired or reacquired their language skills through formal study and travel. The remaining 41 persons indicated that they were unable to carry on a conversation in Korean or Chinese, although many knew isolated phrases or words.

Yet even those informants who were fluent in the Chinese or Korean language could face challenges to their authenticity as "real Chinese" or "real Korean." Joan felt that however great her language and other cultural skills might be, she would ultimately never quite be accepted as "true Chinese," given her American upbringing:

> We grew up speaking Taiwanese at home—my parents insisted on it. I'm also good at Mandarin, I studied it in college and then when I was in China [for six months]. [That must make it easy for you, when you visit Taiwan?] Oh yeah. But I still can't pass for a local Chinese. I guess there are subtle things, mannerisms, phrases that come from growing up there. It's clear that I'm an American. Chinese immigrants, the new ones who just arrived, are the worst about it. [What

do you mean?] They're like: "Oh, you're so American. You speak Chinese well, but you're still an American." In their eyes, you're never quite Chinese, you're not Chinese enough.

For some informants, childhood experiences of being condemned for their "inadequate" Chinese or Korean language skills had been so powerful as to cast a deep and negative pallor on their general attitude, their feelings about being Korean or Chinese. Ken, a Korean American, was raised in Los Angeles during the 1960s and 1970s, at a time when the Korean American community there was still small and composed almost entirely of immigrants. Ken spoke of being constantly disparaged by the Koreans he encountered, who berated and teased him for not speaking Korean. His sense of frustration and anger at this treatment was only compounded by his experiences in Korea during family trips there:

> I grew up with a lot of anger toward Koreans. I believe the situation is changed now, because there are more Korean *Americans* [U.S.-born or -raised Koreans]. But when I was growing up, it was just Korean immigrants, who are very national-istic. It was the same when we visited Korea. I remember being teased and scolded for not speaking Korean. It was like I was a traitor to the motherland or some-thing. I'm at a much better place with all this now. But at the time I was angry. I felt like, "Why are you blaming me for who I am?"

To summarize, then, among the family messages of race that were conveyed to my informants was an emphasis on ethnic consciousness and pride—the coun-sel to "remember and be proud that you are Chinese/Korean." The message was, at least in part, an effort to counter the traumas of racism; in effect, to build self-esteem and provide to the young a positive sense of identity in the face of racial denigration. One way the message did this was to emphasize, however implicitly, the importance of their ethnonational identity as Korean or Chinese *over and above* their Asian one. For my informants, experiences of racism tended to involve their identity as Asians, reflecting their racial categorization as Asian in the dominant society. In a sense, emphasis on Chinese or Korean identity was a way of dismissing the significance of these attacks, of generating distance from them. Other studies of new immigrant populations have also noted this parental strategy, of emphasizing to children the importance of their ethnonational ori-gin rather than their racial identification (Fernandez-Kelly and Schauffler 1994; Waters 1999). When the imposed racial label is a highly stigmatized one, with many costs, immigrant parents may be especially driven to urge their children to look to their ethnonational heritage.

For my informants, the message of ethnic consciousness and pride was informed by a primordial blood-centered ideology of Chinese or Korean membership. Their accounts highlight both the power of this primordialism and its contradictions, the dilemmas it posed. "Blood" affirmed the second generation's claims to full and true Chinese or Korean membership, but it was not able to entirely deflect or negate the questions and suspicions that surrounded these claims.

Achievement and Education

Another family message concerning race was that children should focus on achievement. That is, my informants' parents urged them to compensate for the disadvantages of their racial identity by being "twice as good," outshining their peers in their achievements. This counsel was applied in a variety of specific activities, including music and sports, but it was most powerfully directed toward academic achievement. Doing well at school was presented as an effective means to achieve socioeconomic status and rewards in the United States and to overcome the racial barriers to such achievement. In an important sense, this message affirmed the ideology of the American dream—that socioeconomic success is possible, open to all those who strive for it.

In the popular press, the generally high rates of academic performance among Asian Americans are often explained with reference to their cultural traditions, in particular that of Confucianism. What has received less press are the ways in which this cultural predisposition toward education has been supported by the conditions of Asian immigration itself. Among these conditions, as described in Chapter 1, are the fact that post-1965 Asian immigration has included large numbers of highly skilled and educated persons. Such persons are likely to be familiar with formal schooling processes and to be conscious and optimistic of their significance for occupational achievement. In addition, higher education in Asian countries is highly competitive; by comparison, the greater educational opportunities in the United States has been a driving force, a major motivation for many Asian immigrants for coming to this country in the first place (Liu 1992). These conditions help to explain the familial emphasis on education that my informants so often related to me.

While the question of why Asian immigrant families place importance on education has excited much interest, the question of *how* parents convey and affirm the importance of education to children and the specific ways in which they do so has received less scrutiny. My informants' accounts highlight the ways in which emphasis on education was presented as a racial strategy. That is, their parents suggested that academic achievement was a way of overcoming the racial exclusions and barriers in the United States, of "making it" in spite of them.

Some informants recalled that their parents advised them to "do well at school" after incidents of racial taunting and teasing. We see this in the account of Jenny, a Chinese American in her mid-thirties who grew up in a white, middle-class suburban area outside of Los Angeles. Her family, she explained at some length, did not emphasize or give much explicit attention to the cultivation of Chinese traditions and identity. But her parents did urge her to do better than the others, often as a way of comforting her after she had been teased by other children: "My parents didn't really stress Chinese culture when we were growing up. I mean they were never like 'go go Chinese,' that kind of thing. But there was one thing that they said constantly. When we were little kids and people made fun of us, they would say, 'You have to prove that you're better. You have to do better than them at school and everything you do. Because people have these perceptions, you have to prove them wrong. You have to do better.'"

Curt also spoke of being counseled by his parents, after encounters with hostile schoolmates, in similar ways. A Korean American in his late twenties, Curt grew up in a middle-class area of Los Angeles that was at the time largely white but was experiencing an influx of minorities. His parents had urged him to not respond to the racial harassment at school by fighting, but rather to focus on outshining his fellow students in his achievements, especially in schoolwork:

> There was a time in school, I think it was sixth or seventh grade, when I was getting into fights almost every day because of name-calling. There wasn't a day I remember that I wasn't called "chink" or "Jap" or something like that. People assume that Asians will not respond aggressively if they're picked on. That may be true of other Asians, but it's not true of Koreans. Once I came home with a black eye. My parents were upset; they were afraid I'd get a bad reputation with the teachers. They told me I'd always stick out in this society and so it was important to not bring attention to myself by fighting. The best thing was to work hard and do well at school, to be twice as good as an American at what I do.

While in some situations parents would give a child the message of achievement and education after the child's experiences of racial marginality, in others they did so after recounting their own such experiences. That is, parents worked to bolster their counsel of school achievement to their children with references to their own experiences of exclusion and hardship. They deployed these references to remind and perhaps convince their children of the reality of racial barriers for Asians in the United States, and thus to emphasize the need to compensate for these barriers through added achievement. John, a Korean American, recalled how his father had sought to instill in his children a sense of awareness of the realities and the power of racial divisions in the United States. Education had been the answer, the "panacea"—an assessment that John himself generally shared but with some reservations:

> My parents had a hard time when they first came here—they were not always treated well. My father used to tell me that I would be treated differently by Americans because I was Korean, because I looked different, I wasn't white. And to a certain extent of course, he was right. His answer to that was: education, education, education. [Why do you think he emphasized education so much?] It's always been important to them, and I think that's true for most Koreans, it's part of the culture. It's one of the main reasons why my parents moved to America, so their children could get a good education. Their attitude is that education is a panacea for anything and everything. It will get you more respect, more money. It's not that I don't believe in all this, but I've also gotten to realize that there's a limit to what education can do for you.

The account of Sonia, a Korean American, highlights the ways in which parents raising children in economically privileged circumstances could feel it to be especially important to teach their children about the reality of racial impediments in the United States. By providing their children with a family history of struggle and discrimination in the United States, they could give their counsel to do well at school a special urgency and edge. Drawing on this history, they could urge their children to not be lulled into a false sense of security but to be aware that whatever their own sense of a situation might be, the playing field was not actually level—they would have to work much harder than others to receive the same rewards.

Sonia recalled how her parents feared such complacency among her younger siblings, who had grown up amidst the wealth and privilege of Beverly Hills. Unlike Sonia herself, they did not remember the family's early years in the United States, when they lived in a run-down apartment in central Los Angeles and struggled through a series of failed business ventures before achieving their first success:

> You may get a certain impression of me, knowing that I went to high school in Beverly Hills. But I grew up knowing what it took for my parents to get to that point. It's different for my little brother and sister. They weren't here for the early years. My mom and dad, they always say to them, "Don't take anything for granted here. Remember that you're Korean, that people are going to treat you different no matter what; you have to prove yourself all the time. You have to do well at school; Americans may get away with not doing well, but you won't."

Even as my informants described ways in which "doing well at school" had been presented to them as a racial strategy, they also spoke of it as an expression of cultural tradition—the values and beliefs carried by their parents from the homeland. This interpretation of the message clearly resonated with and drew upon popular understandings of Asian success. But it also allowed my informants to talk about their conflicts with their parents.

Seen as an expression of cultural tradition, the message of academic achievement could be interpreted in the context of the conflicts over tradition that were so central to my informants' relationships with their parents. As I have described earlier, in the classic immigrant narrative, relations between immigrant parents and their children bear the scars of the collision of two worlds—the traditional and the modern. My informants recalled that, in a variety of ways, the message of academic achievement was embedded in the currents of this intergenerational culture clash. They were not necessarily rejecting the message or viewing it negatively—on the contrary, most said that they appreciated the value that their parents had placed on education. Rather, the message was for them part of the complexity of their relationships with their parents, and in particular, the conflicts over tradition that were central to these relationships.

The notion of "tradition" in family life had diverse connotations for second-generation Chinese and Korean Americans and was judged in a variety of ways. Pyke (2000) has noted the operation of a monolithic image of the "Normal American Family" as an interpretive framework, a means for young Asian Americans to gauge their own family experiences.[2] Similarly, holding a highly generalized notion of the "American family" as a conceptual counterpoint, my informants often described their childhood families as "traditional." This connected them to a morally upright and honorable way of life and gave them a positive sense of distinction from those who had grown up in American families. But they also associated their families with authoritarianism and rigidity—family dynamics that were, in critical ways, deficient and unsatisfying in comparison to American ones.

Cori, a Korean American, spoke at some length of her feelings about growing up in a home where education had received such a high priority. While affirming its value, she also resented the manner and means by which her parents had emphasized education; these had clashed with her ideas about how family relationships should operate. She described Korean family culture as authoritarian, in comparison to that of the American family, which provides children with the freedom for self-discovery. She spoke disapprovingly of the psychological pressures and tactics exerted by her parents, which included linking her school performance to their approval and also using it as a measure or evidence of her respect for them. Cori was also critical of the extent to which her parents had emphasized formal education to the exclusion of other life skills:

> I think in this culture, in America, parents give kids a little more freedom and let them sail on their own and learn on their own, and sometimes that's a little bit too much space and sometimes it's not. I think in the Korean culture we just obey our parents. You don't, like, learn for yourself. You don't, you know, discover for yourself little lessons that you learn just from growing up. I think studying was a huge stumbling block for us. More so for me than for my sisters because their grades were better.
>
> I was a B student in an A-plus household. I had fights all the time with my parents about grades and other things. They took it almost like a sign of disrespect to them, if you didn't get straight A's. If you wanted their approval, you got

2. Pyke (2000) notes that against the contrast of the Normal American Family, the Korean Americans and Vietnamese Americans she interviewed felt that their own relations with immigrant parents were deficient, lacking in expressive love and psychological support. But when it came to issues of filial care and collectivist family traditions, the pendulum swung the other way—it was the Normal American Family that came up short.

straight A's. I understand that my parents thought that education would make our life easier. And I'm really glad they taught me the importance of education and doing the very best at whatever you do. That's a valuable part of Korean culture and I want to hold on to it. But there are other things that are as important as schoolwork, like knowing how to socialize with people, how to get a point across well in a conversation.

Similar themes appear in the account of Ben, a Korean American whose childhood experiences we explored earlier in this chapter. In reproaching him for his poor grades, Ben's father had used not only guilt but unflattering comparisons between his performance and that of his siblings. The result was a deep-seated fissure in Ben's relationships with his brothers:

I'm the rebel, the black sheep in the family. I'm the only who didn't go to college, to law school, business school. I'm not proud of myself for it, it's just how things happened. My father tried—he punished and lectured about how if we didn't do well, then everything they had sacrificed was not worth it. It was very typical Korean, you know how the parents push the guilt on you. My parents are actually not all that educated, but I think it's a Korean thing, this obsession with education. I was the baby of the family, kind of spoiled, especially by my mother. But I grew up in the shadow of my sister and brothers who were the straight-A students, the super everything. My dad was proud of them. I get along with my sister, but to this day I don't get along with my brothers.

Some informants spoke of the message of achievement in education in the context of the general rigidity and "strictness" in their family life. That is, the message of achievement was part of a larger set of well-defined rules and expectations of conduct that were restrictive and confining. Some also dwelled on how, in the absence of frank and open communication between parents and children, these rules and expectations were not subject to either review or debate. In short, the message of achievement was embedded in traditional and undemocratic family patterns.

Duncan, a Chinese American in his late thirties and a doctor, appeared to have fulfilled the academic and career expectations that his parents had held before him as far back as he could remember. While he expressed an appreciation for their emphasis on education, he had resolved to raise his own children differently, in a more "open" family environment:

My parents were pretty strict—there wasn't a lot of open communication, discussion. They told us to study hard and expected us to do it. It was very Chinese in that way. American kids get away with a lot more, and when they don't, they can argue with their parents about it. For us it was basically: "Go to school, do your homework, help out Mom and Dad." [How did you feel about it?] Usually it was fine, but I was sometimes resentful. There are important lessons that my parents taught me, like the value of a good education. With my children, I want to pass that on. But I want a more open relationship, more communication.

Joan, a Chinese American, said that as a child she had resented "being Chinese." Her parents' emphasis on her academic performance had been part of the restricted freedoms with which she had associated Chinese culture while growing up. But in retrospect at least, Joan was also appreciative of the expectations with which she had been raised:

When I was young, being Chinese was a thorn in my side. It was very difficult because there were so many rules. You had to spend so many hours studying, you had to bring home straight A's. We had a rule in the house that we couldn't speak English, we had to speak Taiwanese. My dad was very strict about it. I remember once being spanked for speaking English. He came into the room, and my sister and I were speaking English. So that was kind of a big deal.

My parents were just very very strict, and I just attributed that to their being Taiwanese. We weren't allowed to go to dances, or if we could go, we had to be home by 10:30 instead of 12:30 like everybody else. Or we couldn't sleep over at friends' houses. I mean, just even the little things, like my mom wouldn't let us wear makeup, so I had to go to school and put it on there. She didn't want us to wear high heels, and everybody else was wearing high heels. And they didn't want us to date, and so I was always having to make up stories about where I was going.

I remember always just being restricted and not being able to do what I wanted to do, and I always thought, well, you know, "If I were American, I wouldn't have these problems." I remember, I think in sixth grade, my parents found this essay that I had written. [Laughing] It was about why I wished I was American and not Asian. My dad called the whole family, sat down, and said, "Okay now, I want you to be frank and tell us what you're not happy about." Later I found out that there are obviously parents who are really strict who aren't Asian, but at the time that's what I thought.

Now that I have more perspective on it, I see that there were real advantages to how my parents raised me. I'm glad I speak Taiwanese, I'm glad my parents pushed me to do well. American families swing way on the other side of the pendulum. I guess what we need is more of a balance.

For some of my women informants, the conflicts over tradition that surrounded the message of achievement were focused on the dynamics of gender in their families. That is, their memories of the message were accompanied by memories of conflict and resentment about traditional and unequal expectations and standards of treatment for males and females. Here it is important to emphasize that these recollections were of tremendous range and variation. Some of my informants, for example, spoke of growing up in families that were quite committed to treating sons and daughters in the same way, while others recalled being treated differently in ways that were quite minor and perhaps very subtle. For example, Wai Han, a Chinese American, remembered growing up with a sense that her place in the family was different from and less important than that of her brother, although she could not quite put her finger on why she had felt this way.

For Brenda, however, the differences were quite blatant. As a result, she grew up with a certain sense of anger, one that had, for a time at least, caused her to be rebellious and dismissive of her parents' counsel, including that of doing well at school. A Chinese American, Brenda grew up in central Los Angeles:

> I did not like being Chinese when I was growing up. The whole traditional Chinese gender role thing was very prominent in my family. There were different rules for the sons and daughters as far as curfew, dating, and housework. We [she and her sisters] did a lot more housework on a day-to-day level. And as we started getting older, I resented it. As far as education, we were all pushed to do well, but it was more serious for my brothers. And then there was the whole Chinese eldest son thing. My older brother was like Buddha or something—he got everything he wanted. I went through a rebellion, I guess a typical teenage thing. But for a while there, I was trying to get away from the whole Chinese thing. I slouched off at school. I was so angry about things.

These kinds of family tensions gave the parents' message of academic achievement an embattled flavor. But ultimately perhaps far more threatening to the message were the doubts of the second generation about the very efficacy of education as a racial strategy. In some ways, a conceptual tension within the message itself encouraged such doubts. As I have shown, the message to do well at school was offered as a racial strategy, a way of overcoming the obstacles of race in the United States. As part of the message, parents tended to speak of racial barriers as a chronic and inevitable part of American society—hence they and their children would always be outsiders by virtue of race. But the message of academic achievement required an affirmation that achievement was possible in spite of race. To put it simply, race in the message was both intractable and possible to overcome. As I have argued earlier, the message was essentially affirming of the American dream, but with its insistence on the intransigence of racial barriers, it also, in a sense, challenged it.

Accordingly, my informants often spoke of questioning the idea that success at school was the solution—the means to overcome racial barriers to socioeconomic achievement. For some informants, in particular those who grew up in socioeconomically disadvantaged neighborhoods, doubts about the message were encouraged by the often negative orientation of their local peers toward schooling. That is, reflecting the oppositional stance of the youth cultures of such communities, these informants had grown up with a peer message that contradicted the message conveyed by their parents: that school efforts were not worth it.

In such situations, parents often had to make a particular effort to effectively convey the message to do well at school. Wayne, a Chinese American in his early thirties, grew up in New York City where throughout his childhood his mother, a widow, had worked long hours as a seamstress and janitor to support her three children. She demanded that her children do well at school and stay away from the gangs and drugs of the neighborhood, reminding them constantly of the occupational rewards that education was sure to bring. Wayne both admired his mother's faith in education and saw it as naïve:

> My mother, bless her soul, is a little woman—but powerful. I'm in awe of her
> for raising three kids on her own. We were brought up strictly; study was a priority. I remembered being punished for not doing my homework. Some of the
> neighborhoods we lived in were pretty bad—crime, drugs, gangs. Mom would
> say, "You're not going to go near that, you're going to study. If you study, you can
> go to college and get a good job." She would say, "If you do well at school, even
> though you're Chinese, you can get a good job." She had a huge, almost naïve

faith in education. I respect it. Maybe because she had so little herself, she saw it as a great thing, an opportunity.

Like Wayne, many of my other informants assessed their parents' belief in education as naïve. Somewhat ironically, when the parents invoked their own struggles and hardships as a way of convincing their children that they needed to work extra hard, their argument could also, unintentionally, generate pessimism about the possibilities for overcoming the disadvantages of race through achievement in education. Cori, a Korean American whose account of her parents' emphasis on education we have already seen, spoke of witnessing discrimination toward her father and feeling disillusioned as a result. She had grown up in a small town in Illinois where her father had an ob/gyn medical practice:

My mom and dad were very upbeat, they were very positive about opportunities in America, at least for us. But I'm more cynical, I saw what my father went through. My father, you know, pretty much delivered half the town. Where we live, it's very rural, and there's not a lot of money, and my father is really my idea of what a doctor should be. He hasn't raised his rates since God knows how long because a lot of the people in our town are on welfare, a lot of Medicaid, a lot of uninsured. And being an ob/gyn, that's, you know, very touchy because of the malpractice issues. But my father would take anybody because they needed help.

Then a general practitioner moved in a couple of doors down, a white doctor. Even though my father had done all this great service for so long, there were people who just abandoned him and went to the general practitioner. And you know, it really hurt me, because all this time they'd been going to him. And my father offered really good care. My father went to all the conventions, learned how to do all these different laser surgeries that only, like, two percent of ob/gyns know. He was so proud that even in a small town he could give them the best service. I think it's, you know, a loyalty thing, where he felt betrayed. Even if he served these people for eight years, ten years, or whatever, they so easily just left to go to a white doctor.

Mindful that their own histories might foster just such disillusionment, some parents, as recalled by my informants, emphasized at the time that their situation, as immigrants, was fundamentally different from what their children would face. While they themselves perhaps had college degrees from their countries of origin, their children would have the more highly valued academic credentials from the United States. Growing up in the United States, the parents realized, the second generation would also not have the foreign accents and other immigrant markers that had impeded their own success here.

Cynthia, a Chinese American, as we have seen, grew up hearing her father's accounts of facing discrimination in the engineering company where he had worked as a young man. When he told his children that they could "expect to face racism," he drew on those experiences. But he also told them that without the burden of a foreign accent and with the legitimacy of American schooling, they would be better equipped to overcome the disadvantages of their racial status than he had been:

> Because of all the discrimination he felt, my father told us that it was difficult to go far here if you were Chinese. My dad is not the silent Asian type either. He's always talking, arguing. He's very smart. He reads a lot, not just in science and engineering, but everything. But he does have an accent, and I know that was the reason they gave for not promoting him; it had nothing to do with job performance. He used to tell us, You can expect to face racism. [Did he say anything about how to handle the racism?] He told us to work hard, study hard, make it as difficult as possible for people to get away with the racism. He did say that it would be different for us, since we didn't have the accent and we were educated here.

Similar ideas were described by Jamie, a Korean American, whose childhood family memories were deeply marked by family tensions and conflicts centered on her mother's inability to practice medicine in the United States, despite the fact that she had been a physician in Korea. When Jamie was growing up, her mother had returned to Korea to work for periods of time, leaving the family behind in the United States. "I wouldn't say my mother was bitter about not being able to practice here," she told me, "but she was frustrated. We were the bitter ones. It affected us in so many ways. My mother really pushed us in education. She said that it was going to be easier for us because we were growing up here. We were not going to have the language problem. And our college degrees would be from American universities, not Korean ones."

To summarize, then, among the family messages of race recounted by my informants was the message to do well at school, to compensate through academic success for the disadvantages of their racial identity. The message was a deeply contested one, intertwined as it was with the complexities and conflicts of family life, especially in relationships between parents and children. Not surprisingly, none of my informants was inclined to dismiss the message outright, not even those who identified themselves as having been mediocre or apathetic students. But while generally acknowledging and accepting of the idea that success at school would foster occupational success, my informants at the same time felt much skepticism about the scope of that promise. Education did perhaps compensate for race, but the question was how much—perhaps not as much as the message promised.

■ *Childhood Histories and the Identity Dilemmas of Race*

Childhood was the history, the past that helped to make and define the identity dilemmas of the second-generation Chinese and Korean Americans I interviewed. Their childhood histories were broadly organized around the narrative traditions, symbols, and language that have been part of popular understandings of the European immigrant experience. But they were not a simple echo of these understandings, and in fact they departed from them in significant ways. A sense of racialized exclusion from established conceptions of *American* was a common theme. Childhood marked the beginning of an awareness of the difficulties of being American, given an Asian racial identity.

Within the family, members of the second generation encountered messages of race—lessons and ideas about how to deal with the experience of racialized exclusion. Among these messages was the counsel to retain a sense of consciousness and pride in being Chinese or Korean when faced with racism. Echoing a theme that has emerged in other scholarship on new immigrant families, parents urged children to resist incorporation into U.S. racial schemes by maintaining a continued commitment to their ethnonational identifications. But my informants also spoke of growing up with a sharp awareness of the uncertainties of their Chinese or Korean membership. They could draw on the powerful symbol of blood to affirm this membership, but they still faced ongoing challenges to their authenticity as "true Chinese" or "true Koreans."

My informants also remembered being counseled by their family elders to do well at school, to compensate for the disadvantages of minority racial status through academic achievement. Underlying this emphasis on education, and especially the ability of parents to effectively convey it to children, is the middle-class background of many post-1965 Chinese and Korean immigrants. But also of relevance are some broad features of immigrant life in the United States.

The first of these features is a basic, if deeply contested, belief in the American dream—the idea that if one is willing to work for them, opportunities for success exist in the United States (see Hochschild 1995). As persons who have *chosen* to move and resettle in the United States, immigrants have a certain predisposition toward belief in the ideology of the American dream. Relatedly, immigrant adaptation strategies are often marked by a *generally* accommodationist approach to the dynamics of American economic and racial stratification. They are, to put it simply, more rather than less likely to emphasize accommodating to and working within the system as it is, rather than directly challenging it or disengaging from it.

Underlying this accommodationist approach is an ability to detach themselves from the negative appraisals received from members of the dominant society. Comparing "voluntary migrants" with "involuntary minorities," Ogbu and Gibson (1991) note that the former are more likely to react to experiences of discrimination by dismissing them and not internalizing them. As Waters (1999) notes in her study of West Indian immigrants, immigrants often have the resource of the "memory of a homeland to take the sting away" (144). To these observations I would also add the point that immigrants are, generally speaking, a politically and socially vulnerable group, due to their legal status and the ambiguity with which others may view their belonging in the United States. There are, then, a variety of ways in which the conditions of immigrant life can generate an accommodationist stance toward the dominant society.

An accommodationist stance was part of the message of education that my informants recalled in their memories of growing up. The message advocated a strategy not of distancing or turning away but rather of engaging with the institutions of the dominant society. The message also tended to privatize the dilemmas of racial exclusion; the appropriate response to racism was essentially a private one, of individual and familial efforts. Relatedly, the message was consonant with the ideology of the American dream—the idea that it is possible for anyone, however modest or disadvantaged their beginnings, to "make it" in the United States.

But if the message of education affirmed for my informants the ideology of the American dream, it also cast a shadow of doubt over it. Somewhat ironically, with its simultaneous affirmation of the inevitable realities of racial exclusion, the message contributed to the skepticism, the doubts of second-generation Chinese and Koreans about the accessibility of the American dream to those who are not white.

CHAPTER THREE

The Everyday Consequences of Being Asian: Ethnic Options and Ethnic Binds

> One of the first things we notice about people when we first meet them
> (along with their sex) is their race. We utilize race to provide clues about
> *who* a person is. . . . In US society, then, a kind of "racial etiquette"
> exists, a set of interpretative codes and racial meanings which operate in
> the interactions of daily life.   (Omi and Winant 1986, 62)

IN THE UNITED STATES, racial identities, ascribed on the basis of perceived physical characteristics, work as markers or signals in everyday social encounters. As Omi and Winant (1986) observe, *race* is a basic reference scheme, one that offers commonsense and taken-for-granted assumptions about the person encountered—what she is like, how he is likely to behave, and so forth. Race, then, is part of the social terrain of identity—the backdrop of opportunities and constraints against which individuals negotiate their affiliations with others and their understandings of themselves.

This chapter is about the everyday, routine, and expected experiences that accompany one's racial identification by others as Asian. Drawing in particular on my informants' accounts of informal social encounters with persons of non-Asian origin, I explore the ways in which they experienced the identity marker of "Asian race" in their daily interactions. Unlike some who today have come to be defined in an official sense as *Asian American,*[1] my informants have been widely and consistently labeled by others as *Asian* not just in bureaucratic forums but also in the course of informal social encounters.

For these second-generation Chinese and Korean Americans, the everyday consequences of "being Asian" were such as to contribute in important ways

---

1. Persons of South Asian origin, for example, while falling under the official rubric of *Asian American,* are not popularly labeled or seen as *Asian* (see Kibria 1998).

to their sense of being in an *ethnic bind*. In general, as they basically identified with the ethnic American model, they expected to have ethnic options;
that is, they expected that the dominant society would not impose an ethnic
identity on them. The dashing of this expectation produced an ethnic bind—
a powerful if ambivalent and at times uncertain sense that ethnic identity was
for them not a voluntary matter, at least not in the same way that it was for
such European-origin groups as Italian Americans and Irish Americans. Nonetheless, if the picture that emerges is one of constrained ethnic options, it is also
ultimately about achievement. Through contest and negotiation, my informants
worked to achieve some measure of ethnic options—to gain control over the
dynamics of their identity.

■ *The Issue of Race and Ethnic Options*

Given their relevance to the issue at hand, let us at this point briefly review the complex distinctions between race and ethnicity. *Race* is a system of
power, one that draws on physical differences to construct and give meaning to
racial boundaries and the hierarchy of which those boundaries are a part. Racial
boundaries reflect the relations of power from which they emerge. That is, the
dominant group plays a critical role in erecting racial boundaries, through the
definitions and conditions that it imposes on others. In contrast, *ethnic* boundaries involve the emergence of "perceived common ancestry, the perception of
a shared history of some sort, and shared symbols of peoplehood" (Cornell and
Hartmann 1998, 32). Critical, then, to the conceptual distinction between race
and ethnicity is the self-conscious sense of group membership that the latter
implies.[2]

Many scholars today argue that racial minorities in the United States do
not have the same kinds of choices with respect to ethnicity that whites enjoy
(Espiritu 1994; Tuan 1998; Waters 1990). The considerable latitude that whites
enjoy in this respect is highlighted by *symbolic ethnicity,* a particular quality of
ethnic attachment that has been observed among third- and fourth-generation
descendants of European immigrants. Symbolic ethnicity is a voluntary type of

---

2. As Cornell and Hartmann (1998) note, in reality, the boundaries of race and ethnicity overlap. For
example, racial groups are often ethnic groups, reflecting the processes of ethnicization that are set into
motion by the creation of racial boundaries.

ethnic attachment that is centered on ethnic symbols, is highly subjective and intermittent in character, and entails few if any sustained commitments (Gans 1979). As emphasized by Alba, it is characterized by a high degree of choice, in terms of how and even whether to identify with a particular ethnicity: "It is not only that individuals can choose to identify or not, and choose also precisely which elements in an ancestry mixture to emphasize and how important an ethnic identity should be for them, but they also have a wide latitude of choice when it comes to the manifestations or expressions of ethnicity" (1990, 303).

In sharp contrast to the symbolic ethnicity of white ethnics, for racial minorities racial identity powerfully marks and constrains the process of defining their ethnic affiliations. This is vividly highlighted by the identity experiences of black Americans. Reflecting the operation of the "one-drop rule," or the rule of hypodescent, Americans with any African ancestry at all tend to have only the option of a black identity (Davis 1991). The option of choosing which particular element of their multiple ancestries to emphasize is not easily accessible to them. The ability of the black racial label to overpower other ethnic identities is highlighted by the experiences of black immigrants from the Caribbean, who often find their specific ethnonational identities (such as Haitian) to be unacknowledged and unaccepted during interactions outside their ethnic community (Waters 1994). Ethnic options are also constrained by the forces of discrimination in the dominant society—for example, in the area of housing—which work to solidify the boundaries of the black community and limit the ability of individuals to move outside of it. As a result of these restrictions, those who are labeled *black* are relatively constrained in their ability to organize and express their ethnicity in ways of their own choosing.

The study of Asian Americans offers an opportunity to expand our understanding of the dynamics of race and ethnic options. As nonwhites, Asian Americans' experiences are set apart from those of members of the dominant racial group. At the same time, their race and ethnic options are shaped by their distinctive history and location in the United States. Among other things, Asian Americans collectively bring to the puzzle of race and the new immigration (see Chapter 1) the phenomenon of prominent ethnonational identities. Not only do most Asian Americans tend to identify themselves as Japanese American, Vietnamese American, and so forth, but however imperfectly, unevenly, and uncertainly, American society itself to some extent recognizes that Asian Americans are divided along ethnonational lines. For example, the fact that Japan and

China are different countries is not an unfamiliar idea in American life. As we will see, this general recognition of ethnonational divisions among Asian Americans was important for my second-generation Chinese and Korean American informants in their negotiation of their ethnic options.

■ The Production of "Sameness": The Racialization of Ethnicity

"When I watched *M*A*S*H,* I was often enraged by a supposedly Korean person wearing a Vietnamese-style hat wandering around in a Japanese-looking village mumbling nonsensical syllables that were supposed to be Korean," says Los Angeles attorney T. S. Chung, a Korean American. "Americans may not think all this amounts to much. But let me ask this question: How would you feel if a Korean TV producer portrayed an American as a Mexican in a Canadian village mumbling sounds in German or French?" (Kang 1993).

For nonwhites in the United States, their racial identifications are often understood by others as ethnic identifications. In other words, Americans often assume that a person's "race" is not simply a category of reference that has only limited meaning to her or him, but rather a signifier of meaningful membership in a community of shared ancestry, history, and culture. Accordingly, my informants remarked that their "looking Asian" could work for others as a cue or sign of their *pan-Asian ethnic identity,* or membership in a generalized Asian ethnic community. They responded to this assumption in a variety of ways, depending on their assessment of the situation at hand. But it was invariably a matter of complaint, referred to as a "mistake" made by others and a source of some frustration. Not surprisingly, their efforts to correct the mistake involved the assertion of their Chinese or Korean ethnic identity—the claim of "I'm *Chinese*" or "I'm *Korean.*"

Underlying the assumption of pan-Asian ethnicity is the *racialization of ethnicity,* or the processes by which various elements of an ethnic identity, such as the labels, practices, and symbols associated with it, acquire racial meaning and form. Through these processes, the distinctiveness of specific ethnic identities such as Chinese or Korean is downplayed and dismissed.

For my second-generation Chinese and Korean American informants, the racialization of their ethnicity was, for the most part, a taken-for-granted part of their lives. But it sometimes revealed itself in particularly vivid ways. Cori, for example, described a particular episode from her childhood that had come to symbolize for her the significance of an Asian racial identity and how it could overpower her ethnic identity in the eyes of others. Cori was the Korean American in her late twenties who grew up in a small, largely white, working-class town in Illinois where her father practiced medicine:

> In my town they had no clue about different cultures or anything like that. They asked my family to pose for a picture in the town paper wearing native garb, and of course our family obliged. It turns out that the occasion was Chinese New Year. We were on the front page of the small daily newspaper next to recipes of egg rolls and a little article about how it was Chinese New Year. We were their token Oriental family. Chinese, Korean, it was all the same.

Cori noted that the incident might have been a case of a simple error, of mistakenly supposing her family to be of Chinese rather than Korean origin. But this explanation was less than convincing to her because she and her family were not strangers but long-term residents of the town, well known to most in the community. In fact, as the only obstetrician in the area who had for several years delivered most of the town's babies, Cori's father was quite a prominent figure. All of this made her feel that the townspeople saw *Chinese* as synonymous with a generic Asian identity. The specifically Korean origin of Cori's family, whether their neighbors knew about it or not, were largely irrelevant. They were Asian in a generic sense, and so profiling them in the paper as Chinese was not inappropriate.

Among the processes that surround and sustain the assumption of pan-Asian ethnicity is the *racialization of ethnic labels,* whereby terms that refer to specific ethnonational groups acquire racial meaning and form. For example, Cori's account suggests that the townspeople saw and understood *Korean* and *Chinese* in synonymous and interchangeable ways, as generalized references to those who were racially Asian. In general, it is not uncommon for racial minorities to experience the racialization of designations that have meaning for them in ethnic terms. For example, in certain parts of the United States, *Mexican* is sometimes used as a general term to refer to all persons of Latin American descent rather than specifically persons from Mexico. Such usage works not only to affirm a generic racial identity for those involved but also to effect a certain transformation in the meaning of these terms. *Chinese* and *Japanese,* for example, come to signify a generic Asian identity rather than a specific ethnonational one. In the face of homogenizing racial processes, distinctions of nationality and ethnicity become irrelevant.

Virtually of all my informants had, at one time or another, been called *chink* or *Jap.* By their very nature as racial slurs, these names are also generalized Asian designations; they are used against all Asians, regardless of ethnicity, as expressions of hostility, and those who use them are for the most part unconcerned about making distinctions between Asians. Eugene, a Korean American in his mid-twenties, spoke at some length about his experiences of these slurs and how they reflected the fact that, in the eyes of "Americans," Asians were all "the same." Like many of my informants, he made it a point to distinguish experiences of hostility from those involving honest mistakes or genuine confusion about his ethnic origins. In the latter type of situation, he was more inclined to correct the person by letting him or her know that he was actually of Korean origin:

> Americans don't see the differences between Asians; to them, we're all just a big yellow blob. When I think of all the times I've been called "Jap" or "chink." I remember once when I was little, a kid called me "chink," and I told him, "I'm Korean." I was stupid, as if he cared, as if it made a difference to him. I haven't been called names recently, but there are times when I've been taken for Japanese or something. [What do you do? Do you set them straight?] It depends of course. If someone's calling you names, they don't care. Korean, Japanese, what's the difference to them. If I feel that there's an honest mistake going on, I will try and explain that I'm Korean. It depends on whether the person wants to know, to learn more.

Closely intertwined with the racialization of ethnic labels is what may be called the *racialization of ethnic traditions,* the processes whereby cultural symbols and practices associated with a particular ethnic group become incorporated into a racialized and imagined cultural tradition. Thus, as in the incident that Cori described, egg rolls and Chinese New Year come to be seen not as specific Chinese practices but as generic Asian ones. Hayano (1981) has noted that mass culture and the consumption industries, inclined as they are toward a certain type of homogenization, play an important role in this racialization of ethnic traditions. The production of "Asian culture" in the popular media, he notes, can have a bizarre result: a mishmash of discrete and unrelated aspects of different cultural traditions strung together. "What is served to the American public by the popular mass media," he observes, "is a kind of everyman's Oriental, where filial piety, sukiyaki, Confucianism, kung fu, flower arrangement, pigtails and kimonos are representative of an all-purpose Asian" (170).

For my informants, the racialization of ethnic culture gained particular visibility in situations in which they were thought to have knowledge of Asian cultural practices, perhaps imagined generic ones or perhaps those specifically associated with societies other than that of their parents. Karen, a Chinese American, recounted that her largely white and male work group had assumed that she was acquainted with Japanese cultural norms. Japanese culture, as part of a generalized Asian culture, was something that Karen had to know about since she was Asian; it was something with which she was naturally connected:

> At work once we were negotiating a deal with a Japanese company. At a meeting of the engineering group, people looked at me and said, "Hey Karen, tell us how we should deal with Japanese so that we get what we want." I was like, for God's sake, get a consultant or someone who knows about these things, but don't look at me. I told them, "You guys, I'm Chinese. Plus I was born and raised here." But it was amazing, some of them didn't hear me. The manager said to me, "Okay, but Karen, you have to admit that you probably have a better sense of the way Japanese culture works than we do." I really like the manager, he's a sweet guy, but I wanted to strangle him.

Mi Ra, a Korean American, also recalled incidents in which others assumed that she had knowledge of an Asian culture with which she actually had no particular connection. Many of these incidents had occurred during a time in college when she had briefly worked as a waitress in a Thai restaurant. Customers frequently assumed, because she was working in a Thai restaurant, that she herself must be Thai. But this assumption also had a racialized dimension when customers refused to revise it despite her best efforts, thus displaying an unwillingness to recognize distinctions among Asians:

> When I was working at the restaurant, the customers thought that I was of course Thai. They asked me questions about Thailand, and I would have to explain that I was Korean. That was *very* surprising to them. I remember there were some Thai paintings, embroidery pieces on the wall. And a table of customers asked me to explain what the story there was, what it was about. It was obviously a Thai reli-

gious myth. And I said I didn't know, I would find someone who did. They were almost disbelieving. And I remember this one guy stupidly said to me, "Korean and Thai art and literature are the same or very similar." I wouldn't say his attitude was typical. But what bothers me is when people won't listen to you. You can tell them that you're *Korean* till you're blue in the face, but they couldn't care less. It's all the same to them.

Such incidents were particularly memorable to my informants because of the persistent quality of the assumptions being made—the dogged unwillingness of others to recognize an ethnonational identity even when informed of it. While these kinds of incidents did not seem to be unusual, my informants' efforts to challenge assumptions of their pan-Asian ethnicity were in fact often successful. That is, others were willing to accept or at least not overtly challenge their efforts to correct them, to point out that they were Korean or Chinese rather than Asian. Sung, a Korean American, had such an experience:

Of course I've been mistaken for other things: Oriental, Asian, Japanese, Chinese, even Filipino when I was out in the Midwest. Is it a big deal? Not usually. I usually make it a point to say, "No, I'm Korean." And unless we're talking about real assholes, people will generally go along with what you tell them. I mean, what are they going to say—"Oh no, you're not Korean, it doesn't matter to us that you're Korean." That might be what their mentality is, but they're not going to express it.

There was another type of situation, as well, in which the racialization of ethnic tradition could become visible to my informants. These were encounters in which others read or interpreted Chinese or Korean symbols or practices as "Asian." Michelle, a Korean American, described one such encounter, which was particularly memorable and dramatic because the person involved apparently refused to acknowledge that she had made a mistake:

My daughter [in fourth grade] has been learning traditional Korean dance at our church. She danced at a talent show in school. Afterward, the teacher came up and congratulated me. She said how nice it was that Susan was learning "Asian dance." Asian dance? What's that? I looked at her and said, "It's traditional *Korean* dance." Her attitude was basically: Yeah, whatever. It's very annoying when people won't accept who you are. It's like they won't take your word for it.

Michelle's account highlights an important way in which an Asian racial identity can constrain individuals' ability to display or engage in cultural symbols and practices and have them be accepted and defined by others in ways of their own choosing. Much as Michelle found it difficult to convince the teacher that her daughter was performing Korean dance, other informants found that Korean or Chinese traditions ran the risk of being interpreted by others as "Asian" in a generic sense. Explaining to non-Asians that such traditions were actually Chinese or Korean could sometimes require some active effort on their part; that non-Asians would immediately accept it was not something that they could simply take for granted.

Renee, a Chinese American, was quite conscious of the effort she had to make in order to have others recognize various Chinese practices as Chinese rather than as generically Asian. In light of her newfound interest—in fact, her "obsession," as she put it—with "discovering" her Chinese roots, this recognition was particularly important for her:

> When you ask me how I feel about being called Asian, I have to say that it depends. It doesn't bother me a lot. But I don't like it sometimes. When I talk about Chinese food or something like feng shui—everyone's talking about that now, I don't like it when people call it Asian. What's important to me is *Chinese* culture, *Chinese* heritage. I think Americans can't tell the difference between Asians, I mean some of them can't be bothered with it. With them you have to hammer it in, it's Chinese, Chinese, you idiot.

■ Intra-Asian Affinity, Accountability, and Strategies of Disidentification

Embedded in the assumption of pan-Asian ethnicity is another assumption: pan-Asian affinity. In other words, based on an assumed shared membership in an Asian ethnic community, Asians themselves are perceived as likely to connect or get along with one another in special ways. Among my informants, resentment of this idea of intra-Asian affinity was widespread, often co-existing, however, with a sense that persons of Asian origin did indeed share something special.

For Jane as for many others, what was particularly troubling about the assumption that "Asians get along" was the fact that it was imposed by non-Asians. A Chinese American in her early thirties, Jane was highly involved in Asian

American political groups and organizations. During the time of our interview, she was working as an academic counselor in a university in California, where she specialized in counseling Asian American students. Her large and diverse circle of friends included many Asian Americans of varied national backgrounds. Yet when confronted with the idea that persons of Asian origin, regardless of ethnicity, naturally get along with each other, she felt frustrated. She saw it as detracting from her ability to choose and define her bonds with other Asian Americans on her own terms:

> I remember in college they put me in a room with a Japanese American girl. On the housing form they had asked me about personality, sleeping habits, things like that. This girl and I had absolutely nothing in common; I was a night owl and she was a morning person. She was into classical music and I was into funk and jazz. It was really obvious that they put us together because we were Asian. The fact that she was Japanese and I was Chinese American meant nothing to them. There were only Caucasian girls in the suite, so we were the two Asian girls in one room. To me, this is a kind of racism, assuming that I had something in common with her. Asians do share things, but that's up to us, it's not for others to tell us when we should get along. [If the roommate had been Chinese American, would you have felt differently?] I still might not have wanted to room with her, but at least the common background would have been a real thing.

Joan, a Chinese American in her late twenties, had grown up in a small town in a rural part of New Jersey. Echoing incidents described by many others, Joan recounted that in high school, friends had tried to fix her up on a date with a Japanese American student. Part of her frustration at the time, she recalled, stemmed from the fact that the student seemed to conform to negative stereotypes of Asian men and was thus not someone whom she wished to date. But she also recognized that a racialized assumption was at work in her friends. The bitter history of Japan-China relations, so prominent in her parents' consciousness, was not part of the calculations of her friends, who saw only similarity:

> In high school my friends tried to fix me up with this Japanese guy all the time. I thought, "Why are they doing that? Just because he's Asian?" I was thinking, "Oh my God! This guy is like a geek! How can they do that to me?" [Didn't you say something?] Yeah, I did. I mean, I said things like, "Oh God, not him!" It became a standing joke. No one, and to some extent I would include myself in this,

was exactly conscious of what was going on. It was a kind of racial stereotyping: "Oh, you're Asian, so that means you have to go out with an Asian." And he was Japanese, so it was not like we were culturally coming from the same place. My parents would have freaked to hear of me with a Japanese guy. I mean, anything but that! But my friends were like, "Oh, it all makes sense, your families will be so happy."

My informants' frustration about the idea of intra-Asian affinity was magnified whenever they encountered the related notion of *intra-Asian accountability:* the idea that all persons of Asian descent, regardless of their specific ethnonational origins, can be held accountable or to blame for all things Asian, since they are all, in some fundamental sense, the same: fellow ethnics. Not surprisingly, being held accountable as Asian could be extremely powerful in generating consciousness of the significance of race and in particular of an Asian racial identity.

The issue of hate crimes against Asians, as symbolized by the Vincent Chin case, has accordingly been an important one for the development of the Asian American movement, a spur to solidarity among Asian Americans. Vincent Chin was a Chinese American who was beaten to death with a baseball bat by white auto workers in Detroit in 1982. The auto workers were angry at the Japanese, blaming them for the demise of the U.S. car industry. Vincent Chin's attackers did not care about any distinctions between Japanese and Chinese; for them, Vincent Chin was simply an Asian. Recognizing the ethnically indiscriminate nature of the attack, various Asian-origin communities banded together to protest the extraordinarily light sentences (a fine of $3,780 each and probation) meted out to the perpetrators of the crime.

For second-generation Chinese and Korean Americans, then, an important aspect of the marker of "Asian race" is a generalized Asian culpability, by which one may be held responsible for the alleged sins of a group with which one perhaps has little or no identification. It was not uncommon for my informants to be accused by strangers in streets and other public spaces for the problems supposedly caused by various Asian groups. While the specifics of the accusations varied, the theme of "Asian invasion," of Asians as a foreign presence threatening to somehow take over the United States, was a common one.

We see this in the account of Wai Han, a Chinese American, of an incident that took place in Orange County, south of Los Angeles. In recent decades, with the influx of immigrants from Vietnam, this largely white, upper-middle-class southern California enclave has become a prominent center of Vietnamese American settlement. Orange County is now home to "Little Saigon," a bustling commercial district that is a national hub of Vietnamese American life. One day Wai Han was in a crowded supermarket when she accidentally bumped her grocery cart into that of an elderly white woman. The woman launched into a torrent of accusations, to which Wai Han at first responded with complete incomprehension:

> I bumped into her cart when I was trying to get by her. I think funnily enough I was in the ethnic foods section. She raised her cane at me and said we were taking over the country. All we foreign types did was come over to America and take advantage of American kindness by stealing welfare money. We weren't grateful to America for helping out in our war. Oh no, no—instead we were hell-bent on destroying America. When she started saying these things, I was thinking, "What is she talking about? And why is she saying them to me?" Then when I kind of figured it out, I thought, "What do I have to do with these things?" Vietnamese, Chinese, it's all the same to them.

Because of the potential for violence in such situations and for other reasons as well, my informants responded to them in many different ways, ranging from simply ignoring the accusations to aggressively challenging them. At times they engaged in a strategy of disidentification—using various clues or signals to distance themselves from the perceived "problem group." In *Stigma,* Goffman (1963) described processes of disidentification from stigmatized identities, involving the careful control of information about the self presented to outsiders. Central to these processes are "disidentifiers," which he describes as "sign[s] that tend—in fact or hope—to break up an otherwise coherent picture . . . in a positive direction desired by the actor" (44). In an analysis of intraethnic Asian disidentification (i.e. the distancing of members of one Asian ethnic group from another), Hayano notes that the disidentifiers or signs used by Asian Americans today (in contrast to the past) tend to be of a verbal nature, involving disclaimers, jokes, and so forth:

> Historically, differences between the Japanese and Chinese were marked by what could be classified as stigma symbols: hair styles, clothing, foreign accents, food, residence, and religion. Because these obvious symbols of ethnic identity are not

as pertinent today, this has laid the groundwork for more ethnic confusion and the greater use of disidentifiers. But other than displaying placards (which were used in the past), disidentifiers today are more verbal than visual. When social situations arise as to require an explanation, ethnic disidentification among Japanese-Americans takes place mainly through disavowals, flat denials, voicing stereotypes of other Asians, apologizing with the "we-all-look-alike" jokes, or in maintaining an ignorance, not being "wise" about things Chinese (1981, 165–66).

During the 1980s and much of the 1990s, Americans popularly identified Japan as an economic threat—a formidable economic force and an aggressive competitor to the United States. Like many others I interviewed, Eugene, a Korean American, was particularly bothered by the experience of being associated with and blamed for the activities of Japan. He had grown up with vivid and horrific stories of the atrocities committed by the Japanese in Korea in the first half of the twentieth century. Now, whenever he found himself implicated in anti-Japanese sentiment, his response was to vigorously disidentify. Not only did he tell others of his Korean identity, he tried to educate them about the bitter history between Japan and Korea:

> You know, what bothers me the most is being seen as Japanese. It freaks me out. Someone makes a negative comment about the Japanese for their economic policies, and they look at me to see if I'm offended. [What do you do when that happens?] I talk, I don't just stand there and take it like some silent Asian. I say, "I'm Korean, I'm *Korean*. And don't you know that Koreans despise the Japanese for the way we were treated by them?"

Simon, a Chinese American, also expressed frustration at being implicated with the Japanese. Like Eugene, he made it a point at times to disidentify by letting others know of his Chinese origins and the deep-seated divisions between Japan and China. But he also expressed ambivalence and uncertainty about how he should respond. He was deeply aware of the racialized character of the anti-Japanese sentiment that he encountered:

> You know, there's been a lot of anti-Japanese feeling because of their involvement in the American economy. Our neighbors have talked about it, they blow off steam, and then they look at me, like I'm involved. Sometimes I make it a point to say I'm Chinese. [They don't know?] Well, they do and they don't. I can relate to some of what they say. But some of it is just plain Japan-bashing. It's

about jealousy: "Those goddamn gooks are doing better than us—how can that be?" And when they do that, they start seeing all Asians in those terms. So where does that leave me? Does that mean I should defend the Japanese, just because people think I'm one of them? Do I have anything in common with Japanese? The fact of the matter is that simply because of the way I look, I'm affected by these things.

Meg, a Chinese American, had worked for a summer as a youth counselor in a summer school program in a largely African American neighborhood in Los Angeles, an area that also had a number of Korean immigrant small businesses. Korean-black relations, which were already tense in general, had been especially so in the aftermath of the killing of Latasha Harlins, a 15-year-old African American, by a Korean immigrant grocer, Soon Ja Du. In this environment, in anticipation of what could happen, Meg affirmed her Chinese origins and used a preemptive strategy of disidentifying from a Korean identity:

> It was after the Latasha Harlins case. It was before the riots, but there were already a lot of bad feelings against the Koreans. There were some problems, some Korean businesses had been attacked. My mother and sister thought I was insane to go into that area as an Asian. Nobody is going to stop and ask you for an ID to check if you're Korean or Chinese. But the media exaggerates, I think it doesn't give enough credit to the black community. I enjoyed it for the most part, and I learned a lot. [You didn't feel hostility because you're Asian?] Yes, but I think being Chinese did make a difference. I think I did make an effort to talk about being Chinese, more than normal. Especially at the beginning.

Such strategies of disidentification highlight the importance of ethnonational identity for the second generation in maneuvering around the racial terrain of identity that they faced. In general, the effectiveness of disidentification as a strategy depends on the individual's ability to convey the idea that a hostile person's appropriate focus of interest or animosity is properly targeted elsewhere, on a different collectivity, of which one is not a part. The acts of disidentification that I have described here were made possible and at least to a certain extent were effective because of the ethnonational identities of my informants and their understood significance, however uncertain, both for themselves and for others.

But these accounts also reveal that highlighting one's ethnonational identity entails effort. In the face of an assumption of racialized homogeneity, my informants had to make a constant effort to ensure that the significance of their ethnonational identity was not lost on others. For them, being able to choose one's ethnic definition required some work. Furthermore, as highlighted by the tragedy of Vincent Chin, the results of such work were fundamentally uncertain. That is, regardless of how hard one tried, there would still inevitably be times and situations in which one was "just another Asian."

■ *The Achievement of "Americanness"*

In the spring of 1995, Americans seemed mesmerized by the televised trial of the athlete celebrity O. J. Simpson, who was accused of the double murder of his ex-wife and another man. Lance Ito, a Japanese American, was the presiding judge in the trial. In the midst of the trial, Senator Alfonse D'Amato of New York appeared on a radio talk show in which he did a mocking imitation of the judge (whom he referred to as "little Ito") in a circa–1940s Hollywood Japanese accent, complete with broken English. Many Asian Americans expressed dismay at the incident. Ito, a third-generation Japanese American, was born and raised in the United States and spoke English in what can only be described as a standard American accent. But for D'Amato, the most obvious and preferred aspect of Ito's persona to be ridiculed was his presumed foreignness. Ito's Asian racial identity was enough to irrevocably mark him with a foreign accent and demeanor.

As suggested by the D'Amato incident, prominent among the racial meanings that surround Asians in the United States is the image of the foreigner, or unassimilable alien—a presence that is fundamentally and unalterably outside of, if not diametrically opposite to, what is American (Lowe 1996; Hsu 1996). My informants' accounts shed light on the everyday character and consequences of foreignness—the routine and expected ways in which being seen as foreign marked daily interactions. Among these was the seemingly innocuous and frequently heard question, "Where are you from?" While this question may be intended as an inquiry about one's regional origin in the United States (e.g. "Are you from southern California?"), when asked of Asians it is often implicitly understood as a question about nationality and origins. In fact, informants told me that if they answered the question in local terms (say, "I'm from Boston"), it could be followed by the query of "Yes, but where are you *really* from?" The frequency of these questions varied little between the experiences of my California and Massachusetts informants, but they had a more persistent quality in the latter. That is, perhaps because of the larger and more visible presence of Asian Americans in California, both in the past and today, Californians may have been more able to easily recognize that the Asian-origin person facing them was from the United States, while residents of Massachusetts may have been, relatively speaking, less willing or able to revise their assumption that he or she was not.

My informants understood and responded to the query "Where are you from?" in varied ways, depending on their assessment of the motivation of the questioner. In some situations they interpreted the question as innocuous or even positive, as an effort on the part of the questioner to avoid making generalizations about Asians and to establish a specific ethnic identity for the individual involved. But at other times, when the question seemed devoid of such intent, my informants interpreted it simply as an expression of the assumption that all persons of Asian origin are foreigners and are not American.

When faced with the "where are you from" question, Hea Ran, a Korean American, vigorously worked to educate questioners about the errors of their thinking, even though, as she acknowledged, it placed her at risk of being seen as a bothersome person:

> I think it's really important for people to realize that we're not foreigners. That's a really big misconception because I get the question all the time: "Where are you from?" And it hurts me, it offends me. People probably think I'm nitpicking and paranoid, but lately I say, "Excuse me, I think what you mean is 'What is your ethnicity.' As far as my nationality, I'm a U.S. citizen. As far as my ethnicity, I'm a Korean American."

While Hea Ran responded by challenging the questioner's underlying assumption, others spoke of playing with it. In her work on third-generation Chinese and Japanese Americans, Tuan (1998) has noted a similar response, of "playing the ethnic game," when faced with the "where are you from" question. For example, Jane, a Chinese American, dealt with queries about her origins by playing with them: "I kind of laugh it off now, this whole business of where are you from. I mean, what's the point of being sensitive? If I'm asked, 'Where are you from?', I say L.A. 'Where are you really from?' South Pas[adena]. 'Oh yeah?'

Yeah, the corner of Huntington and Figueroa. I refuse to give in, I just go on and on."

Jane's responses are an example of what may be called *racial identity play*,[3] a term that I use to refer to the self-conscious manipulation, by those on whom it is imposed, of the marker of race and the assumptions and meanings about identity that that marker signals. Depending on the situation, the signaled notions of identity may be overtly negated, affirmed, or some combination of both. But the hallmark of racial identity play is that the individual who is being labeled uses or manipulates the labels in order to essentially turn the tables on the labelers. Through racial identity play, then, he or she gains a measure of control and perhaps advantage over the assumptions that others are making about her or him, while all the time maintaining an understanding of their socially constructed character. The work of Shrage (1996) suggests that what I have described as racial identity play may have an educative function. That is, depending on the particular course that it takes, it may expose the marker of race as well as the assumptions that surround it. As Shrage notes, such acts can de-essentialize racial and ethnic categories and the norms and ideologies that are a part of them:

> [P]articular systems of race and ethnicity in the United States naturalize themselves by setting up certain illusions of continuity between skin pigment, genealogy, race, ethnicity, character, behavior, ability, aspirations, dispositions, and so on. How might these illusions be interrupted so that we might glimpse how blacks and whites, Jews and Gentiles, are made by the operation of racial and ethnic norms, rather than born naturally possessing their notorious racial and ethnic traits? If these illusions of continuity are created, in part, by conforming to socially conventional interpretations of skin pigment and genealogy, then these illusions might be destroyed by attempts at transgressive interpretations of these facts. (1996, 196)

Particularly powerful in making visible to my informants their presumed foreignness in the eyes of others were situations in which they were assumed to lack knowledge of mainstream American culture. Simon, a Chinese American,

---

3. My use of the "play" concept is inspired by the work of Thorne (1993) on children and gender. She uses the metaphor of play to capture the active and ongoing character of the social construction of gender, a process in which children are active participants and not just subjects. Like Thorne, I caution against the connotations of triviality that are part of the word *play*, given the often extremely serious and nontrivial consequences of the racialized assumptions that undergird racial identity play.

had an encounter with a stranger who immediately mistook him for someone who did not speak English. He was shaken by the mistake, which served as an unwelcome reminder that he could not escape his minority identity:

> I'm not usually very conscious of being Chinese. When I am conscious, it's because I've been reminded of it. But like the other day I was in a gas station, and this lady was looking for directions. She came up to me and said, "Do you speak English?" I was really kind of surprised, taken aback—it actually took me a minute to figure out what she was talking about. And I felt like, What the hell is she talking about? I can barely say a few words of Chinese.

Not surprisingly, my informants were highly aware of the use of disidentifiers to neutralize or at least deflect the assumption of foreignness. Disidentifiers can involve many different kinds of symbols, such as language, dress, demeanor, and social associations (that is, the identity of the person[s] with whom one is seen or associated). The importance of one or another of these disidentifiers will vary, depending on the particular identity and the stigmatized meanings from which one is disidentifying. For example, research on the experiences of middle-class black Americans suggests that dress is an important disidentifier of associations with the urban underclass, which is among the meanings that surround a black racial identity in the United States today. In this connection, Cose (1993) notes that "prudence dictates dressing up whenever you are likely to encounter strangers (including clerks, cops and doormen) who can make your life miserable by mistaking you for a tramp, a slut, or a crook" (55–56).

The accounts of my informants suggest that language is also an important disidentifier of foreignness. During some encounters with strangers, they could immediately deflect their presumed foreignness by speaking fluent and unaccented English. Yet at the same time, the ability to speak American English was not as definitive a marker of a nonforeign identity as one might expect it to be. For my informants, it was not at all uncommon for them to receive compliments on how well they spoke English. Underlying such compliments is the idea that the person is not a native speaker; she or he has deliberately learned the language rather than naturally picked it up. For my informants, then, these compliments only highlighted the presumption of their foreignness; the reality of their English-language skills collided with the alien connotations of their Asian racial identity.

A situation recounted by James, a Chinese American, highlights the signifi-

cance of language as a marker as well as the presumed disjuncture between looking Asian and speaking American English, itself a reflection of the assumption
of foreignness:

> I don't think I have any kind of Chinese accent. In fact, I got chosen by the
> military to make a voice message. They were looking for a straight nonaccented
> male voice, and I did a voice audition for them. They didn't see any of the candi-
> dates, and they chose me. They still have never met me. The guy I was working
> with said, "Here's a bunch of midwestern white guys, probably looking for the
> white authoritative male. If they met you, they'd fall over when they saw you were
> Chinese."

In the first few minutes of my interview with him, Paul, a Chinese American, described himself as a chameleon and a "shape shifter"—like one of the
alien characters on the science fiction show *Star Trek: Deep Space Nine*. A highly
successful marketing executive in a large Los Angeles entertainment corporation, Paul had, during his adolescence, been through many different stages. He
described a "white surfer dude stage," a "cool black stage," a "New York Jewish stage," and an "artsy moody European continental stage." During each of
these stages he had successfully manipulated his presentation of self to create a
persona that was in keeping with the identity that he was trying to cultivate.

Paul's acute interest and experience in cultivating different images made him
especially conscious and articulate about disidentifiers. He first began to consciously use them in high school, when he wanted to establish himself as American and not Asian. While he saw his family background as culturally "very
American," among peers at school, this identity was something that had to be
purposefully achieved. Paul was, in retrospect, critical of these past efforts, which
he now saw as a futile attempt to deny his Asian identity:

> I wanted to be an American like everyone else. And the thing of it is that I was
> actually completely American. At home we had cornflakes and spaghetti and
> watched *The Brady Bunch*. Because you're Asian, everyone assumes that you're dif-
> ferent. So I think it was in junior high that I concentrated on fitting in. I dressed
> cool, I learned how to dance, I became the class clown. There were a few Japanese
> and Chinese in my school, and I looked really carefully to see how they would
> act, and then I would do exactly the opposite. And it worked! I was one of the
> most popular kids in school. I realized then that I was really good at projecting

different identities. I could copy hand gestures, accents, you name it, down to the smallest detail. I was young and stupid. You can't deny your Asian heritage.

Opinions vary as to whether Asian Americans should cultivate such disidentifiers of foreignness, as well as the effectiveness of the strategy of using them. Across these opinions, however, cuts an awareness that the achievement and acceptance of an American identity requires constant vigilance and work. David, a Korean American, was somewhat extreme in his feeling that when the identity markers of language, dress, and demeanor were used correctly, they could virtually wipe away the assumption of Asian foreignness. But he also recognized that for persons of Asian origin, the achievement of being seen as like "any other American" was not an easy matter, certainly in comparison to the experience of whites:

People tell me that I'm *the* most Americanized Korean they've ever met. [How do you feel about that?] Hey, it doesn't bother me. I've never felt that I've been discriminated against for being Korean. I mean, I talk like an American; I don't have broken English. I act like everybody else. In terms of how I walk and talk and act, you can't tell me apart from any white on the street. That helps me to be accepted. Granted, I think it's harder for me as Asian than for, say, someone who's white who doesn't have to worry about these things at all.

Michelle, a Korean American, also spoke of how it was important to "walk and talk like an American" in order to be accepted in the dominant society. But unlike David, she saw these disidentifying strategies as effective only to a point; they could not completely erase the significance of an Asian racial identity. Her words also highlight that being accepted as American was understood to be part of a process of upward socioeconomic mobility. That is, for second-generation Chinese and Korean immigrants, the task of disidentification from "foreignness" had important implications for socioeconomic status:

My husband [who is Korean American] and I feel like it's important to give the kids strong Korean roots. But we also want them to have all the advantages, some of which we didn't have growing up in an immigrant family. There are certain things about the American culture, little things, that you don't pick up so well if you grow up with parents who are from another place. Like how to dress in a way that's completely appropriate, how to behave in a completely appropriate way in different kinds of social situations. I remember going to a friend's house in high school—she was white and from this very wealthy family. I was uncomfortable, I didn't know how to behave. I remember thinking, "So this is the way white people live."

So if you know all the little almost invisible things about American culture, you're likely to have an easier time. You're accepted better. At the same time, I want my kids to know that no matter what they do, there are places and times where they're just not going to be accepted because of their skin and eyes and the way they look. Because of that they shouldn't try too hard.

■ *Immigrants as Mirrors of "Foreignness"*

These accounts call our attention to the ways in which for the second generation, being seen as American required constant work; this identity was for them achieved and provisional rather than taken for granted. In speaking of this work, my informants sometimes observed that immigrants of Asian or Chinese/Korean origin could complicate it for them. Their attitudes and feelings, it should be emphasized, were complex and multidimensional. Not surprisingly, they sometimes expressed a deep sense of empathy and identification with immigrants. But such persons could also become a group from which to establish distance and perhaps even to blame, when the immigrants seemed to threaten their achievement of "Americanness," contributing to and reinforcing, as they did, the image of Asians as foreigners.

The resentment that U.S.-born Chinese sometimes feel toward Chinese immigrants is the focus of the play *FOB* (1990) by the Chinese American playwright David Henry Hwang. The acronyms *FOB* (fresh off the boat) and *ABC* (American-born Chinese) are terms that Chinese Americans use widely to refer to immigrants and U.S.-born Chinese, respectively. At the center of Hwang's play is the loathing that the U.S.-born Dale feels toward the immigrant Steve. For Dale, Steve acts as a mirror, reflecting back an image of how others see him—as "Oriental" and "foreign"—rather than how he sees himself. The immigrant becomes a foil for Dale's insecurities and ruminations about affiliation and belonging. As the play begins, Dale is ranting and raving about FOBs:

F-O-B. Fresh Off the Boat. FOB. What words can you think of that characterize the FOB? Clumsy, ugly, greasy FOB. Loud, stupid, four-eyed FOB. Boy FOBs are the worst, the pits. They are the sworn enemy of all ABC—oh, that's "American-born Chinese"—of all ABC girls. Before an ABC girl will be seen on Friday night with a boy FOB in Westwood, she would rather burn off her face. FOBs can be found in great numbers almost anyplace you happen to be, but there are some locations where they cluster in particularly large swarms. Community colleges, Chinese club discos, Asian sororities, Asian fraternities, Oriental churches, shopping malls, and of course, Bee Gee concerts. How can you spot a FOB? Look out! If you can't answer that, you might be one.

By reflecting back to them their presumed foreignness in the eyes of others, Asian immigrants could become for the second generation an important focus of disidentification. In other words, in their attempts to negate their own presumed foreignness, the second generation also tried to dissociate from immigrants. Thus some of my informants described situations in which they had avoided having contact or establishing relationships with Asian immigrants, for fear that the latter's "real foreignness" might reinforce, in the eyes of others, their own.

Lily, a Chinese American woman in her early thirties from the Boston area, described such a situation. She felt resentment toward a female co-worker who had recently arrived from Taiwan, fearing that she might affect her own image. Lily may also have seen the new co-worker as a competitor on the job (although she did not say so). Eventually, Lily's attitude did change; she came to recognize that her resentment was unfair, an expression of prejudice against immigrants:

> My first job out of college was in the sales and marketing department. I was the only Asian in our section. And then they hired a woman in the department. She was from Taiwan, she'd been in America for just a few years. She fit all the stereotypes. She was this passive quiet type and she spoke with an accent and dressed superconservative. I remember being cool, not so friendly. It was completely irrational but I felt, "She's spoiling it for me." I avoided her at first. She comes here and she feeds into all the stereotypes that don't have anything to do with me. But eventually we did become friends. I've developed a better attitude about it. [How did that happen?] I thought about it more, and I talked with my Asian American friends from college. It's really prejudice against immigrants; there's so much of that in this society that we all learn it.

Young Min, a Korean American who worked in a bank, also worried that his own image in the workplace might be affected by the presence of co-workers who were recent Asian arrivals. He avoided social associations with the immigrants and made an extra effort to act in ways that would distance himself from stereotypes of Asians. Like many other informants, he stressed the importance of using different terms to refer to foreign and U.S.-born, such as "Chinese" and "Chinese American":

> There are a few Asians at work, but I don't hang out with them. I make a point to not do that. [Why is that?] They're Chinese—if they were Korean it would be a little different. Plus they're Chinese from China, not Chinese Americans. There is a Chinese American [U.S.-born or -raised] in our department, and we get along well. She stays away from the other Chinese too. They speak Chinese, and I don't think she does. And they have a reputation for staying in their own little group and not being very outgoing. I just don't want to get into that whole scene. I don't want to be associated with it.

As we have seen, disidentification involves, in essence, establishing one's difference from the "other." In establishing their distance from immigrants, my informants frequently drew on popular stereotypes of Asians to construct a homogenized and unitary picture of the Asian immigrant, a construction that, more often than not, was tinged with hostility.

Matthew, a Korean American in his mid-twenties, was raised in Virginia and was now living in the Boston area. In asserting how different he was from "them," he drew on two popular stereotypes of Asians in contemporary American life: that of the serious, nerdy, passive, colorless Asian, awkward and naive in social matters; and that of the nouveau-riche Asian, the "JOJ (just off the jet)" Asian (as another informant called it): wealthy, flashy, crude and quite definitely out of sync with American norms of decorum and behavior. "A lot of the Asian guys from Asia," he remarked, "you know, not people like me who grew up here, fit the stereotype. First you have the engineering major, with glasses, real quiet and boring. Or there are the ones who are totally into the Euro scene: flashy clothes, a lot of money, talking on the cellular phone. I don't fit into either."

Despite some differences in emphasis and image, the remarks of James, a Chinese American, about Asian/Chinese immigrants had a similar flavor to those of Matthew. James, a man in his late thirties who was living outside of Los Angeles, in the San Fernando Valley, associated new Asian immigrants with Monterey Park, a city in the Los Angeles area that has been called "the first suburban Chinatown" because of its large Asian-origin population. James asserted that when it came to new Chinese immigrants, the popular stereotype of Chinese as bad drivers was true. More generally, he paints an unflattering picture of the young male Asian immigrant as "showing off money," enmeshed in a subculture whose rules of public conduct violate his own:

> I identify with some Asian people who've grown up here and are basically American like me. But with a lot of Chinese I can't relate. You go to areas of L.A. that are primarily Asian, like Monterey Park, and it feels different. Those areas have a lot of recent immigrants. You go into an area like that, and you see more tripped-out cars. You see more young guys who are trying to be cool. You see more smokers. The phrase that comes to mind is *too hip Oriental:* someone who is just too much into his car, too much into his clothes, which dance place to go to on the weekend. A lot of it is just showing off money. And that whole stereotype of the Chinese being lousy drivers seems true when you go into those areas.

James's remarks highlight the powerful and complex ways in which issues of class fold into processes of disidentification. His scorn for the Asian immigrant, we sense, is about not only his[4] foreignness but an absence of the cultural capital—the requisite signs and behavior of being middle class. In other words, it is not just about not being American but also about not being middle-class American.

Another important theme in the homogenized construction of immigrants was Asian gender traditionalism. My informants remarked upon the male chauvinism of Asian cultures, as reflected in the attitudes of Asian immigrant men. If they focused often on immigrant men, they implicated immigrant women, too, for their tolerance and even acceptance of male chauvinism.

Michelle, at the time of our interview, was a homemaker in her late thirties who was married to a second-generation Korean American like herself. Both while growing up and as an adult, Michelle was embedded in local Korean immigrant communities, which makes her remarks particularly interesting. She, her husband, and her children were deeply involved in a close-knit Korean church community in the Los Angeles area, one with many recent immigrants. At several points in the interview, she expressed a strong sense of identification with Korean immigrants. But at one point she also made an effort to distinguish U.S.-born Korean American men from Korean immigrants:

---

4. I use *his* here deliberately, since James talks in particular about male immigrants, focusing on images of masculinity.

I always swore I would never marry an immigrant, and I'm glad I didn't. You can always tell who the guys from Korea are. They walk like this. [She gets up and struts, shoulders wide and jiggling, head held high.] They're on top of the world, and women are second class to them. "No, I won't allow my wife to work. I'll decide the way my girlfriend should dress, where we go out for dinner." [Are you talking about Korean men in Korea or here?] It's still there with Korean men who've grown up here, but not as much. I do feel that the men from Korea give the 1.5 and second-generation men like my husband a bad name. I guess there was never any real danger of my marrying a Korean immigrant because most of them end up marrying women from Korea. They [the women] will put up with these guys.

For Michelle, the differences between immigrant and nonimmigrant Korean American men were clear, but for other women informants, the differences were not so clear: the male chauvinism of Asian culture was reflected also in the attitudes of second-generation Asian American men. For them, the issue of Asian male chauvinism could serve to distinguish not only immigrant from nonimmigrant Asian Americans, but also Asian American women and men.

For this reason, Katie, a Chinese American, was vehement about not going out with Asian men, U.S.-born or otherwise:

I'm not interested in Asian men—my experience in that department hasn't been that great. They want you to cook and clean and wait on them—actually wait on not just them but their parents too. They don't want their women to work, especially in a job that's better than the one they have. [You find that with Asian American men?] Yeah, even the ABCs [American-born Chinese]. I went out with three guys like that, and all of them were just really male chauvinist.

For my informants, then, immigrants were at times a focus of disidentification. While the specific complaints they raised about immigrants varied, from male chauvinism to nerdiness, the informants generally seemed to feel that immigrants could aggravate the "foreignness" that was signaled to others by "Asian race." Issues of social class also played a role, introducing another complex layer of meanings. That is, informants' desire to distance themselves from immigrants could be based not only on their aversion to "foreignness" but on their own class identification. Thus the recent increase in immigration of persons from more modest class backgrounds may be an aggravating factor, an additional reason to distance from immigrants. But as we have seen, even relatively wealthy Asian immigrants could be a target of disdain, not so much for their lack of money but for their cultural behaviors, which were perceived as inappropriate to middle-class American life. Finally, disidentification could play into the relations of Asian American men and women, reflecting and reinforcing tensions between them.

It is important to emphasize that my informants' less than hospitable attitudes toward immigrants are by no means exclusive to them or to Asian Americans generally. On the contrary, such attitudes are quite a common aspect of the intergenerational dynamics of many ethnic communities, especially those whose ranks are being replenished by new immigrants. Gutierrez (1995) has noted this phenomenon in his historical study of the attitudes of Mexican Americans (i.e. U.S.-born Mexicans) toward Mexican immigrants: "[F]rom their point of view, the mass immigration of so-called backward, un-Americanized illegal aliens [from Mexico] reinforced the negative stereotypes Anglo Americans held about all Mexicans, regardless of citizenship status" (2). In general, then, immigrants are often seen by U.S.-born fellow ethnics as providing an unwanted mirror, a reflection of how they wish not to be seen by others. For Asian-origin persons, the reflection of "foreignness" produced by immigrants is perhaps particularly vivid and troubling, given prevailing images of Asians.

■ *Authentic Ethnicity: "You Must Speak Chinese"*

"Foreignness" not only cast doubt upon one's membership and belonging as American, it also marked the operation of race as an identity marker by signaling *authentic ethnicity.* That is, the dominant society assumes that second-generation Chinese and Korean Americans, as "foreigners," have ties to a community and culture that is either located or rooted well outside the United States. These ties are assumed to be strong and genuine in character—authentic rather than contrived or fake. This assumption reflects what Weston (1995, 90) has called "a cultural preoccupation with authenticity in U.S. life."

My informants became most aware of this assumption of ethnic authenticity at times when a non-Asian American would ask them to translate or interpret Asian, Korean, or Chinese cultural practices, or to prove or display their ethnic cultural knowledge in some fashion. Duncan, a Chinese American in his late thirties, said he felt aggravated that others assumed that he knew certain things simply because he was Chinese. He identified the assumption as a kind of stereotype, but decided that it was not worth battling:

> The other day a group of us were going to lunch with some guys from out of town who were here for a convention. There was a discussion about where to go, and a Chinese place was suggested. Someone looked at me and said, "Duncan, is that good?" Of course I didn't know, I don't know every Chinese restaurant around here. It's the same when you go to a Chinese restaurant and people expect you to choose the food and order for them. They expect you to speak to the waiter in Chinese. [What did you do when you were asked about the Chinese restaurant?] I guess I told them it was okay. With little stereotypes like that, it's easiest not to fight them. There are a lot of bigger battles in the world that are worth fighting over.

Curt, a Korean American, also described situations where people made assumptions about his knowledge of Korean culture. While he generally interpreted their queries as expressions of simple and benign curiosity, he was also aware that they helped to create a context in which his Korean ancestry could not be ignored:

> I don't have an accent—there's nothing about me that's obviously Korean. But in people's eyes, you're always Korean. I was in a meeting about a contract; it was all white. I don't know if you do this, but being a minority I always count how many whites and people of color there are when I walk into a room. Everything went well. Then they started asking me, "How do you say this in Korean? What's the weather like in Korea?" I guess they were curious—there was nothing really wrong with it. But like I said, you can't ignore being Korean. It's not something you can ignore, because others won't let you.

Not surprisingly, given its potency as a cultural marker, language figured prominently in my informants' experiences of their expected ethnic knowledge. Those who did not speak much Korean or Chinese were particularly conscious of the power of this expectation. Kyung Sook, a Korean American in her early twenties who grew up in Boston, described her knowledge of Korean as "childlike"; what she did know was mainly "domestic-type" activities and phrases, such as the names of foods and simple instructions like "go to bed" and "it's time for dinner." One powerful childhood memory was of an incident involving her presumed knowledge of the Korean language:

I regret not speaking the language. People expect that you will speak it. There's a time that stands out in my mind. It's not a big thing, but it kind of traumatized me. I remember when I was about nine, we were living in Brookline then. And they brought two Korean kids, a brother and a sister, into class. They had just come from Seoul. Everyone looked at me. The teacher called me over to the front to help explain things to them. And I remember I couldn't. I mean, I did say a few things, but I couldn't translate what the teacher was saying. At first they wouldn't believe me. [Who wouldn't believe you?] The kids in the class mainly, but also the teacher. You know, people just assume, "You're Korean—you must speak Korean."

Similarly, non-Asians also sometimes reinterpreted ethnic symbols and practices in the light of an assumed authentic ethnicity, presuming that those symbols and practices had a more genuine and authentic quality than even the informants themselves understood. Katie's non-Asian friends imagined her family's celebration of Chinese New Year to be far more elaborate and exotic that it was in reality:

For Chinese New Year we have a special dinner. When I was younger, my aunts and uncles would drive down from San Francisco. It's not as big a deal as Americans think it is, at least not in my family. I remember friends going, "Oh, it's Chinese New Year. You must go home and do all kinds of exotic worship and rituals, the whole nine yards." It was just a dinner that was fancier than usual.

Situations where non-Asians read "ethnic authenticity" into certain aspects of an Asian American's life are, for obvious reasons, especially fertile ground for racial identity play. When non-Asians would make assumptions about my informants' ethnic authenticity, it was easy enough for them to play into it—and when they did so consciously, with an understanding of the play involved, racial identity play occurred.

Dave, a Chinese American in his early thirties who was working as a graphic design artist, laughingly related to me a story from his college days. While he was attending an arts college in northern California in the late 1970s, he played with the assumption of his ethnic authenticity so as to enhance his chances of getting dates:

When I went to college, the hippie influence was still there. I remember some funny stuff in college. At one point I was smoking a lot of dope, and I bought a whole shelf of books from a used bookstore on Zen Buddhism and Eastern philosophies. You know how it is in a dorm, kids wandering in and out of each other's rooms, looking at each other's things. Because of those books, I got a reputation as being an expert on Oriental religions. I played into it, especially because the girls, I mean the women then were taken in with the whole Oriental mystique. They liked the idea of an Asian guy with long hair who was hip and seemed to know these deep Eastern things. Of course it was all a game. I was stoned out of my mind a lot of the time. Except for what I read on my own, I knew as much about that stuff as the next person. I was raised by a mother who was a devout evangelical Christian. It was all fire and brimstone. There was nothing like Zen philosophy there.

Matthew, a Korean American in his early twenties, also recalled playing with the assumption of authentic ethnicity, but in his case the play had the effect of subverting rather than affirming the assumption. Matthew and four friends from his high school days—one Chinese American, one Korean American, and two Jewish Americans—liked to play around with the assumptions of racial identity that others made about them. In one case, they played with the assumption that Asian-origin men would tend to date from within their group. For Matthew and his friends, the delight that came from racial identity play derived in part from their sense of regaining control over the force of others' assumptions:

> The five of us—we like to do crazy things. One of the Jewish guys, Tom, is more Asian than any of us. He majored in East Asian Studies in college, he speaks Chinese, and he has a Chinese girlfriend. In fact, he's in Hong Kong at the moment. We go to Chinese restaurants, and the waiters look at us, the guys with the Asian faces. Then one of the white faces in the group starts zipping off our order in Chinese. It's fun to see the surprise.
>
> All of the Asian guys in the group like to go out with white women. And Tom goes out only with Asians. We've gone to parties, and the three of us Asians have taken white girls, and the two Jewish guys have taken Asian women. What's funny is people's reactions. They assume that I'm with one of the Asian women, and then when they find out I'm with one of the white women, they get embarrassed.

Jenny's account of racial identity play has a different flavor from those described thus far. During her college years, she visited a boyfriend's family in the

Midwest, where she engaged in racial identity play in order to make an uncomfortable situation tolerable, even amusing. In her account, the presumption of authentic ethnicity is closely nested within the larger one of "foreignness":

> They [her boyfriend's family] had weird ideas. It was like a cartoon. Their sense of what was Chinese was like a caricature. It was annoying at first, and then I decided to have some fun with it. [What did they do that was weird and annoying?] "Look, Jenny, we made some rice for you, and here's a bottle of soy sauce, because, you poor thing, that's all you've ever eaten." Or "Tell us about what it's like in China. What's going on there?" And of course, "Where did you learn such beautiful English?"
>
> It was too much work to correct them, and I got a kick out of going along with it, making up details and exaggerating. Like, I would pretend to know so much about China. I suppose it was a little mean—they were nice, simple people. But what was I going to do? I don't think correcting them all the time was an option. Even if I did, I'm not sure they would have gotten it.

The assumption of ethnic authenticity was an important part of my informants' experience that ethnicity was for them not a voluntary matter. Part of this ethnic bind was a sense of pressure and obligation to cultivate their ethnic identity. That is, the idea, held by non-Asians, that Asians will have a substantial and genuine knowledge of their ethnic culture produces a sense of pressure on persons of Asian origin to actually meet this expectation.

But if the assumption of authentic ethnicity produces pressures to cultivate ethnic identity, it also, somewhat ironically, can raise questions about the legitimacy of such cultivation. The *authentic,* as popularly defined, implies that which is organic and natural rather than deliberately created, the desire for which is driven, as Halter (2000) notes, by "the search for an idealized and fixed point in time when folk culture was supposedly untouched by the corruption that is associated with commodity development" (17).

My informants, accordingly, felt a certain tension between the pressure to cultivate and the suspicion that cultivation would produce something that was false and artificial rather than genuine. In short, their attitudes about the active cultivation of their Chinese or Korean culture and identity were highly ambivalent. They could even level the charge of "born-again Chinese" or "born-again Korean" against those who had *become* Chinese or Korean in some deliberate fashion.

Reflecting her exceptionally strong views on this subject, Kyung-Sook's words were especially expressive of this ambivalence:

> I'm not one of these people who's rah-rah Korean. Now if someone asks me if I speak Korean, I don't beat around the bush. I say, "No, I don't." That's it, *fini*. I've seen a lot of "born-again Koreans," people who have had almost nothing to do with Korean culture all their life suddenly become completely Korean. They surround themselves with Korean people, make an effort to learn the language. [That hasn't appealed to you?] No, it seems fake. I'm more focused on the political issues facing minorities in this country.

For my informants, the assumption of authentic ethnicity complicated issues of ethnic identity in another, perhaps even more fundamental way. The meaning and significance of their identity as Chinese or Korean were, for them, issues of ongoing concern. They had grown up with primordial or "blood" conceptions of Chinese/Korean membership that had supported their understandings of themselves as true Chinese or Koreans. But as second-generation persons, they had also grown up with the doubts and challenges of others, especially fellow ethnic immigrants and nationals, as to how genuinely Chinese or Korean they were. The assumption of their authentic ethnicity as they experienced it in everyday encounters with persons of non-Asian origin added to the complexity of the currents and pressures that marked this issue for them.

■ *Authentic Ethnicity and Ethnic Identity Capital*

In my informants' accounts thus far, the expectation of authentic ethnicity, even if perhaps an occasion for racial identity play, comes across as largely unwanted and constraining. But the expectation of ethnic authenticity could also be an occasion for advantage and opportunity. Among the benefits of authentic ethnicity is the insurance that it provides against the possibility of slipping into the homogeneity and vacuity of the mainstream. The normality that is implied by an unhyphenated American identity seems to have a quality of blandness, of being ordinary. The symbolic ethnicity sought by white ethnics may, at least in part, be understood as an attempt to ward off this slippage into the humdrum, the boring (see Waters 1990).

As we have seen, my informants found the expectation of authentic ethnicity to be a source of some frustration, highlighting as it did their distance from the ethnic American model, in particular the choice to be or not be ethnic. But this very inability was not devoid of advantage. It could add an element of spice to one's identity, a note of interest. Brenda, who related to me at some length how she had not liked "being Chinese," also spoke of her growing appreciation of the benefits of a Chinese identity: "I've come to realize that being Chinese is something good. When you're younger, you don't want to stand out—you want to fit in. Now that I'm older, I want to stand out; being special and different is a good thing. I mean, there's so much emphasis on diversity out there."

Others observed that an ethnic identity, particularly a genuine and thus distinct one, was especially advantageous in light of the contemporary emphasis on diversity and multiculturalism. The assumption of authentic ethnicity allowed them to assume a central and legitimate place on the stage of multiculturalism, as it has been popularly defined. That is, as true ethnics, they were very much part of the diversity that multiculturalism celebrates and affirms.

Lillian, a Chinese American, noted that during informal conversations with others—especially, one would assume, non-Chinese others—she could assume a position of knowledge and authority about events in China:

> There is a perception that I'm wise about China and its culture, more than I actually am. People assume that I speak Chinese fluently, when I actually don't. I don't think it's a hard cross to bear. With all this emphasis on multiculturalism, I think having a unique background is held up as a good thing. [Can you think of a specific instance when someone assumed that you knew about Chinese things?] Ah, I remember after the student uprising in China, some of the people at work looked to me for information, for guidance. That's not a bad position to be in. I actually did know more than they about what was going on, and that was only because I was reading the papers very carefully, more closely than they were.

I suggest that for the second generation of Chinese and Korean Americans, the presumption of authentic ethnicity is tied to their *ethnic identity capital,* by which I mean the opportunities, broadly speaking, that accrue to them from others' *perception* (whether justified or not) of them as a member of an ethnic community and hence able to tap into the social capital[5]—the connections, soli-

---

5. Drawing on the work of Coleman (1988), I use *social capital* to refer to the resources that inhere in social relationships, "those aspects of social structure . . . that can be used by the actors to realize their interests" (398).

darity, and other resources of that community. In some sense all those who are judged to be ethnics, especially genuine ethnics, have ethnic identity capital, but the character and significance of that capital varies across groups. Some ethnic communities, because of their social and economic position and resources, may be expected to generate greater ethnic identity capital for their members than others.

For both Chinese and Korean Americans, the implications of possessing ethnic identity capital are generally positive. Although the Asian economic crisis of the late 1990s has undoubtedly complicated the picture, American society continues to generally perceive East Asian societies as economically powerful—a perception that generates ethnic identity capital. This is perhaps especially the case for mainland China, which is widely identified as a formidable if at the moment unrealized economic (and political) force. Chinese and Korean-origin communities in the United States are today also understood in generally positive terms with respect to their economic and social resources. They are often seen as upwardly mobile, model minority communities and, in some parts of the country, an increasingly visible and prominent presence, economically and politically speaking.

Ethnic identity capital can thus accrue from perceived connections to Asia. Four of my informants described job situations in which they had found themselves being pushed, in one way or another, toward the Asian or specifically Chinese/Korean aspects of the business. Sung's account of such *ethnic channeling* is particularly striking. A Korean American, Sung spoke little Korean and his parents had not done much to teach him Korean cultural practices. Soon after joining a large multinational financial investment firm in Los Angeles, he found himself assigned to its East Asia section, and eventually to the Korea segment of the section. On the one hand, Sung felt pressured by and resentful of the presumption that he was suited for the Korea section, especially since he had come in with an interest in Latin America. But he also recognized the opportunities that the situation presented:

> In college I was very interested in Latin America. I took classes on the politics and economy of the region. I knew more about Latin America in a real sense than about Asia. I speak Spanish too. But as soon as they see an Asian face, they think, "Aha, that's where he belongs." [Could you have told them you wanted to work on Latin America?] Yeah, I did during the job interview. But even though I com-

plain, it is an asset. I'm given a lot of leeway and responsibility. And I am learning. I've been to Korea now many times, and my speaking ability has improved.

Ethnic identity capital may also accrue from a person's perceived ties to Asian, or perhaps specifically Chinese/Korean, communities in the United States. Eugene, a Korean American, was working in a bank in the Los Angeles area, providing financial services and investment advice to customers. One day the manager asked him to target Korean Americans in his work, a request with which he was not entirely comfortable:

> There is an expectation. Soon after I came on board, I was told to try and cultivate Korean clients. They didn't tell me that in the interview, so I was a little pissed. That's not to say I mind being seen as Korean. I am actually very Korean-identified. I belong to a Korean church, a lot of my friends are Korean, and my parents are very traditional old-style Korean. But that's exactly it, I don't want to mix my business life with all that.

What makes the operation of ethnic identity capital especially vivid in these and other situations is the clashes involved, between an individual's self-perception and desires and those of others. But in other situations, ethnic identity capital was something my informants actively pursued and cultivated. In general, they commonly made active use of ethnic identity capital.

It is important to not simplify the complexity of pressures and motivations that underlay this deployment of ethnic identity capital. One could choose to use it to build a career in response to the experience and realization that one's opportunities were otherwise blocked—the "glass ceiling" in the workplace. Nor should we view the mobilization of ethnic identity capital in jobs as driven by simple or narrow self-interest. It could involve the desire to provide services to one's ethnic community, to help and empower it, and more generally, to make a positive difference in the lives of others.

■ Ethnic Options and Ethnic Binds

In comparison to their predecessors, the lives of Asian Americans today are less constrained by institutionalized forces of racism and segregation. But if the ability of Asian Americans to exercise ethnic options has improved, it nonetheless remains limited. Reflecting the privileges of their middle-class status, my informants expected to exercise ethnic options in much the same ways as European Americans. But these expectations were often challenged. Others accepted their legitimacy as American only uncertainly and provisionally, and supporting it required their ongoing efforts.

And part of their ethnicity was simply not optional. Unlike the white ethnics who practice symbolic ethnicity, they could not, in the perceptions of others, slip in and out of "being ethnic," into a nonethnically marked American identity. The realization of this inability was central to my informants' sense of being in an ethnic bind: that ethnicity for them was a binding and involuntary matter.

If my informants found their ethnic options to be constrained, however, they also worked to expand them, to gain control over their identification. To this end, they marshaled important identity resources, related to their socioeconomic and other characteristics. For example, as persons born or raised in the United States, they could successfully use the identity marker of speaking American English to dispel the presumption that they were foreign. Another strategy was to assert an ethnonational rather than a racial identity ("I'm Korean, not Asian"). For immigrants from the Caribbean and Latin America, ethnonational identity (Haitian, Cuban) is an important basis of resistance to incorporation into the established racial schemes of the United States, especially when such incorporation brings with it a stigmatized identity (Fernandez-Kelly and Schauffler 1994; Waters 1999). For second-generation Chinese and Korean Americans, too, the ethnonational identities of *Chinese* and *Korean* are important tools in their efforts to negotiate and to resist incorporation into the racial identity of *Asian*. The effectiveness of ethnonational identity as a counterpoint to racialization was clearly enhanced for them by the fact that most people in the dominant society understand, however vaguely, the significance of national boundaries in Asia. In other words, along with its pervasive tendency to "generalize Asians," American society also recognizes the ethnonational diversity of Asians.

CHAPTER FOUR

College and Asian American Identity

The term Asian-American identity encompasses on the one hand a strategic politics, and on the other a limiting trap for the expression of diverse ethnic cultures.   (Takagi 1994, 239)

At first glance, the premise of a common identity seems not to apply to Asian Americans, given their diversity. Yet among many of my friends of various Asian ancestries who socialize with one another, a definite sense of a shared background and culture has developed. For some, it flows from having been immigrants. For many others (myself included), it largely derives from our American experience—our racial features in a predominantly white society, our two-culture (or multiculture) lives, and our treatment by the mainstream.   (Hing 1993, 175)

FOR MY SECOND-GENERATION Chinese and Korean American informants, being labeled *Asian* by others was a routine and everyday experience. This kind of shared experience of imposed "Asianness" has been identified as a driving force behind the transformation of the label *Asian American* into something more than a bureaucratic category. In this chapter I turn my attention to processes of *pan-Asian ethnogenesis,* or the development of an Asian American ethnic collectivity, one whose members self-consciously understand themselves as belonging in an Asian American community. I focus on my informants' accounts of their college years, which for many of them were a time of especially sharp and explicit engagement with the idea of being Asian American. It was often in college that they encountered for the first time the possibility that *Asian American* was not just an identity imposed from the outside but a notion to be actively embraced.

Current scholarship on ethnic identity in general emphasizes its multiple, fluctuating, and situational character (see Hall 1996; Nagel 1994). A given individual may have more than a single ethnic identity, and the relative significance of one identity over another will shift across different times and situations. This issue is important to keep in mind, as we consider the emerging significance of Asian American identity for second-generation Chinese and Korean Americans. The general pattern that I encountered among my informants was of increasingly affirmative engagement with the identity of *Asian American,* in the college years and especially beyond. The growing significance of Asian American identity did not, however, mean that my informants did not sometimes reject it or engage in vigorous critiques of it. Nor was the rising significance of Asian American identity, for them, necessarily accompanied by a rejection of their ethnonational identity as Chinese or Korean. These varied and cross-currents were all part of the broad canvas of identity on which, for them, the meaning and significance of being Asian American emerged.

■ *Asian Americans, Race, and the Post-1960s Campus*

The traditional college years, the late teens through the mid-twenties, are years of extraordinary maturation and growth. These are the years when many young people leave home, often for the first time, meet very different kinds of people (also often for the first time), come upon previously unheard ideas, and have the opportunity, and indeed the task, of defining for themselves and others who they are — what they think, the values they hold, their place in a world beyond the one in which they grew up (Sidel 1994).

As Sidel suggests in this passage, college is culturally expected, especially for middle-class Americans, to be a time of self-exploration, of engagement and concern with issues of identity. Since the late 1960s, the construct of *Asian American* has increasingly become something that students of Asian origin confront during their college years. In the following section I briefly explore the context of these confrontations — that is, the conditions that accompany the negotiation of *Asian American,* as an aspect of affiliation and identity, on the contemporary U.S. college campus.

Among these conditions, race is generally prominent and highly visible as a subject of social and political division. Underlying the racialization of the contemporary campus are important demographic shifts, including the fact that since the 1960s, the number of minority students attending college has greatly increased.[1] While this increase has not been uniform across all types of institutions and has not affected all minority groups equally, it has nonetheless transformed the overall racial composition of the American college population. Drawing on a 1991 report issued by the American Council on Education, Loeb (1994) notes that "students of color presently number 1 out of 6 at 4 year colleges and 1 out of 5 if you count two-year community colleges" (190).

This growth in numbers has been especially sharp for Asian Americans. Between 1984 and 1995, the number of Asian Pacific Americans enrolled in higher education institutions rose by 104.5 percent, with comparable figures of 5.1 percent for whites, 37 percent for African Americans, and 104.4 percent for Hispanics.[2] Students of Asian origin have also been an important part of the growth in the foreign student population on U.S. college campuses.[3] In comparison, then, to the post–World War II period, the Asian-origin college population since the 1960s has been not only larger in size but also more diverse, in terms of such variables as ethnonational origin and immigrant versus later-generation status.

The rise in minority student numbers has been accompanied by the heightened prominence of race as a subject of division and controversy on college campuses. In recent times, race has been at the core of most of the major controversies within higher education, controversies over curriculum and course content as well as faculty hiring and student admissions policies. These issues are "hot buttons" in a campus environment that has often been described as divided, with race a prominent aspect of that polarization. There have, for example, been disturbing reports of rising harassment and violence against minority students.[4] Thus a *New York Times* article, after describing the hostilities experienced by

1. Minority enrollment rose from 6.4 percent in 1960 to 13.8 percent in 1977. And in 1995, 11.7 percent of those obtaining bachelor's degrees were minority students, and 16.8 percent in 1994 (Hune and Chan 1997; Takagi 1992).

2. According to Hune and Chan (1997), in 1994, Asian Pacific Americans constituted 4.8 percent of those obtaining bachelor's degrees. And in 1995, 60 percent of Asian Pacific Americans attending college were enrolled at four-year institutions; 80 percent were in public institutions.

3. According to Sidel (1994, 42), Asians have constituted about half of the foreign student population in recent years.

4. Between 1986 and 1990, the National Institute against Prejudice and Violence monitored incidents of "campus ethnoviolence" at approximately 250 colleges and universities across the country (Sidel 1994, 8). They found that about 20 percent of minority students experienced some form of attack during an academic year, with many experiencing several. According to the report, "Campus ethnoviolence covers the spectrum of violent acts including potentially lethal assaults, classroom and dormitory harassment, personal insults, graffiti, property damage, and so on" (Sidel 1994, 8).

black students following the acquittal of O. J. Simpson (a verdict that blacks and whites viewed in sharply divergent ways), concluded that "the overall picture of racial relations on campus is one that seems to get more brittle as time goes by" (Applebome 1995).

A related aspect of the contemporary campus environment that has recently received some attention is its balkanized character (Levine 2000; Takagi 1992). That is, in ways that violate expectations of racial integration, the apparent trend is for students to engage in social activities that are divided along racial lines rather than those that are not.[5] Campus advocacy groups that are focused on particular student populations have grown in both number and size. More generally, both in formal organizations and in informal socializing, students increasingly tend to stick to their own racial groups: "A quick glance at the local eateries on campus is more suggestive of segregation than integration. Blacks sit with blacks, whites sit with whites, Asians sit with Asians, each group clustered at separate tables" (Takagi 1992, 62).

Popular stereotypes and images of Asian students provide, I suggest, a glimpse into some of the ways in which Asian Americans have been located in these currents of racial division and tension. One stereotype that is most likely to affect the Asian-origin college student is that of Asians as the model minority group. They are seen as "good students," an assumption that is bolstered by the realities of Asian Americans' generally favorable grade point averages and SAT scores (see Takagi 1992, 60). This image of the academically competent and motivated Asian student is posed *in contrast* to that of other racial minorities, especially blacks and Latinos. Among other things, the image suggests that a certain fissure exists between the experiences of Asians and those of other racial minority students. Because of this image, for example, Asian American students are far less likely than black and Latino students to be accused of having been admitted to the school unfairly, on the basis of racial preference rather than merit.

But if the image of the meritorious student works, in this respect, to shield Asian Americans from the kinds of hostilities that other racial minorities have

5. Observers have also noted contradictions in the state of race relations on college campuses. Spitzberg and Thorndike (1992), drawing on a study of higher education by the Carnegie Foundation, assert the following: "We found that individual minority and white students interact substantially. Students have friends from other racial and ethnic backgrounds and most residence halls and organized extracurricular activities are integrated. . . . Despite this evidence of friendly interaction, we also found evidence of racist attitudes and substantial racial and ethnic separation" (32–33).

experienced on the post–civil rights campus, in other respects it facilitates certain kinds of hostility. In general, the "good student" image has meant that Asian Americans are, on college campuses, not only admired but also resented and disliked. They are the "damned curve raisers," generating competition and making the struggle for academic grades more difficult for everyone else. With their high GPAs and SAT scores, they are also felt to be taking up too many of the scarce slots in admission to selective colleges and universities. The ensuing sense of resentment toward Asians for flooding the college gates is captured by the emergence, in informal student cultures, of such phrases as "Made in Taiwan" to refer to MIT and "University of Caucasians living among Asians" to refer to UCLA (Takagi 1992, 60).

The reputation of Asians for academic achievement is expressed in the popular image of Asian students as nerds—studious, serious, shy, mathematically inclined, and lacking in social skills and outside interests. But another, seemingly contradictory set of stereotypes is also at work today: those that are centered on the supposedly essential "foreignness" of the Asian student.

One of these stereotypes is the image of Asian students as clannish and cliquey, sticking to their own kind and doing everything in groups—a proclivity that is seen to be deeply contradictory to the individualism of American culture and hence foreign. Seen in terms of this stereotype, Asian students become more than just a part of the balkanized college campus—they become, in effect, *a cause* of it.

Another stereotypical image is that of the frivolous and well-to-do Asian, an image that is associated with the presence, within the contemporary Asian immigration stream, of some persons from wealthy, elite backgrounds. Here the Asian student is alleged to be not only cliquey but also focused on parties and conspicuous consumption and obsessed with the display of material goods (especially clothes and cars) that will gain him or her status within the clique. The particular markers (like clothing styles) that are part of this status game are further affirmations of Asian Americans' "foreignness" when they are out of sync with those of mainstream American culture.

Last but not least, a final stereotype is the one that associates Asian culture and Asians generally with gender traditionalism—supporting male dominance and enforcing separate standards for men and women's behavior. All these stereotypes, as we will see, were an important part of my informants' negotiations of Asian American identity in college.

Critical to understanding the development of Asian American identity on college campuses today is the presence of pan-Asian or Asian American institutions in these environments. The complex racial currents endemic to campuses have energized but also challenged the development of these institutions. Today as in former years, colleges continue to be important centers of pan-Asian organization and activity. Thus pan-Asian student associations that aim to bring together students of varied Asian ethnic origin for political and social events are a part of many if not most college campuses today. The courses and programs in Asian American studies have been expanded, and student centers devoted to Asian Americans have been established.

These institutions have been important vehicles for the dissemination of what may be described as an *official ideology of pan-Asianism,* an understanding of Asian American community that is based on the founding goals of the Asian American movement and that has since become its official ideology. In essence, official pan-Asianism defines *the Asian American community,* based on the shared racial identity of Asian-origin persons in the United States, as a single community united by strategic political interests. Rooted in the civil rights struggles of the 1960s, it emphasizes the bond that Asian Americans share with other oppressed groups of color and, relatedly, the importance of mobilizing Asian Americans in a larger struggle against racial oppression (Dirlik 1996; Espiritu 1992; Yanagisako 1995).

The recent growth of Asian American studies programs and course offerings has strengthened pan-Asian institutions on college campuses. The growth in numbers of Asian-origin students has facilitated the efforts of Asian American activists to seek and expand resources for pan-Asian institutions on campus. Moreover, amid all the racial divisions and tensions of contemporary campus life, Asian-origin students may find that the fellowship and resources offered by pan-Asian organizations are especially appealing to themselves.

But at the same time, many of these same developments are also challenging to the growth of pan-Asianism. As noted earlier, as the Asian student population has grown, it has become more internally diverse, most notably along the lines of ethnonational origin and of immigrant versus later-generation status. This growing diversity raises questions about the ability of pan-Asian campus organizations to appeal to and draw in Asian-origin students, given their vast range of backgrounds. As Espiritu and Ong (1994, 302) have noted in their analysis of pan-Asian organizations, membership in these groups tends to be U.S.-born and middle-class and hence representative of only a relatively select segment of the Asian-origin population. More generally, the diversity of the Asian American student population suggests a heightened potential for intra-Asian conflict and division within its ranks. Among other things, it has created the possibility that for many Asian-origin students, organizing along ethnonational lines would be more viable and appealing than organizing along pan-Asian lines.

■ *College and the Development of Asian American Identity*

In this section I explore the college histories recounted to me by my second-generation Chinese and Korean American informants. The majority of them were college-educated, having attended college at some point in the period between 1975 and 1995, with a large cluster in the 1980s (see Chapter 1). They attended a wide range of specific colleges and universities, many but certainly not all of them located on the East and West Coasts. Their institutional environments varied tremendously in terms of numbers of all minority students, including those of Chinese, Korean, and other Asian origin. The schools also varied with respect to their policies on and approaches to issues of race, diversity, and multiculturalism. My informants who attended college in the 1980s and 1990s in California, for example, were the most likely to have found themselves on campuses with a significant Asian-origin student presence as well as Asian American studies programs and centers.

My informants' accounts of their relations to pan-Asian or Asian American affiliation and identity in these years are informed by two thematic tensions. The first involves their conflicting impulses of *acceptance and rejection* of *Asian American* as a basis for affiliation and identity. The second centers on the specific notions of *Asian American* that the Asian American movement self-consciously advanced: the ideology of official pan-Asianism, and the contrasting ideology of ethnic pan-Asianism, which defined *Asian American* in broadly ethnic terms, as a community of shared culture and life experiences.

In general for my informants, these thematic tensions were part of the situational flux that marked their approaches to *Asian American*. For example, those who said they accepted Asian American identity could also, depending on the circumstances, speak of rejecting it, sometimes sounding much like those who generally rejected *Asian American* as a basis for affiliation and identity. Similarly, my informants understood the boundaries between official and ethnic pan-Asianism to be porous rather than rigidly separate.

At the same time, these two thematic tensions also represented differences among my informants in how they related to being Asian American. On a continuum of acceptance and rejection, some were more accepting of an Asian American identity than others, and they also differed in the degree of their identification with the ideologies of official versus ethnic pan-Asianism. To be sure, these differences were by no means carved in stone—changes in outlook along the continuum were a vital part of the life histories they recounted to me, as were redefinitions of the continuum itself. These shifts and changes were a vital part of the complex and emerging picture of Asian American identity that I uncovered.

The informants who accepted *Asian American* as a basis of affiliation and identity during their college years suggested, in their accounts, that they had followed two different, albeit crisscrossing paths to that acceptance. One path was to join a pan-Asian organization on campus, and the other was to join a pan-Asian social circle—a group or network of friends of varied Asian origin. In the next section I explore these paths of acceptance, then move on to look at the accounts of those informants who rejected Asian American identity in college.

■ *Joining Pan-Asian Organizations*

About one-third of my informants said that they had joined and become actively involved in a pan-Asian organization during their college years, usually for the first time in their lives.[6] Most of these informants attended college on the West Coast, and they also tended to be Chinese American rather than Korean American.

The organizations joined were, for the most part, associations with a broad agenda of bringing together students of varied Asian origin for political and social activities, with names such as Asian Students Alliance and Asian American Students United. Membership in pan-Asian organizations with a more specific

---

6. My definition of *active involvement* includes those who, at minimum, indicated that they had attended meetings and participated in activities on a fairly regular basis. There was great diversity in the scope of this involvement, ranging from those who simply met this minimum requirement to those who assumed positions of leadership and responsibility.

focus (like the Asian American Christian Fellowship and the Asian American Business Students Organization) were cited but tended to figure less prominently in the accounts. About half of my informants who were active in a pan-Asian organization were also active in an ethnic-specific association (like the Chinese Students Association), highlighting the fact that membership in both types is not mutually exclusive.

My informants often described their joining of the pan-Asian student organization on campus as a point of transformation, a watershed event in their lives that marked a shift in their attitude toward Asian American identity. In general, it signaled a shift from rejection to acceptance of their own "Asianness"; what had been an unwanted label, something to deny, now became something to embrace. This sense of transformation is conveyed by Paul, a Chinese American in his late twenties who grew up in a predominantly white area of northern California. Shortly after arriving at a California state college in the mid-1980s, Paul joined the Asian Student Union, attracted by its aura of political excitement as well as the character of its members, who defied the stereotypes of Asians as nerdy that he had been battling in his own life:

> It was in college that I first stopped denying who I was, that I was Asian. I joined the Asian Student Union and became very involved in that. I remember the first meeting, it was a real experience, all those years of denial, I just felt it slipping away. [What made you go to the first meeting?] They had a reputation, very exciting, very radical. Really militant. I didn't always like that, I didn't believe in everything they wanted to do. But I liked it too.
>
> [What kinds of things did the group do?] Well, we protested things like negative media portrayals of Asians, which I'm still very interested in. And we belonged to a Third World Students Association, which was comprised of the various groups like La Raza and the Black Students Union. So we met to go over the various issues that were important, you know, like racism, like the college not giving enough support to minorities.
>
> It's not that those things weren't important to me, but I was more interested in the social aspect of it. Yeah, I think maybe that's what was going on. It was a very positive experience for me because I think I became more proud of who I was and more comfortable. I finally met some cool Asians. I met Asian American men who were into sports, who were smart, they could dance and they weren't nerds. You know, they were very interesting people.

A wide variety of events and circumstances induced my informants to become involved in pan-Asian organizations on campus. While for Paul it was at least in part a desire to get to know "cool Asians," for others the trigger to involvement was an encounter with racial hostility on campus, or a general desire to become politically active. Particularly striking were the many informants who said that a notable individual or class had provided them with the decisive push. For these informants, a mentoring relationship with a staff or faculty member who was involved in Asian American organizing on campus was critical.

This was the case for Wayne, a Chinese American who attended a small private college in the Midwest in the late 1970s and early 1980s. Wayne spoke of how a staff member, the coordinator of the Asian American Alliance on campus, had nurtured his self-awareness and inspired him to become involved in Asian American organizations and activities:

> I was part of the Asian American Alliance at ——— College. And I think that has given me a certain depth of understanding about the world that I wouldn't have had otherwise. [How did you come to be involved in the Asian American Alliance?] I was just having such a horrible time my first year. I was very homesick. I was uncomfortable. I think some of it has to do with ethnicity and some of it with socioeconomic class. I wasn't used to being around wealthy kids.
>
> I started occasionally going to lunch with the coordinator of the alliance. He was Chinese American, like in his thirties. Looking back, I can see that he was giving me counseling. I mean, I could have gone to psychological services, but I could trust this guy. I could just sit in his office, and we would talk. Soon he started asking, "Why don't you come to one of our meetings?" I wasn't sure at first. But that's how I got involved.
>
> And I found it really pulled together a lot of what I was going through. We organized panels on interracial dating and hate crimes. We had dance parties. And we had this Asian American theater group that I later became part of. I'm still quite active in the Asian American arts movement, organizing workshops, raising money for theater, that kind of thing.

Echoing Wayne, Lily, a Chinese American, recalled that Mary, a dean at a private university in the Northeast, had been an important influence for her. Mary, a Korean American, had been a role model for Lily and was uniquely able to mediate on her behalf, when it came to her parents:

When I walked into ——— University, Mary was someone who would seek out
the Asian families. She made an effort to come and talk to my parents. And parents, of course, loved the fact that any dean would come and talk to them, let
alone an Asian dean. I went to see her later. My dad was saying, "Do something
practical. Take economics courses." I wasn't doing well at all. Mary said, "What
do *you* want to study?" I said, "Psych, but what about my parents?" She was the
one who said, "It doesn't matter what you take—I want you to get your grades
up." So then I could go back to my parents and say, "Look, this is what the dean
said." And my parents, not being the ones to challenge authority, went along
with it.

Mary tried very hard to put some unity around the Asian population. I took
Chinese, which was taught by a white woman. I took some sort of Asian American course—the readings were like *The Woman Warrior,* and we had to keep a
journal. And then there were speakers. Mary pushed the issue, so if you wanted
to explore your identity, you could do that.

There were a couple of racial incidents on campus at the time I was there. And
I started writing letters to the editor and stuff. I showed them to my parents, and
my mother, like, freaked out. She was like, "Don't make waves." I went to Mary,
and she said, "Oh, don't worry about that." She was a good older person who
understood a lot of the cultural issues.

For some informants, a particular class in Asian American studies was the
critical event, the spur to involvement. Here the experience of the course itself
was the point of transformation, the critical watershed in the development of
a person's Asian American identity. Philip's account of such a class is especially
dramatic. A Korean American who attended a state university in the Northeast
in the 1990s, Philip enrolled in an Asian American studies class:

I was a biology major, then economics—and really unaware, apathetic politically.
A friend talked me into taking an Asian American studies course—it was the only
one offered at that time. It was an amazing experience. I came to see the world in
a different light. Things that hadn't made sense before kind of fell into place. The
subtle racism that Asians face, things I couldn't quite put a finger on before. And
the instructor was a very dynamic guy who had been involved in Asian American studies for a long time. He was passionate and charismatic, and kind of drew
everyone in. I still have friendships from that class, it was a very special experi-

ence. But that was how I started to get involved in Asian American issues, that was how it started.

As Philip's account suggests, my informants' transformations toward *Asian American* had multiple dimensions, involving not only the development of political consciousness and activism but also the formation of important social relationships with other Asian Americans. That is, involvement in pan-Asian organizations brought with it participation in pan-Asian friendships and social networks.

When Soo Kee joined the pan-Asian student group on his campus, a large state university in New England in the late 1970s, the repercussions were both political and social in nature and were apparently deeply intertwined, indeed virtually seamless. A Chinese American, Soo Kee described an intoxicating atmosphere, one in which the Asian American campus organization provided an umbrella for socializing, self-exploration, and political activity, all mixed together in heady and exciting ways:

> College was a fantastic experience as far as bringing my Asian American awareness to the surface. Because when I was growing up, there was no such thing as the Asian American movement. But at ———, that part of me became very strong. I got quite involved with the Asian American Students Association, with their cultural and political events. We protested. There was an Asian American studies program at the time that they were going to cut, so we protested. We did a lot of soul-searching academically, culturally, otherwise. We talked about racism, about stereotypes against Asians. We hung out together. I got to know Asians from different backgrounds, Japanese, Filipino.

Like Soo Kee, Greg found that joining the pan-Asian organization in his college affected his friendship circle in important ways. A Chinese American, he attended a large state university in the Midwest in the early 1980s. He was motivated to join the Asian American Coalition in response to encounters with racial hostility on campus. Thus while the political activities of the coalition were of the utmost importance to him, the friendships that he had developed through it were also very important:

> I joined the Asian American Coalition after the first year. Initially I was not interested, but then when I got to college, my freshman year, that was probably the

first time I've experienced any kind of racial hostility against myself. There was frat row, and I remember slurs. That was the first time I ever got called a "chink," you know. I mean, that was just a word I had heard about before that. And it made me pretty angry; I decided to get involved.

[What was that like, the Asian American coalition?] We organized workshops, speakers, events on Asian American literature, hate crimes. We were also friends. They weren't my only friends, but it was socially pretty important for me. Most of the people I keep up with from college are from that group.

By contrast, a few informants emphasized the decidedly political rather than social character of their involvement with pan-Asian organizations. It was, in fact, the emphasis on political activity that had made these organizations far more appealing to them than the ethnic-specific associations on campus (like the Chinese Students Group). This was the case for Cori, a Korean American who attended a private university in New England in the late 1980s and early 1990s. For her, the Asian American organization on campus was a vehicle for progressive activism on behalf of minority groups. Its activities stood for her in sharp contrast to those of the Korean student groups on campus, which had, she thought, a "party focus."

Cori's remarks caution us against overgeneralizing about the circumstances and impact of joining a pan-Asian organization. But they do not, I believe, ultimately argue against the idea that joining such an organization tends to be accompanied by the development of pan-Asian friendships and incorporation into pan-Asian social networks. In one sense, the vehemence with which Cori denied the social character of her political involvements underlined the fact that it could be and was often so for others; she was the exception to the rule:

The Korean student groups, I didn't really get along with. I was more involved with the Asian student groups because they were more political, educational, and the Korean groups were purely social, really into parties. I mean, I had individual friends who were in the Korean groups, but I never felt they were worth my time. I never understood the point. I can be social without a group, I can meet Asian people without a group.

So I got involved with the Asian Student Union. I learned a lot about the history of Asian Americans by attending talks and just listening to people who were really involved in community work. Like, I remember going to something on the Japanese American internment, and I remember talking with people about hate crimes against Asians. But I worked a lot with the other minority groups, the women's groups, the civil rights groups. At the time there was a lot of anti-Asian violence against the Cambodian population. So I helped with a campaign to protest and to build awareness against that.

Reflecting her involvement in pan-Asian organizations, Cori's understanding of *Asian American* was colored by the official ideology of pan-Asianism and the notions of shared racial and political interest that are so vital to it. But among those who spoke of the pan-Asian organizations as not just a political but also a social activity, glimmerings of a different, more culturally oriented view of Asian American affiliation, of ethnic pan-Asianism, were more apparent. In these cases, relationships with other Asian Americans provided the basis for an understanding of *Asian American* in not just political but also cultural terms.

An understanding of Asian America as a social and cultural community appears in the account of Steve, who joined the pan-Asian organization on his campus as a strategy for coping with the new social environment of college and for creating a comfortable social niche for himself. A Chinese American, Steve had grown up in the Chinatown area of Los Angeles and attended a private university in California in the mid-1980s:

> It was a whole new world. I mean, it was my first exposure to the Anglo population. It was a big culture shock—I mean, just figuring out how to deal with different kinds of people and cultures. I guess I was shy, naïve. You know, the Chinese culture is not one for being real extroverted, whereas a lot of the Caucasian people I meet are more aggressive. And so it was just totally new, just trying to meet people and working with people. And then at ———— University you kind of end up doing what you grow up doing: You stick with your own type. I joined the Asian Students Organization, and I met a lot of people. They weren't just Chinese, but Koreans, Japanese.
>
> [How did you feel relating to these other groups?] You mean, like Koreans and Japanese? We discovered a lot in common as Asians. Like the culture we had been raised with, the value on education, kind of a similar outlook on life.

Sam, a Korean American who attended a large state university in California in the late 1970s, also developed a sense of the cultural commonalities of Asian Americans through his membership in several pan-Asian groups in college:

My social life in college basically centered on Asian Americans. My freshman year I joined the Asian Coalition, got really active at one point. I took Asian American studies courses, and I was active in the Asian American Bible Studies Group my first and second year. My friends were from these activities, so I had a lot of Asian American friends, mostly Japanese American and Korean American, a few Chinese and Indian. I found a lot more in common with them than with Caucasians. [How do you explain that?] It's the way we look, the history we share, and the culture. The Asian cultures have a lot in common: respect for the elderly, taking care of your parents.

Sam leaves somewhat vague and unspecified here the boundaries of Asian America and the nature of its commonality, thus giving the impression of a broadly based and inclusive collectivity. But other informants pointed out that it was with some Asian-origin persons rather than with others that they had felt a common background and worldview. The variable of immigrant versus later-generation status was prominent here: informants often spoke of having cultural commonality with other second-generation or later-generation Asians like themselves rather than with immigrants.

We see this in the words of Brenda, a Chinese American who attended a large public university in California in the late 1970s and early 1980s. She was quite active in the Asian Alliance, as a result of her general inclination toward political activism and her desire to better understand her upbringing and experience as the child of Asian immigrants. The sense of belonging in a pan-Asian community that she came to feel had been centered around relationships with American-born Asians:

> I was very active in the Asian Alliance, helping to draft a constitution, organize programs. I just kind of went all out with Asian activities during college. I took an Asian American studies course that was very eye-opening. I got a sense of the history of Asians in this country, the history of racism, and the need for political action. [What do you think attracted you to all this?] Well, I've always been politically aware, involved. Being in college, being in California, I think you're bound to start thinking of these things. But I think it was also to better understand the generations before me, so I could better relate to or understand them. If I look at it honestly, it was probably more to search for ways to help them better understand me, so they would have some respect for my opinions and values. I just didn't know where my parents were coming from. I needed to meet other people

who were going through the same experience. I think it was really important for me to be with American-born Asians. That's where I felt at home, that there was some real connection going on. I wanted to read about the second-generation experience, study about it.

■ *Developing an Asian American Social Circle*

I turn next to a set of informants who accepted Asian American identity but did not become involved in pan-Asian organizations. Their social life in college, they said, was centered around a friendship network of Asian Americans of varied ethnicities but for the most part of Japanese, Chinese, and Korean origin. When I asked these informants about the absence of their involvement in pan-Asian organizations, most indicated that they were not necessarily averse to such involvement. They had rather lacked opportunity, time, or sufficient interest in the particular activities of the available groups. Though not exclusively so, many of these informants were among those who attended college in California, thus suggesting that a significant Asian American presence was important to the development of this pattern. In contrast to the previous set of informants, no significant disparities between Chinese and Korean Americans were apparent here.

Where informants who had joined pan-Asian organizations had described undergoing dramatic shifts, even transformations, in developing an Asian American social circle, these nonjoining informants tended to describe a smooth, unremarkable process in which an Asian American social circle had "just happened." For Wai Han, a Chinese American who attended a state college in California in the mid-1980s, college friendships had been primarily pan-Asian or Asian American. At first she had been extremely busy at school, experiencing the pressures of both classes and jobs. Forming and maintaining friendships with non-Asians had required some active effort, while friendships with Asian Americans had developed in a natural, almost organic fashion. She felt a greater sense of social ease and receptivity with Asian Americans:

> I was working and didn't have a lot of time. I lived at home part of the time. My friends were from classes. They were all Asian. I mean not just Chinese but Korean, Japanese. It wasn't planned, it just happened. I've noticed that Asians are more receptive to me in terms of friendships. It may be they feel like I'm less apt

to decline any conversation or any attempt at conversing. There's also the sense of familiarity in terms of looks. You know that people see you the same. I think there's kind of a tie that comes out of that. We've talked about it, about how it's different in relationships with whites because there isn't that connection.

By contrast, George, a Korean American, turned to an Asian American social circle as a response to the pressures of the campus environment, and so his account has a more deliberate quality. At the Ivy League University he attended in the 1970s, he found the white students to be stand-offish and unreceptive to him, but relationships with other Asian American students were easy and comfortable:

> I found myself mainly with Asian American friends. In fact, there were three of us who were really close and they used to call us the Three Musketeers. Interestingly, one guy was Chinese American, the other was Japanese American, and of course I was Korean American. Maybe it's because ——— University is such an old, conservative, white place. But we felt more comfortable with each other. I found a lot of the students snobbish, unfriendly.
>
> Asian Americans tend to have more in common, you know. They have similar views on education and family. Similar family experiences, like pressure from parents to do well when you're growing up. When we talked about how we'd been raised, we were always amazed at the similarities. Plus we were pretty serious students. We were the nerds, you know.

Meg's social life in college involved mainly friendships with Asian Americans, and her reflections upon them were marked by references to ethnic pan-Asianism. She shared a common background and hence felt empathy with other Asian Americans, related to common growing-up experiences such as conflicts with parents over dating. Meg, a Chinese American, attended a private university in California in the early 1990s:

> I've thought about this before. I think it would have been good for me to have had a variety of friends. But psychologically, I didn't feel comfortable around Caucasians. I felt more in control of the situation when I was with other Asians. There's a common background there with Asians. The other day my friends and I were talking about how whenever we got together, we always asked each other about how our parents were, how the family was, that kind of thing. And how that just wouldn't be a normal topic of conversation for whites. Also, all our growing-up

experiences were the same — "You can't date until you're this age," or your parents disapprove of you dating this type, that type. We all understood that. My girlfriends especially.

[What was the ethnic background of your friends? Were they Chinese, or—]
Oh no. It was real mixed, all kinds of Asians, Japanese, Koreans. There was like a Chinese student crowd, and there was the CSA [Chinese Students Association]. I guess I could have been involved, but I felt a lot more comfortable with Asians. A lot of the Chinese crowd was not very Americanized. They're very different from me. More into the group thing, the material thing. You know, parties and stuff. I wouldn't fit in.

As I have noted earlier, my informants sometimes seemed to define notions of shared Asian culture and worldview in quite specific ways, carefully defining their boundaries. Meg, for example, made a point of differentiating her pan-Asian social circle from the "Chinese student crowd" on campus: she associated her circle with U.S.-born Asians, and the "Chinese student crowd" with foreign-born Asians. She felt no sense of kinship with the foreign-born, who had not had the experience of growing up in the United States.

Similarly for Sandra, the second-generation experience — that of growing up in the United States as a child of immigrants — was an important part of what tied her to other Asian Americans of her generation. A Korean American, Sandra attended a private women's college in the mid-1980s. (It is important to note that the working-class Asian immigrant history that she invokes here does not capture the socioeconomic diversity of contemporary Asian immigration.)

I would say the whole immigrant experience really brought us closer together. It's like they know what it's like to have parents who do not speak the language fluently, who are handicapped culturally and verbally. And they know what it's like to see their parents working seven days a week and in these often dangerous settings or every kind of blue-collar work like dry cleaning. So I think that common experience ties us together. Or the fact that we do share just this rich heritage, and there are these kind of overlaps to our history. Definitely we share that bicultural experience where we feel more comfortable with English, yet when we go home we have to adjust.

I think when you're talking about people who were raised here, we share a lot of that, but not necessarily with people who came here when they were older. But I think there is high emphasis on education and emphasis on whatever you're doing—you have to be diligent and industrious. Family values—yeah, that seems to be a given. It's like a common thread.

Although in far more muted or less explicit ways, informants sometimes, in their reflections on the commonalities of Asian Americans, spoke of differences between themselves and persons of other Asian ethnonational backgrounds. It is possible that, during our interviews, my own South Asian origins constrained them from openly discussing how some Asian origin groups had more in common than others. But even in the face of this possible constraint, they did sometimes mention ethnic differences. Commonalities of race and culture were, they felt, most pronounced among persons of East Asian descent, specifically of Chinese, Japanese, and Korean origin (due to similarities in physical characteristics as well as overlaps of history and culture, especially a tradition of Confucianism). George, the Korean American who previously recounted developing a pan-Asian circle in college, made this point:

> My friends were Japanese, Chinese. Of all the Asian groups, Koreans, Japanese, and Chinese have the most in common. [In what way?] Everybody gets us mixed up; they can't tell us apart. [That doesn't happen with a Vietnamese or Filipino?] It can happen, but it's less likely, especially if you're talking about Asians looking at each other. It's much easier, I think, to tell a Korean from a Filipino person than Chinese. It's also that there are common roots for Koreans, Japanese, and Chinese if you go way back. Like our writing is from the same family. And the cultures are based on Confucianism.

Taken together, these accounts begin to sketch the contours of a particular understanding of Asian American community. While those who joined pan-Asian organizations created a certain synthesis and interplay of the official and the ethnic ideologies of pan-Asianism, those who socialized informally with other Asians clearly preferred an ethnic pan-Asianism in which shared race and culture, and a common personal history and worldview, were at the heart of Asian American community. According to ethnic pan-Asianism, because Asians have a shared racial identity in the United States, they had all had the experience of being racially labeled and lumped together as Asian, and being stereotyped as nerdy, foreign, and so forth. They also shared an Asian culture, marked by certain orientations and values, such as an emphasis on education, family, and work. My informants understood these dual commonalities of race and culture within the framework of the classic immigrant narrative, in which the second generation grows up in two different worlds—the ethnic and the American—with all the attendant conflicts. The particular significance of Asian American community stemmed from the intersections of this particular history, of growing up in two worlds, with the commonalities of Asian race and culture.

My informants, then, were describing critical differences between official pan-Asianism and ethnic pan-Asianism. Both ideologies acknowledge that race and racism are part of what brings and holds persons of Asian origin together. But ethnic pan-Asianism does not explicitly associate race with the shared political interests of Asian Americans or with the notion of Asian American as a strategic political community—rather, it emphasizes the shared *personal* histories and outlooks produced by race. Certainly it has the potential to make such a recognition—the boundary between official and ethnic pan-Asianism is porous. But in ethnic pan-Asianism, such recognition remains a potential rather than a clearly articulated notion.

Ethnic pan-Asianism, put simply, lacks the emphasis on race that marks official pan-Asianism, which assigns a central, chronic, and systemic role to race in defining the very meaning of *Asian American*. Ethnic pan-Asianism filters the impact of race through the lens of the classic immigrant story, a filtering that mutes and neutralizes the significance of race. At the same time, ethnic pan-Asianism emphasizes a shared Asian culture, while official pan-Asianism is critical of efforts to construct *Asian American* as a cultural community, mindful of the realities of diversity among Asian Americans.

■ *Rejecting Pan-Asianism*

I turn now to my informants who identified themselves as *not* having been involved either in pan-Asian organizations or in pan-Asian friendship groups and networks during college. They offered several explanations for their lack of involvement, varying in degree of self-conscious or active choice. Some, for example, spoke of a lack of opportunity or appropriate circumstances. But others chose to actively reject Asian American affiliation outright.

Many of those who rejected Asian American affiliation explained their choice by saying that they had chafed at the artificiality of the Asian American construct, in particular at the notion of community that it implies. This artificiality critique was voiced by many of my informants, but it was especially clear and stark in the accounts of those who said that their social life in college had been dominated by friendships with fellow Chinese Americans or Korean Americans and, in some cases, accompanied by involvement in a Chinese or Korean student organization. These informants, more often Korean Americans than Chinese Americans, rejected *Asian American* in favor of *Chinese* or *Korean American* as a basis for their identity and community. In essence, they understood *Asian American* to be a weak and relatively insignificant basis for identity and community—a construct that was artificial and externally imposed, in contrast to the more natural, primordial ties and solidarity of specific ethnonational groups such as Chinese or Koreans.

Susan, a Korean American who attended a state college in California in the early 1980s, was among those who rejected pan-Asianism as artificial. For her, pan-Asian friendships were far less important than Korean friendships. College had been a time, she said, when she had come to identify more strongly as Korean. This transformation had come about as she had encountered, for the first time in her life, Korean-origin peers who were, like herself, Americanized:

When I started going to ———, I was really anti-Korean because I thought all Korean men or boys were really chauvinistic and domineering, like my dad. Or really wimpy and nerdy. And I didn't really have respect for Korean girls because my sense was, they didn't have any ambition in life. They just wanted to marry right and to gossip about clothes, boys, that type of thing. They weren't conscious about other things that were going on. I don't know where I got this idea, but I was really dissatisfied with Korean women.

So I had this stereotype of Korean women, and I used to tell myself, "I'm not going to hang out with Koreans when I get to college, because they're so narrow-minded and they only speak Korean and they don't assimilate." But then once I got there I met Koreans, and they encouraged me to join their Korean student organizations and stuff. I realized that it was kind of a bonding that almost comes naturally. I think I realized my identity, and I also realized that not all the Korean kids fit the stereotype. There were Korean kids just like me who grew up in predominantly white neighborhoods and had a lot of white friends. They weren't all nerdy or chauvinistic. We could relate to whites really well.

[So your friends in college were mainly Korean American?] Yeah, I mean, there were so many Korean Americans there that I didn't need to go beyond that. I mean, I had a lot of friends. I did have some Chinese and Japanese friends I met through a pre-law Asian students group. But still, with Koreans it's different. I feel like there's a natural attraction. With other Asians, it's more artificial.

If Susan found *Asian American* to be artificial because it lacked a kind of primordial underpinning of natural attraction, Jeff, a Korean American, rejected it because its sense of common interest seemed to him falsely constructed. Jeff's perspective on this and many other issues was deeply affected by the 1992 Los Angeles riots, during which the small store owned and operated by his parents had been attacked. Jeff attended a private university in the Northeast in the early 1990s, and for him as for Susan, the transition to a primarily Korean American social circle had taken place during college. But for him this transition had been triggered by a growing sense of discomfort with and alienation from the predominantly white social groups around which he had initially organized his social life:

I would say that the first time that I started feeling a close bond with Koreans was in college. It's funny because when I started, in my freshman year, I joined a white fraternity, and I was fairly active. I didn't really participate in any of the Korean functions, and I guess the Koreans called me whitewashed. Then I had a good friend who was part of that Korean clique. By my second year, I kind of assimilated into the Korean crowd. It wasn't easy at first because they had labeled me as whitewashed. [What happened with the fraternity?] I was less and less involved. I was one out of three Asians in a very large organization, and it felt strange. It was subtle, but I don't think I was accepted. So my friends were pretty much Korean in college, and it's been that way since then. I find it's more comfortable.

[Is that also the case with Asian Americans from other groups? Do you have other Asian friends?] No, not really. I mean, I had acquaintances in college who were Chinese, that kind of thing. I can't say I had more in common with them than with whites or blacks or whatever. It's a mistake to think there's any real bond going on there. We speak different languages, have different perspectives. I was in college during the riots. I remember reading right after the riots about how the Chinese and Japanese communities in L.A. were just unfazed. I mean, it didn't concern them—it was a Korean problem. You know, I just don't see that there's too much in common going on there. Why do we have to go around pretending that Asian Americans are the same?

Jeff's resentment of what he felt to be the pretense of Asian American unity was echoed by several other informants. Some had encounters with pan-Asian groups and activities that made sharply visible to them what they perceived as the fictional nature of Asian American community. This was the case for Terry, a Chinese American who attended a state college in California in the early 1980s. Unlike Susan and Jeff, Terry had grown up with Chinese American friendships, having been raised in the Chinatown areas of San Francisco and Los Angeles. In college, her experience with an Asian American student organization and its internal tensions was disappointing for her and made her feel that Chinese were more similar, culturally and in other respects as well, than Asians in general. It is of note that she simultaneously qualified this notion of a natural Chinese bond by recognizing generational divisions among Chinese, and by highlighting her sense of ethnic affinity to American-born Chinese in particular:

> Most of my friends were Chinese, I felt more comfortable socially with Chinese. [How about Asian friends, I mean, from other Asian groups?] I did have some Asian friends in college who were not Chinese. At first I went to the Asian Students Association. But it was very political. One group would say, "We're not getting represented, we want a voice." I couldn't get into it, I couldn't see the point. I find it less stressful with Chinese; I'm talking mainly American-born Chinese. We have the same history, we grew up with the same superstitions, foods.

Several informants echoed Terry's general sense of discomfort with campus pan-Asian organizations. Some complained of the progressive or "radical" political agenda of the pan-Asian groups, with which they disagreed and which only confirmed for them the fake, contrived character of *Asian American* as a basis for identity and community. Bill, a Chinese American who attended a private university in California in the early 1980s, found the progressive political agenda of the pan-Asian groups on campus to be unconvincing and in fact distasteful. While he was not very interested in the Chinese student groups either, in the latter half of his college career he found himself in a "Chinese clique." Besides connoting to him a certain economic glamour, Chinese ties, he said, were natural and primordial—rooted in blood:

> In college I stayed away from Chinese for a long time. I mean, I didn't go looking for Chinese. The Chinese Students Association was not very interesting to me. Neither were the Asian student groups. They were too crazy, always spouting off

about oppression. I really think this whole Asian thing is overplayed. In the last couple of years, I got into a Chinese clique. It was a change—I'd spent all this time avoiding Chinese. And then it seemed kind of exciting. China is such a booming area economically. I felt kind of drawn to it. I think it's like they say, being Chinese is in your blood.

If some informants rejected the Asian American construct for its artificiality, others dismissed it as "stifling." This particular criticism was most commonly voiced by those who described themselves as "not ethnically oriented" in college, more or less unconnected with the Asian, Chinese, or Korean American communities on campus. As many took pains to assure me, this lack of connection did not mean that they had no individual friends from these backgrounds—it was just that the social groups, networks, and associations to which they had belonged could not be characterized in racial or ethnic terms. Still, while many spoke in general terms of having "diverse friends" from varied backgrounds, their accounts also tended to indicate that friendships with white students were what prevailed.

According to this group of informants, the *Asian American* construct was stifling because of its opposition to individuality and to the exercise of freedom and choice in affiliation and identity. In their view, Asian American communities collectively embodied qualities and traits that were antithetical to individualism, such as clannishness, group conformity, and gender traditionalism. Second, they felt that the very fact of prescribed membership challenged individuality itself. That is, the fact that one was expected to belong to Asian American group(s), regardless of how one felt about it, was stifling. In a sense, then, they saw *Asian American* as an expression of racism, rooted in the imposed label of *Asian.*

For Gordon, a Chinese American, the expectation held by other students of Asian origin on campus that he would join an Asian group were particularly troubling. He refused to join, and other students labeled him as a "banana"— someone striving to be white and denying his true heritage. His discomfort was only compounded when his white friends teased him about belonging to the "Asian crowd." These dynamics, along with his negative impressions of the Asian student groups (he found them closed-minded and too serious) meant that the very idea of *Asian American* made him feel claustrophobic:

It was very strange at ———— University because that was the first time that I was surrounded by other Asian people. And it was kind of funny, but I felt uncomfortable with it. [How did it make you feel uncomfortable?] I never really looked at myself as Asian. Well, I never really looked at myself as anything, you know, growing up in this white suburb. When I got there, I was solicited to join the Korean Club and the Chinese Club and the Asian Club.

But I had never grouped myself as Asian or Chinese or anything like that. And so it was just something new. I met a lot of them, and it really turned me off. It's the closed-mindedness, to the point where they kind of shun other people. It's kind of mean to say, but I didn't enjoy being with them. They were—they were typically Asian. They were—they were not very fun. They were very serious.

[Were these people mainly Asian immigrants? Foreign students? Or were they raised here?] Both—I didn't see a huge difference there. I would get a lot of flak from both sides. The Asian group, they would give me a hard time—"Hey, why aren't you hanging out with us? Are you a banana?" My [white] friends would kid around about it and ask me why I wasn't hanging out with the Asians. They were joking, they knew I wouldn't fit in with the Asians.

Ben, too, was repelled by the perceived cliquey and conformist character of Asian campus communities. Soon after he began speaking of his experience with his fellow Korean students, he slipped into talking about Asians in general. Ben attended a private university in the Northeast for a year in the early 1990s, before dropping out and joining the armed services:

These Korean guys came up to me and said, "Why aren't you hanging out with us? Why aren't you part of the gang, the Korean posse?" I was thinking, "Are we still in high school? A Korean posse? Is this for real?" It was too stifling—I didn't want to be part of some group. I think it's important for people to be themselves. You always see these Asian people in a group, everything's a group.

My female informants in particular tended to express an aversion to traditional male-dominant gender roles, in order to explain why they had steered clear of the Asian, Chinese, or Korean communities on campus. Katherine, a Korean American who attended a private university in the Northeast in the early to mid-1980s, began by speaking specifically of her experiences with the Korean Students Association, but then moved on to Asians in general. What she felt to be the male chauvinism of Asian men, along with the general Asian emphasis on group activity, led her to stay away from all Asian groups in general:

I had a really broad group of friends. We had a rooming group of ten women, and we looked like the United Nations. Puerto Rican, Japanese American, Jewish American, a woman from Seattle, two black women from the South. I did find, though, that I couldn't hang out with Koreans who were in Korean groups; that wouldn't work for me.

I went to the Korean Student Association meetings, and I felt like they were pointless. The men pretty much led the meetings. Basically I really like Asian women, and I don't really get along with Asian men. There are few Asian men who are willing to let down all preconceptions about women — I've even seen that with a lot of really liberal, well-educated Asian guys. And I seem to break a lot of the stereotypes about Asian women. In any case, the whole group thing drove me nuts.

Jane's concerns about gender traditionalism were focused less on the behavior of Asian men than on that of the women who were part of the Chinese student groups on campus. Not only were the women deferential to the men, she said, but they were also frivolous and focused on ostentatious material displays. Coming as she did from a modest financial background, she was particularly offended by these material displays. A Chinese American, she attended a private university in California in the early 1980s:

I was working and going to school at the same time. I had a scholarship, and I felt a lot of pressure to do well. You know, I had basically gone to an inner-city school, and I don't think the academic standards had been too high. I had to work really hard to get good grades. I was on scholarship, but financially it was still not easy. So socially I wasn't all that active, until about my third year. My close friends were people I met in class, pretty much Caucasian.

[Did you join any Asian or Chinese student groups?] No. I did have a Chinese friend who dragged me to a couple of meetings and a dance organized by a Chinese group. It was a real turn-off. I was almost offended in some ways. It was a big status thing — expensive clothes, cars. And I didn't like the whole male-female dynamic. It was too much like the delicate Asian flower waiting for the man to sweep her off her feet.

Men informants, too, voiced complaints about an excessive "party focus," particularly in relation to the Chinese or Korean groups and organizations on their campuses. Sung, a Korean American, was turned off, he said, by the "drinking club" atmosphere of the Korean Students Association. He also felt no sense of connection to the Asian American organizations on campus, disagreeing with their political agenda and feeling a lack of space for dialogue within them. All of this only enhanced his tendency to associate the idea of Asian American affiliation with conformity and the restriction of free choice.

His friends, he said, were a diverse group (a point often made by informants who criticized what they saw as the cliquish and conformist character of Asian groups). A diversity in one's friendships thus became a kind of proof of one's individuality and one's ability to make choices apart from groups:

> My friends in school were really just a motley crew, and that was something I really liked. I wasn't interested in the Korean Students Association, which was a social thing. I mean, it was like a drinking club, a place to find a future wife— that kind of thing. It was like a fraternity. [How about Asian American groups?] I went to a couple of Asian American meetings my first year, but the agenda that they had just didn't sit well with me. I mean, I couldn't get all that interested in what they had to say. They were very much oriented toward trying to frame the Asian American experience using a language or way of describing things that is similar to civil rights. There was no room for disagreement, for dialogue. You know, I thought it was kind of a stretch. African Americans have been screwed in this country for a long, long time, whereas the Asians have generally been treated better.

The accounts of the informants presented in this chapter so far are dominated by negative impressions and reactions to Asian student groups on campus. A somewhat different perspective was provided by Connie, a Chinese American who attended a state college in California in the late 1970s and early 1980s. Having grown up in a largely Chinese neighborhood, she self-consciously set out at college to meet persons from other backgrounds. These efforts had, she felt in retrospect, paid off, teaching her to feel comfortable with different kinds of people. Thus while for her, Asian American affiliation did not have the kinds of overtly negative connotations that other informants described, she nonetheless associated it with limitations, with restriction on choice. Once again, she too associated a diverse friendship network with free choice, in contrast to the constraints of an Asian or Chinese social circle:

As soon as I got there, I found myself in an Asian clique. These Asian persons that I didn't know came up and invited me to sit with them in the dining hall. And every night we'd eat together and there would be this long table of about twenty Asian Americans — Japanese, Chinese. And then I decided, "What's going on here? I want to meet some other kinds of people." So after my first year I kind of expanded, joined some different groups, and met other people. I had some white friends for the first time in my life, and I had Hispanic friends.

[How did you feel with the other, the non-Asian friends that you made? Did you feel accepted?] Oh yes, absolutely. I think it was really important for me, because I started to feel more comfortable with other people. I have a really diverse group of friends, I can choose to be with whoever I want. If I hadn't made that effort in college, it might be different. I don't feel confined. I feel that I can go anywhere and be accepted.

To summarize, then: Some second-generation Chinese and Korean Americans recalled their college years as a time when they chose not to affiliate with Asian American groups at all, or to understand themselves to be Asian American in some meaningful way. Many criticized the notion of Asian American community as artificial and stifling. Such criticisms, let me emphasize, were extremely widespread. This is not so surprising. As we have seen in Chapter 3, resistance to imposed "Asianness" is a fundamental experience for second-generation Chinese and Korean Americans. As analysts of the Asian American movement have noted, attempts to build solidarity around the very category that has been used to racialize, homogenize, and oppress those within it has inherent and ongoing contradictions (Dirlik 1996).

■ *Developing an Asian American Identity*

Just as my informants responded to the social and identity challenges of the college years in many different ways, some of these differences remained significant to them beyond their college years as well. For example, those who developed a pan-Asian friendship circle during college were more likely to continue to have a social life in which pan-Asian friendships figured prominently.

But other informants underwent changes. The general direction of the shifts described were toward acceptance of *Asian American* as a meaningful identity. After college my informants became more involved in pan-Asian organizations, even those individuals who had felt an aversion to pan-Asian involvements during college. In the years after college they joined pan-Asian groups with a specific focus or membership base, most commonly professional or workplace associations, such as the Asian American Architects Association or the Asian American Resource Network of ———— Corporation. A smaller number joined pan-Asian religious groups—Asian American churches and fellowship groups. Quite notably missing from their adult lives were the progressive and broad-agenda pan-Asian associations of the college years.

This postcollege rise in pan-Asian activity appeared among both my Chinese and my Korean American informants. In college the Korean Americans had been less likely than their Chinese American counterparts to join and participate in pan-Asian organizations on campus. They had also been somewhat more likely to have social lives dominated by fellow Korean Americans. In the years after college, too, Korean Americans were more likely than Chinese Americans to be members of ethnonational-specific organizations. Yet even with these differences, Korean Americans too reported a growing interest and involvement in pan-Asian associations after college.

My informants' growing pan-Asian involvements were the result of several factors, including newly affirmative understandings of the identity of *Asian American* and a self-conscious acceptance of it. Their subjective understandings of Asian American community were marked by what I have called ethnic pan-Asianism, at the heart of which is the idea that Asian Americans have the common ground of race and culture, along with the shared experiences that that common ground implies. In making sense of these new-found commonalities, my informants drew on the conceptual stage set by the ethnic American model and the dramatic narratives, informed by the European American experience, that are a part of it. In the chapters that follow, I further explore the emerging contours of ethnic pan-Asianism and the forces and impulses that inform its development.

CHAPTER FIVE

The Model Minority at Work

Despite years of discrimination—much of it enforced by the federal government—the difficulties of acculturation and a recent backlash against their burgeoning numbers, Asian-Americans now enjoy the nation's highest median family income: $22,075 a year compared to $20,840 for whites. The Chinese have a term for it—"gung-ho"—and the industrious Asians believe they are contributing a needed shot of some vanishing American values: thrift, strong family ties, sacrifice for the children.   (*Newsweek* 1982)

Although I am standing less than a mile from where our family began its life in America, we've come a long way. Our journey was possible because of a deep faith in the essential goodness of mainstream American values; the values of hard work, hope, enterprise and opportunity. Our journey was successful because the Locke family embraces three values: Get a good education, work hard, and take care of each other.
(1997 inaugural address of Gary Locke, Chinese American
and governor, State of Washington; from Wu [1997, 46])

IN RECENT YEARS, as we have seen, Asians in the United States have been popularly identified as the *model minority,* or a minority group that is primed for socioeconomic advancement and success. At the heart of their achievements are, it is said, their cultural predispositions, in particular a strong work ethic and an emphasis on education. While the model minority stereotype is undoubtedly pervasive, its meanings and implications for the contemporary Asian American experience have been a matter of some controversy. Some observers interpret it in a positive vein, seeing it as marking the assimilative potential of Asian-origin persons in the United States. Others, however, see it as symptomatic of the deep-seated and chronic marginality of Asian Americans. In this chapter I explore the effects of the model minority stereotype on those who are its focus. Of particular interest are the ways in which second-generation Chinese and Korean Americans actively respond to the model minority stereotype and negotiate its impact on their lives.

The model minority stereotype has a highly fluid and multidimensional set of meanings. I found my second-generation Chinese and Korean American informants to be struggling at times to resist the label of *model minority*, to ward off its limitations and dangers; they considered it part of their experience of racial marginality in the dominant society. But they also drew on the model minority stereotype in affirmative ways, in their efforts to make sense of and define the position of Asian Americans within the racial hierarchy of the United States.

■ *The Model Minority Stereotype Debate: Assimilation or Marginality?*

The model minority stereotype has, in recent times, been a focus for reflection and debate about the place of Asian Americans in the contemporary American racial and ethnic landscape (see Kibria 1998). The stereotype's most controversial aspect is the notion that it is beneficial to Asian Americans. At first glance, the stereotype does indeed seem to signal that the dominant society accepts Asian Americans as active participants in the American dream: they are "making it" through their own talents and accomplishments. As Hochschild (1995) has noted, the ideology of the American dream implies that those who succeed according to its tenets are considered virtuous, and virtuous success would seem to offer a passport to assimilation, to acceptance by the dominant society and integration into its ranks.

But most academic analyses of the model minority stereotype have been quite critical of its meaning for the Asian American experience. They identify it not as a sign of ongoing Asian assimilation but rather as a vehicle for the expression and perpetuation of racist attitudes toward Asian Americans. Many such analyses urge us to look beyond the sugary veneer of the model minority stereotype and observe its hidden surfaces and meanings.

Okihiro (1994), for example, argues that the model minority stereotype does not, after all, represent a favorable departure from the nineteenth-century image of Asians as a "yellow peril." The "model minority" and the "yellow peril" are actually continuous images, he argues, vitally connected to each other:

It seems to me that the yellow peril and the model minority are not poles, denoting opposite representations along a single line, but in fact form a circular relationship that moves in either direction. We might see them as engendered images: the yellow peril denoting a masculine threat of military and sexual conquest, and the model minority symbolizing a feminized position of passivity and malleability. Moving in one direction along the circle, the model minority mitigates the alleged danger of the yellow peril, whereas reversing direction, the model minority, if taken too far, can become the yellow peril. (142)

As Okihiro suggests, the model minority stereotype, with its yellow-peril roots, can provide both a focus for the expression of resentment toward Asian Americans for their achievements as well as a means of containing the competitive threat posed by these achievements. In both the model minority image and that of the yellow peril, Asian achievement takes on an inhuman, even species-different character.

Takaki (1979), for his part, observes that white workers in nineteenth-century America, when accusing Chinese workers of posing unfair competition, described them as "human machines" and "steam engines" that could work endlessly. Echoing these accusations, current hostilities toward Asians often focus on their inhuman, robotlike, and one-dimensional qualities, underscoring their essential distance from the "normal." For example, in American school and college environments today, Asian American students are often stereotyped as overly studious and socially awkward nerds who raise the grading curve and so make life difficult for everyone else. They then become a legitimate target of resentment.

Critical analyses also point out that the model minority stereotype not only sets up Asians as legitimate targets of resentment but potentially denigrates the scope and significance of their achievements. Takagi (1992), for example, notes that in the race and college admissions debates of the 1980s, Asian students were not only applauded but also described as "good *but limited*" students. This description suggests a competence that is routine, unextraordinary, and limited in scope.

In the corporate sector the limitations of Asian achievement find expression in the "glass ceiling"—the inability to penetrate the uppermost tiers of the corporate ladder (Der 1993; Ong and Blumenberg 1994; Tang 1993; Woo 2000). Suggesting a quiet and routine competence, the model minority stereotype contributes to the dynamics of the glass ceiling for Asian Americans by marking them as "not leadership material."

Other critiques of the model minority stereotype focus on its role in creating a distinction, in public culture and consciousness, between the good, deserving minority—the model minority—and the undeserving minority. Here the stereotype is seen as an instrument of white supremacy, used to pit Asians and other minorities against each other and thus to weaken minority solidarity and power. Relatedly, the model minority stereotype also works to legitimate the absence or failure of programs and measures to address racial inequality (Osajima 1988). That is, since Asian Americans are able to pull themselves up by their own cultural bootstraps, the racial disadvantage suffered by minorities is not in fact structural to American society, and therefore no active intervention is required to remedy it.

The model minority stereotype can thus be understood in quite different ways: as a sign of the high level of acceptance enjoyed by Asian Americans, but also of the resentment that surrounds them and an indication of the barriers that obstruct their integration into the dominant society. But what seems to have been lost in these discussions is the perspectives of Asian Americans themselves. How do they understand the model minority stereotype, and how does it affect their lives? In what follows I explore my informants' experiences and negotiations of the model minority stereotype, with the aim of answering these questions.

My informants related to the model minority stereotype in a variety of ways. Sometimes it represented a template of expectations that others held of them—an idealized picture of how they were supposed to be as Asians. At these times the stereotype was a focus of resistance. But at other times it offered them a way of defining Asian culture and the place of Asian Americans within the social landscape of the United States. At these times, the model minority stereotype was a matter, not of resistance, but of affirmation.

■ *Negotiating the Expectations of "Typical Asian Achievement"*

Stereotypes, for those who are the focus of them, carry with them externally imposed expectations—the given ideas of others about individuals' character, motivations, actions, and behavior.[1] In this section I explore how my informants experienced and negotiated the expectations that arose from being seen as a

---

1. While emphasizing their externally imposed character, this definition does not exclude the possibility that the expectations may also be internalized.

member of the model minority. Contrary to what one might expect, given the at least superficially favorable character of these expectations, my informants very often not only refused to embrace them but resisted them and denied their applicability to themselves.

"I'm Not the Asian Whiz Kid": Falling Short of Model Minority Achievement

In the narrative of socioeconomic mobility that surrounds the Asian model minority stereotype, children play a particular role. Building on the efforts and sacrifices of immigrant parents, the children are expected to do well in school and thus to eventually make their way into a professional occupation. Among my informants, disclaimers or efforts to distance themselves from such "typical Asian achievement" were common. A frequent focus of these disclaimers was their academic talents and career: they would say that their school performance did not measure up to the expectations generally held for Asian students. While they sometimes said they were weak specifically in math skills, at other times they made general disclaimers about their academic achievement. Somewhat to my surprise, such statements were quite common, coming not at all exclusively from those whose biographies indicated explicit disengagement from schooling. Even those who appeared to have done quite well in their formal education made references to having not been a "good student."

This was the case with Duncan, a Chinese American who at the time of our interview was working as a physician. Despite the professional credentials that he had acquired, Duncan felt that he had not fulfilled what was expected of him as a student. "I was never the Asian whiz kid," he told me, "the one in school who got straight A's and perfect SAT scores. I mean, I've done okay, but it was never like that, I was never the smartest kid in class. And people expect it of a Chinese, that they're going to be the super-ace student. Like I said, I've done okay, but I'm not the Asian whiz kid."

As Duncan suggests, young Asian Americans may experience the model minority stereotype as an idealized and evaluative yardstick of achievement. That is, "typical Asian achievement," as it is etched out by the stereotype, becomes a basis for comparison, a standard for judging one's own accomplishments. Since these standards are inevitably generalized and imagined, one could almost inevitably come up short against them: the "Asian whiz kid" to whom Duncan compares himself is impossibly perfect in his or her grades and test scores. This negative comparison then contributes to the student's sense of personal failure, of not living up to expectations for Asians. To be sure, Duncan's disclaiming remarks, like those of other informants, could have been motivated by other considerations, such as the need to defuse the possible resentment of other students and, relatedly, to appear "normal" and not "nerdy." But it nonetheless seemed clear that they also expressed a certain sense of personal failure in relation to the imagined yardstick of Asian achievement.

Soo Jin, a Korean American in her twenties who had recently completed her law degree and started a new job, also spoke of not measuring up to academic expectations for Asians. In her case, family pressures had reinforced the high expectations generated by the stereotype of "typical Asian achievement." As we saw in Chapter 2, my informants grew up in family environments that strongly emphasized doing well at school. These pressures added to the expectations of model minority achievement, in particular to their psychological potency, their ability to impact a young person's self-esteem and generate a sense of failure. Soo Jin recalled:

> For me, one of the hard things about being Korean and Asian is the pressure to be really good at what you do, especially at schoolwork. It's always been a struggle for me. I've always felt like I haven't done well enough. [Why is that? It sounds to me like you've done pretty well.] Asian kids get it from all sides. Your mom and dad, who are probably immigrants, they're telling you to be the superstudent, like, "Get into Harvard." Then because you're Asian and people have this idea that Asians are really smart, you feel like you have to live up to it.

The feelings of failure related by Duncan and Soo Jin were echoed by Ki Hong, a Korean American who was working at the check-out counter of a convenience store at the time of our interview. Ki Hong remarked several times that he was not the "typical successful Asian." He spoke of a troubled adolescence, involving disengagement from school and difficulties with drugs and other illicit activities. But while clearly important, these problems were not the only way in which his life did not fit the Asian model minority picture. His account below hints at the importance of family context, of the socioeconomic status of his parents and the family in which he had grown up. Once they arrived in the United States in the early 1980s, Ki Hong's parents had struggled to support the family of six with a variety of unskilled and low-paying jobs. While they had hoped at one point to open a small business, they had been unable to do so. Ki Hong had a sharp consciousness that his entire family, in their economic situation and prospects, was not "typical Asian." "Most Asians do well at school," he asserted. "Nerdy, you know. I'm not like that though. In high school I got into a lot of bad stuff, like drugs and stuff. Most Asian kids are not like me. I'm different, I guess. Not in a good way, but that's the way it happened. My whole family, we're not like the typical Asians, the engineers or the store owners. We don't have that much money."

We see then that the Asian model minority stereotype, either with respect to academic performance or to familial prosperity, could be an evaluative yardstick for second-generation Chinese and Korean Americans, a standard by which to assess one's achievements. It was moreover a yardstick against which one would inevitably come up short and so feel a sense of personal failure. Such negative evaluations could even generate a sense of Asians as "others"—as persons different from oneself. At several points in the interview, Ki Hong asserted that he was different from "other Asians," whom he portrayed in homogenized terms, as uniformly prosperous and successful, in contrast to his own modest socioeconomic circumstances. A sense of discrepancy from the idealized Asian American experience may be especially sharp for those whose lives clearly diverge from the model minority images of prosperity and success.

The power of the model minority stereotype, especially its ability to make some Asian Americans feel distant from others, could be mitigated by exposure to critical analyses of the stereotype. Those of my informants who had a history of involvement in Asian American studies were particularly aware of its deceptive and negative aspects. Thus Hea Ran, a Korean American, mused on the complexity of her feelings about the model minority label: she felt a sense of failure, but also of anger and frustration: "Asians are supposed to be like this, like so—[What do you mean?] Good at math, good at the violin, supersuccessful. I've felt inadequate, and I think that's a common Asian American experience. But of course Asians are not all successful. That's a myth we're fed by this society."

"Don't Box Me In": Resisting Model Minority Expectations

If my informants lamented that the model minority achievement stereotype produced in them feelings of inadequacy and failure, they also found that disclaiming it could, in contrast, provide an opportunity for self-affirmation. Disclaiming the stereotype could be a way not only of distancing themselves from its expectations but of affirming their individuality, of asserting that they did not fit the standard box. I often detected a certain pleasure, a sense of empowerment on the part of the informants who asserted they were different from what was expected of Asians.

A number of my informants who had in fact achieved said that they had done so but in ways that differed from the stereotype. Cliff, for example, excelled not at academics but at athletic and social activities, which he felt distinguished him from the stereotypical expectations of Asians. While he expressed more than a hint of regret about the academics, his other successes affirmed for him his individuality.

A Korean American in his thirties, Cliff had become a police officer after a brief stint in the military. In his evaluation of his school career, Cliff contrasted himself, as "the jock," to the "Asian kids with straight A's." Implicit in this imagery is the stereotype of the "Asian nerd"—the socially awkward, serious, quiet, and mathematically oriented student. For Cliff as for many others, disclaiming model minority achievement seemed to be in part about disidentifying himself from the image of the "Asian nerd."

> I'm not one of those Asian kids with straight A's, the honors student who plays the violin. I was basically a jock who didn't care too much about school. [How do you look back on that? How do you explain it?] I had a natural talent for athletics. I wish I had been more interested in school, but I was just more into sports. I'm always going against the flow—I'm someone who doesn't go with the crowd.

If Cliff's identity as a jock was what distinguished him from "other Asians," for Dave it was an artistic and, more generally, an unconventional and nonconformist temperament. A Chinese American in his thirties, at the time of our interview Dave was working as a graphic arts designer in a large entertainment company in Los Angeles. Dave saw himself as talented and successful but in a way that was different from what is expected of Asians. "There are a lot of expectations, if you're Asian, that you'll be good at math, you'll do well at school," he told me. "That was not the case for me at all. I'm not that smart, at least in a conventional academic way. I do much better in creative, open learning environments. I eventually found my niche, something I'm really good at, that taps into my interest in art."

Some informants focused not on school performance but on occupational choice as their point of contradistinction from the "typical Asian." After several years of working in the entertainment business, Cori, a Korean American in her late twenties, had become involved in the formation of a film production company. These career choices, she felt, distinguished her from what was expected of an Asian. She also expressed frustration over these expectations, recognizing them as imposed stereotypes. In keeping with her history of political activism in college, she was working to develop an Asian American association dedicated to improving the visibility and status of Asian Americans in film production: "I didn't do the typical Asian thing, not computers, not law school, not an MBA," she told me. "It's been difficult because of the expectations. [Expectations coming from where?] It's what Asians are supposed to do, and a lot of them do. But I have to do what I believe in, draw on my talents. I'm a very extroverted, talkative, unconventional kind of person. It's a stereotype, of course, that Asians are not like that. It frustrates me that we get boxed in."

The model minority stereotype has a fluid set of meanings, and hence the ways in which individuals can use it as a basis for asserting what they are not, are potentially vast in number. For Jamie, images of the model minority Asian evoked "driven" and "ambitious" qualities that she did not associate with herself. Her words also suggest that the model minority achievement stereotype has a masculine character, at odds with the traditionally feminine values and activities of domesticity. A Korean American in her mid-thirties, Jamie was working as a registered nurse. "I'm not the typical Asian," she remarked. "I work hard and I have a decent job, but I'm not driven, ambitious like a lot of Asians. I did think about going to medical school, but I saw all the problems my mother went through and I really want to have a family, children. Those things are much more important to me than a high-powered career."

"I'm Not the Passive Asian": Hitting and Cracking the Glass Ceiling

As we have seen, the model minority stereotype not only applauds Asian achievement but also works to limit its scope, by defining it in particular ways. Among the limitations that it imposes is the suggestion that Asians have a passive, introverted personality style, one that makes them unsuited for positions of leadership. Among my informants, especially those who had a history of employment in professional corporate settings, this presumed passivity was a particularly important focal point for their rejection of the model minority stereotype and its expectations of achievement. My professional informants saw the stereotype's connotations of passivity and introvertedness as an integral part of the glass ceiling—the barrier that they faced as Asian-origin persons to moving up in the corporate world. In many cases the existence of the glass ceiling had driven them to participate in Asian American professional or workplace groups and associations.

The theme of the glass ceiling dominated my interview with John, a Korean American in his thirties. By his own admission, the problem of the glass ceiling had become a personal obsession of sorts—he was determined to overcome it. In college, John had majored in business and accounting. His first job out of college had been in a small accounting firm in Pittsburgh, where he recalled experiencing subtle discrimination. "When I had to do audits in rural Pennsylvania," he said, "I would get offhand comments, uncomplimentary. In terms of the company, I felt that it wasn't outright discrimination but that it was more subtle, like I wasn't given the best assignment, or it took me longer to get the best assignment."

Feeling frustrated, John decided to attend law school, hoping that this additional credential would allow him to avoid these experiences in the future. After completing law school, he relocated to southern California, where he moved through several jobs in different firms in rapid succession, hoping to find a setting that had the right ingredients for moving up. But he repeatedly encountered what he felt was the glass ceiling. He understood his apparent inability to move up the corporate ladder to be a result of a complex variety of factors, including the operation of "old boy networks" organized around elite college attendance. But he also felt that stereotypes of Asians and their personality traits were involved:

> I'm kind of obstinate. I want to know, what does it take to get to the very top in corporate America? There's the glass ceiling—you probably have heard about that. By the second firm, I really started to feel like there was a limit to what I could achieve. [What do you mean?] Well, in the bigger law firms where they control big corporate clients, the network really matters. Chances are the CEO of a major corporation is going to be white, and he probably went to certain schools, maybe he has a Harvard MBA. So he's going to be looking for an attorney he's comfortable with, who's similar to him in background. An Asian might have a Harvard MBA, but he's not going to be white, and chances are he's going to be hooked into different networks. Then there's the whole idea of Asians being book-smart but not politically savvy, and hardworking but not aggressive. Asians are not viewed as leadership material. I think that's very important.

John had pursued many strategies to achieve his goal, including moving from company to company and adding to his educational credentials. But a particularly crucial strategy, he felt, was to consciously project a personality and image that were at odds with the "quiet Asian." He thus made a deliberate effort to be extroverted and to affirm that he was leadership material.

While John remained committed to his quest to crack the glass ceiling, some of my other informants had given up on this task. Some contemplated moving to work for multinational companies in Asia, as a way to avoid the glass ceiling in the United States and also to make use of their ethnic identity capital.[2] Other informants, all men, had set up their own businesses after knocking up against the glass ceiling. This was the case for Bill, a Chinese American in his thirties, who had set up his own computer sales business after working in the banking sector for several years:

> There was the proverbial glass ceiling. Wham! [Gestures toward his face] I couldn't believe it till it actually hit me in the face, I was so naïve coming out of college. It was about working and working and not getting recognition, realizing there was no way they were going to accept a Chinese face giving them orders from the top. Asians don't have that aura of authority. I'm not quiet or retiring, I don't fit the stereotype, but how much did that matter? I was putting in long hours and cleaning up other people's messes and getting no credit for all of it. I was not happy. Period. So now I'm my own boss.

For women, the stereotype of the passive Asian could be especially potent, reflecting the popular associations of femininity, especially Asian femininity, with docility. Renee, a Chinese American accountant working in a large corporation, began by speaking of the favorable attitudes of the management toward Asian workers, but she quickly turned to the subject of negative perceptions of Asians, in particular their presumed passivity. While she did not see herself as passive, her supervisor had reprimanded her for not being aggressive enough in her dealings with others, an assessment that she felt could ultimately inhibit her ability to make it to the coveted position of partner:

---

2. A 1997 article in *AsianWeek* notes a movement of professional Asian Pacific Americans to corporations in Asia: "A growing number of Asian Pacific Americans . . . are capitalizing on the Asian part of their Asian American-ness by going to Asia to advance their careers and explore the promise of a new frontier with unlimited opportunities" (Yip).

[How has being Asian affected you at work?] Maybe in the positive, in that they think maybe I'm smarter than everybody. They think, "Oh, she's Asian, so she's got to be good in math." That probably happens quite a bit around here, because a lot of the people at the top are from the Midwest, where they don't have that much exposure to Asians. But maybe that's part of the reason why we're hiring so many Asians. There is the impression that they're really detail oriented, good with math, and they're going to be good workers. And a lot of them come with good grades from school, although of course that doesn't mean you're good in a practical sense.

But then, to some extent being Asian and being female may affect my career badly because people look at me, and because I'm an Asian female, they think I'm very passive. They think that I'm not going to yell to get what I want. Actually it's true, I'm not going to yell. But that doesn't mean I don't get things done. So I think in that respect it has hurt me because they tell me, "Oh, you're just too nice to the staff. You need to be hard. I really want to see you, like, get mad and yell."

I said to my boss, "I never have a problem getting my work done, so what's the problem? Why do you want me to be yelling at everyone?" It's a perception thing, you know. A white guy could be acting just the way I do, and they wouldn't even notice. But because it's an Asian female, they're thinking, "Oh, you must be passive."

Susan, a Korean American attorney in her thirties, said that her courtroom experiences had been shaped by the assumption of others that she, as an Asian and especially an Asian woman, was quiet and soft-spoken:

I go to court, and most of the time I am the only woman attorney in the courtroom, and almost 100 percent of the time I am the only Asian in the courtroom. And the reason for that has to do with the stereotype of Asians. Asians who go into law tend to do corporate desk-type work; they don't go into court. Asians are not seen as aggressive or outspoken enough. They don't speak loudly or whatever. I mean, there's no such thing as a soft-spoken litigator.

So Asians are not hired to be litigators. Even if they are in the litigation department, they do the background research and writing. But I work in an office where everyone has their own caseload, so I go to court. I think being a woman and being Asian makes you even more soft-spoken and not aggressive, in terms of how people look at you. [How do you deal with that?] I try to make sure I don't come across that way. I have a different personality anyway, but I try to make sure there's no mistake about that.

Other informants too made conscious efforts to ensure that others could not construe their self-presentation and behavior as passive. In some cases, these efforts took on the character of what I have described as racial identity play (see Chapter 3) — the self-conscious manipulation, by those on whom it is imposed, of the marker of race and the assumptions and meanings about identity that it signals.

Eugene, for example, adopted a self-conscious strategy of compartmentalization with respect to the model minority stereotype. A Korean American in his twenties, Eugene was working as a financial consultant in a large investment firm. He played up the notion of the "Asian whiz kid," he said, but at the same time he challenged the stereotype of the shy and retiring Asian. Eugene's references to the issue of accent suggest that one of his underlying strategies was to disidentify from immigrants and the "foreignness" that they represent:

Being Asian is an advantage at work in that they think you're smart, like a whiz kid. I'm no better as a financial consultant than anybody else, but they look at me and they go, "Oh, this guy is so sharp." But I guess I come off a little different from most Asians. I don't have that accent, and I'm not shy. You know, there's that stereotype of Asians: they have a heavy accent and they're shy. So I kind of try to project myself as the best of both worlds: I'm smart, but not shy and I don't have an accent. I try to use whatever I have to my advantage. Whether it's my ethnicity or whatever, I use it to my advantage.

By comparison, Joan's form of racial identity play had a different flavor. A Chinese American attorney, Joan described using a strategy of shock: she would play along with the stereotype of the passive Asian female but then quite suddenly launch a surprise attack. It is of note that while Joan described gaining the upper hand, her strategy could also potentially backfire, generating not cooperation but the hostility and resentment of others:

I guess there's that whole Asian stereotype, because of which they think I'm just going to be a meek, submissive thing, real quiet. It bothers me, but sometimes I get a kick out of surprising people. In meetings I sometimes kind of play them along, letting them think that I'm just a wallflower type. And then—pow! When they least expect it, I get angry, or I start acting and talking in a very aggressive lawyer-type way. There have been times when I've won a point or something just because people are a little taken aback.

These informants all described challenging the assumption of their passivity in a direct and immediate way, by making overt displays of a personality style that contradicted it. But others made challenges of a more subtle and general character, involving their behavior or style of conduct over a prolonged period of time. Women especially often spoke of not wanting to deliberately "act aggressive" in order to combat the passivity stereotype, since it would on some level be false, an act of deception, and at the same time would also mean giving in to the imposed standards of the dominant society.

Sandra, for one, established her authority at work by making a series of sustained actions and decisions rather than by trying to change her outward presentation of self. A Korean American in her late twenties, Sandra was the building manager of a large office complex in Los Angeles:

There are a lot of attorneys in the building. So you know, when something happens, I get a letter within thirty minutes. They know how to get out of an eviction and not pay late fees. They definitely make the job more stressful. It took them awhile to get used to me. My predecessor was the antithesis of me. She was this tall, blond blue-eyed woman. And she was very vocal, very outwardly aggressive. She was the kind of person who would just stroll into a restaurant, and everyone would notice her. She would go up to the attorney having lunch there with his clients and say, "You owe me this money, and if I don't get it, you're in trouble." She was just very tough, the kind of tough blond type, wearing high heels and chewing gum.

I'm much more reserved. And I'm young and Asian, so I don't have that imposing look. At the beginning there was definitely the perception that you could get away with whatever you wanted with me. But now I think it's changed. And I'm glad I haven't done that by changing my personality—I have no desire to be like my predecessor, becoming something I'm not. What happened was that I stood my ground in a number of situations. I was very firm and decisive without making a big show of it. I took a number of actions: I filed some lawsuits, got some evictions going, called the cops on a couple of tenants. [So how do you think the tenants look at you now?] I have good relationships with the building staff and the tenants. I'm friendly, and I like to think that I'm fair and considerate. But no one sees me as a pushover.

My informants understood well that the idea of Asian passivity was a stereotype, an unfair generalization. But even so, the activity of disavowing passivity could also involve distancing themselves from an Asian identity and thereby contributing to the construction of a homogenized Asian "other." Gordon's explanation of why few Asian American medical students elect to go into surgery highlights this point. A Chinese American, Gordon was himself a medical resident in training for a specialization in surgery. He contrasted his own personality style with that of his father, which he felt fit that of the "typical Asian":

There's probably a larger percentage of Asians in medicine than in the general population you know. But there are fewer in surgery, and I think there's a reason for that. As a group, surgeons are more aggressive, more active, more talkative, verbal. I hate to say it, but the typical Asian would not fit into that. Take my dad. I wish I could be half as smart as my dad, but he wouldn't make a good surgeon, he's too quiet. I'm very extroverted, so it fine's for me, even if people have these ideas in their head: "He's Asian so he's going to be quiet." As soon as they meet me, they're going to realize I'm not like that.

In contrast to Gordon's certitude that he himself was different from the "typical quiet Asian," Cynthia, a Chinese American, expressed ambivalence or at least a certain amount of confusion on this point. She affirmed that Asians, unlike herself, are passive, but she also expressed fears that she might not be so removed from this Asian quality. Her words bring to light the uncertainties and difficulties of distancing from a racialized stereotype, for those who are the focus of it:

I hate to say it, but there's some truth to the passive stereotype. Maybe that's putting it too strong, I don't know. When I worked with J.D. [an activist for Asian American issues] in college, she would say, "People just *think* Asians are like this." But to a certain degree I would say that Asian people *are* like that. The people who aren't like that are the ones who are the voice, the people who speak out.

I'm not like that. I'm pretty assertive, at least I think I am. But sometimes I don't know. Around a bunch of white Caucasians, I feel like I'm more Asian than

I thought. I feel like I'm just another Asian person who's submissive and quiet and you can push around. Then when I'm with an Asian person, I can compare myself, and I see that I'm not like the stereotype.

Perhaps because of uncertainties like Cynthia's, the work of distancing one-self from passivity could be intertwined with the work of disidentifying oneself from immigrants. That is, some informants felt that the stereotype of Asian passivity made sense with respect to Asian immigrants and nationals, even as it did not for U.S.-born or -raised persons like themselves. John, whose efforts to overcome the glass ceiling were described earlier, understood Asian passivity to be a reflection of Asian culture and hence likely to erode over the generations, with assimilation into American culture:

> I would say that Asians are not aggressive enough. They work very hard, but they don't like confrontations; you rarely see them saying no. They're just a lot more subtle than that, and I guess it's a different business style. We have quite a few Chinese and Korean clients here. Nobody will ever say no to your face.
>
> Whereas to some extent in the white culture, if you're not confrontational, you're like a pushover. You're too wimpy to be at a high-level position where you make big decisions. I think I have some of those traits. I was brought up in a Korean family, so it's inevitable. But they're not so strong for people like me who were raised here, and in the next generation, we'll barely see them.

Not all of my informants used individualized strategies to overcome the stereotype of passivity—others used strategies of a more collective nature. Just under half of my informants indicated that they were members of pan-Asian as-sociations that were broadly oriented toward workplace and occupational issues. The glass ceiling was a focal point of their concern.

Hyesook, a Korean American, said that it was only after college, when she began working in a corporate setting, that she became consciously aware of racism and the need for Asian Americans to come together as a political bloc. An executive in a large communications corporation, she was a founding mem-ber of a group that brought together the company's Asian-origin managers. The group had given her, she felt, a keen sense of the common concerns of Asian Americans:

> I only became aware of racism when I started working. You're so protected in a college environment. But with work, you start seeing all the subtle ways in which

being Asian does matter, like the glass ceiling. We [Asian-origin managers] started meeting, just informally at first, and then it got to be more organized. We now have seminars and luncheons. We act mainly as a support group, where people can connect and help support each other. We also provide information to the company about Asian American concerns. I've gained an appreciation of what Asians share: the racism and then the cultural issues, like how Asian women have been raised to be quiet.

■

For my informants, then, the model minority stereotype was a template of others' expectations for their own academic and occupational achievements. Given its idealized character, this template could easily result, as we have seen, in feelings of failure, of having not measured up to typical Asian achievement. But these expectations were also often a focus of resistance, as my informants engaged in a variety of strategies aimed at avoiding the template's strictures and limitations. As I have described, such resistance could be accompanied by a general critique of the model minority stereotype, an understanding of it as a form of racism or at least as a set of ideas unfairly imposed upon Asians. It could also be a spur to my informants' involvement in Asian American associations. But their coping strategies could also involve distancing, the assertion that they were not like the stereotype and thus were different from other Asians.

■ *Model Minority Culture, Ethnic Pan-Asianism, and the Positioning of Asian Americans*

For my informants, the model minority stereotype was not only a source of imposed expectations for academic and occupational achievement. It was also a source of ideas about the shared culture and worldview of Asian Americans. These ideas were, in turn, part of the ideology of ethnic pan-Asianism—an emergent set of ideas about the nature of Asian American commonality and community.

At least on the surface, the basic message of the model minority stereotype is a simple but powerful one, rooted as it is in popular American notions of success and merit. Asians, the stereotype says, have a cultural orientation (the work ethic) that makes them able and likely to succeed in the United States. For my informants, these core ideas served at times as materials with which to define what it meant to be Asian American. Reflecting its fundamentally relational character, this process of definition involved constant comparison, both implicit and explicit, of Asian Americans to other groups.

Thus deeply intertwined with my informants' comments on qualities particular to Asian Americans were reflections on how these qualities made them similar to or different from other groups. The process of responding to the model minority stereotype was thus intertwined with the activity of *positioning:* of locating Asian Americans within the social landscape of the United States.

As my informants compared the cultural characteristics of Asian Americans with other groups, they frequently mentioned Jewish Americans. Asians, they often claimed, were similar to Jews in their emphasis on work, education, family, self-sufficiency, and enterprise. Young Min, a Korean American in his thirties who was working as a bank manager, was among those who made this comparison. In his "Asian upbringing," he said, working hard was emphasized, an experience he perceived as shared by Jews. (Like many of my informants, Young Min in his interview sometimes slipped between references to "Asians" and "Koreans," thus giving the impression of a certain interchangeability.) "There's no doubt in my mind," he remarked, "that Asians have an edge at work because of the values they're raised with. My parents left no doubt in my mind that you had to work hard, there were no excuses. There's a similarity with Jews and Koreans. You've probably heard how Asians and Jews get along really well because they have the same values."

Lillian, a Chinese American who was working as a librarian, also spoke of how Asian and Jewish Americans were culturally similar. Like most of my informants, she attributed the origins of the strong work ethic among Asians with reference to "Asian cultural tradition." But her account also highlights the potential for primordialist explanations of Asian cultural tradition. At one point Lillian suggested that the Asian work ethic might be racial in origin — rooted in the givens of biology and genetics:

> I have a strong work ethic that's helped in every job that I ever had, and I think that has Asian roots. Jewish people are raised like that, they're very similar to Asians. I was told, "You have to work, you have to get good grades," [that] type of thing. It just carried on in terms of work ethic and thoroughness. It's my Chinese roots. I think it's cultural, but it could be racial. It could be racial.
>
> I heard of this study where they looked at newborn babies. They picked Chi-

nese babies from San Francisco, all with the same kind of background. They put a little cloth over the noses of the little Chinese babies, who just turned their heads and started breathing out of their mouths. They did the same thing with the white babies, who started to cry and didn't turn their heads.

So there could be some racial type of thing that makes certain people behave a certain way—like my being a quiet person and not making a fuss. A lot of it is cultural. Anyway, I think the roots of my success on jobs has to do with being Asian, being Chinese. I do think so.

The complexity of my informants' understandings of the model minority stereotype is further highlighted by the words of Brenda. Like a number of others, especially those who had been exposed to Asian American studies at college, Brenda was deeply critical of the political implications of the model minority stereotype, particularly its suggestion that Asian Americans are self-sufficient and so do not need government assistance. Her experiences as a social worker assigned to low-income Asian immigrant families made her especially sensitive to the way the model minority image legitimates the absence of social programs for Asian Americans.

But even as she voiced these criticisms, Brenda also affirmed that Asians are specially marked by core values of education, family, and work. To be sure, simply having these values did not guarantee success, as she knew from her dealings with Chinese and Vietnamese immigrant families. Ultimately, however, rather than dismissing the connections between the core values and success, she took a long-term view of their relationship. As in the history of Jewish Americans, she said, many if not all Asian Americans would eventually triumph over the odds, given their cultural orientation:

I've done counseling work with kids, Chinese and Vietnamese kids who are in trouble. Kids who are in gangs, have drug problems, family problems. The idea that Asian Americans are a model minority doesn't really hold up when you look at what's going on in these communities. [You're talking about the idea that Asians stress education, family?] Not exactly. What I'm saying is that not all Asian Americans make it—some are poor. Because of where they're coming from culturally, Asians do stress education, work, family loyalty. It doesn't mean that they're successful. But over time I think it's like the Jewish people here—they do move up, [although] it might take a long time and some get left behind.

My informants also made comparisons between Asian values and the values of American society and culture. But in this case the comparisons were points of contrast rather than similarity. American culture was distinguished from Asian, they observed, precisely by its absence of the core values. The political discourse on "declining family values" in the United States, as popularized by Dan Quayle and other conservative politicians during the 1980s and 1990s, provided an important point of reference for my informants in their construction of this contrast.

Gordon, for one, a Chinese American, painted a grim picture of American society as undergoing moral decay and decline, against which the honorific aspects of Asian culture contrasted favorably: "I was raised with certain Chinese values, like discipline, working hard, honesty," he recalled. "I do feel like those are parts of the Asian culture that are important, that I'd like to keep. They're so lacking in American society. You see the divorce rate and the crime rate, and you know something's wrong."

Gordon's sentiments were starkly echoed by Dave, the Chinese American whom we have met working as a graphic arts designer. "Asians emphasize education and work," he told me. "There is a problem with those things in America today. An American might put in five hours of work on the job and then quit. Asians are brought up differently. An Asian will be trying twice as hard, putting in ten hours."

In these comparisons, my informants, as can be seen, invoked the label *American* in highly general and nonspecific terms. On several occasions I pressed them for more detail about the precise meaning of *American* that they intended. But my efforts did not seem to lead anywhere. For example, in response to my question about whether she meant *all* Americans, Mi Ra, a Korean American, reiterated that she meant "Americans in general": "Asians do have the advantage in the workplace," she had been saying, "of having been raised to value working hard and being disciplined in your work. Americans have that problem, they don't have the same attitude. [Are you talking about all Americans, or some groups?] I'm talking about just Americans in general, I guess, not anyone special."

For Mi Ra as for others, the refusal to be more specific about *American* may reflect a reluctance to name and hence vilify particular groups. But in other contexts, my informants did name particular groups as lacking the core values, in contrast to Asians. This suggests that the very homogenization of *American* was an important part of the comparison here. In other words, it was precisely its generalized quality that made American society the appropriate basis for negative comparison and a contrastive point for affirming that Asians have the core values.

My informants were more willing to speak of who specifically did not have the core values of work and so forth, in contrast to Asians, when the subject turned to affirmative action, a willingness that itself reflected the implicit interminority comparison posed by the model minority stereotype (the "undeserving" versus the "model"). Indeed, affirmative action as a topic turned out to be particularly fertile ground for the drawing of such comparisons.

■ *"Affirmative Action Is Not for Asians"*

In the closing decades of the twentieth century, affirmative action came to represent a "racial hot button," a marker or signal of racial divisions and controversy. As Ong (2000) has remarked, it came to be "the contested boundary defining how aggressive government ought to be to address racial inequality" (314). While the name *affirmative action* officially refers to a broad, diverse, and loosely organized group of measures designed to ensure racial equality,[3] in popular discourse it has come to be more narrowly defined as a system of preferences, in hiring and school admissions, in favor of racial minorities. In general, the 1990s were a period of decline for affirmative action practices. In 1996 California passed Proposition 209, a statewide constitutional amendment that is also known as the "California Civil Rights Initiative," which triggered similar developments across the country (see Ong 2000, 320). Proposition 209 prohibited "preferential treatment" on the basis of race, sex, color, ethnicity, or national origin in the operations of public employment, public education, and public contracting; its practical implication was to prohibit state and local jurisdictions from implementing most affirmative action programs. In 1997 the regents of

---

3. Curry (1996) argues that affirmative action "per se was never a law, or even a coherently developed set of government policies." It has included the enforcement of fair employment practices, government programs regarding the awarding of federal contracts and licenses, and civil rights laws. The Civil Rights Commission has defined *affirmative action* as "encompassing any measure, beyond the simple termination of a discriminatory practice, which permits the consideration of race, national origin, sex or disability, along with other criteria, and which is adopted to provide opportunities to a class of qualified individuals who have either historically or actually been denied these opportunities, and to prevent the recurrence of discrimination in the future" (Curry 1996, xiv).

the University of California voted to uphold Proposition 209, thus setting off important changes in student admissions to the state university system.

As noted by Takagi (1992) in *The Retreat From Race,* Asian Americans have been quite visible in the public debate over affirmative action, especially involving college admissions. In their efforts to bolster anti–affirmative action sentiment, she argues, conservative political forces have successfully made use of Asian Americans by giving publicity to the idea that affirmative action victimizes them. Prestigious colleges and universities, according to this view, often turn down Asian Americans for admission, despite their competitive academic credentials, because of quotas and preferences for other minorities. The implication is then that it is not just whites but also Asian Americans who are the victims of affirmative action.

These claims and portrayals have not gone uncontested by progressive Asian American groups. For example, in 1996 Leadership Education for Asian Pacifics issued a special report attacking Proposition 209 (LEAP 1996). The report aimed to educate Asian Americans about the importance of retaining affirmative action programs and their significance for all racial minorities.

The results of available opinion polls do not show a clear consensus of opinion among Asian Americans about affirmative action. A 1996 poll conducted by *Asian Week,* for example, suggests that Asian Americans are divided, with a slight majority in favor of affirmative action programs. Fifty-seven percent indicated that they were in support of them, compared with 22.8 percent who were opposed and 20.1 percent who had no opinion (*Asian Week* 1996). Such studies also tend to show that, in their support for affirmative action, Asians are somewhere in between whites on the one hand and blacks and Latinos on the other. For example, a 1998 poll of Massachusetts residents showed that 31 percent of Asians supported an increase in affirmative action, compared with 18 percent of whites, 49 percent of blacks, and 53 percent of Latinos (Watanabe and Hardy-Fanta 1998).

My discussions with informants only complicated the picture of Asian American attitudes toward affirmative action that is offered by these polls. To be sure, some were quite definite in their disagreement with affirmative action. But overall, I found the most prominent attitude to be one of ambivalent support.[4] That

---

4. This is not unlike public attitudes in general. Ong (2000) notes that "voters are neither totally for nor totally against affirmative action. Most people accept the fact that racial discrimination has not been

is, many informants said that they were generally supportive of affirmative action but were also not completely sure about it. Their support stemmed from a general recognition of the continued and unjust realities of racial inequality in the United States. At the same time, they felt profound uncertainty about the legitimacy and benefits of affirmative action.

For my informants, the problematic dimensions of affirmative action were thrown into sharp relief by the relationship of Asian Americans, as they understood it, to affirmative action. There was, they felt, a certain distance between Asian Americans and affirmative action, largely because of the Asian cultural values of self-sufficiency and belief in merit, which clashed with a system of race-based preferences. These very cultural values also meant that Asians did not actually need affirmative action to succeed. For these reasons, the Asian American relationship to affirmative action was fundamentally different from that of other racial minorities. For my informants, the issue of affirmative action seemed to provide a forum for affirming the Asian cultural values of work, self-sufficiency, and so forth, in contrast to the values of other racial minorities.

Renee, a Chinese American accountant whose encounters with the glass ceiling we have already explored, spoke of "Asian culture" as contrary to affirmative action, but for blacks and Hispanics, she said, the situation was different:

> There is prejudice, but it's not as prevalent as it used to be. From where I'm sitting, it doesn't look like Asians need it, compared to other groups like blacks and Hispanics. But I think that in general our culture kind of discourages us from taking handouts and that we need to be proud and accomplish things on our own. I mean, I don't see that many Asian people on the street begging. I think a lot of it has to do with, you know, the family pride, because the family will be so embarrassed to see this happen. So in terms of affirmative action, I think the Chinese people just want to do it on their own; they don't necessarily want help from other people.

Jeff, a Korean American in his early twenties who was working for a large corporation, expressed uncertainty about where he stood on affirmative action,

---

eliminated, and many believe that something should be done. At the same time, a growing number find that affirmative action goes too far by forcing white men to bear a burden to remedy a societal problem not of their making. In other words, there is support for anti-discrimination policies, but resistance to giving unjustified preferential treatment" (321).

saying that he had questions about the significance of affirmative action for Asian Americans. Affirmative action, as he understood it, was not relevant to the particular barriers to mobility faced by Asian Americans, such as the glass ceiling. Like Renee, he said that affirmative action was at odds with Asian cultural values. The implied if not explicit comparison here is to other minorities, for whom, it is presumed, affirmative action is more useful:

> In the class I took on African American literature in college, we had a discussion about affirmative action, and I couldn't make up my mind on it. I kind of stood on the fence. I really don't know. I can understand both sides of the argument. I have mixed feelings because I truly believe that as far as Asians, Asian students are some of the brightest in the country, and I think that manifests itself in test scores. I guess what I'm saying is, I'm not sure Asians in particular need it. Then again there are glass ceilings and things like that. But I'm not sure affirmative action helps with those things. Asians succeed without affirmative action, because of the culture, the values, education, family.

Like a number of other informants, Robert, a Chinese American, drew a distinction between his support for affirmative action with respect to college admissions versus jobs—he was more favorably inclined toward the former. Robert was preparing for admission to medical school, and like Jeff, he expressed uncertainty about the relevance of affirmative action programs for Asian Americans. The problems of Asian Americans, he felt, were different from those of other minorities, like blacks:

> I don't know what to say about affirmative action. It's a good thing because there's so much racism. I guess I would make a distinction between college and jobs. Colleges need to create stimulating learning environments; that's different from a job situation, where the employer wants to get the best guy possible.
>
> [How do you think Asian Americans have done with affirmative action?] That's tough, I don't know. Is it relevant for us? Don't think so. Asians make it on their own. Asians are not usually considered an underprivileged minority, at least in southern California; I don't think Asians get preference for jobs. And even when we are, how much does it help Asians? Affirmative action helps to open the door for minorities, like blacks, but the problems of Asians are different. It's the glass ceiling, it's not getting the same pay as whites.

Even as they described their distance from affirmative action, a number of my informants asserted that it was important to preserve this distance, because affirmative action was stigmatizing for its beneficiaries. In fact, they understood affirmative action to be an important element of the stigma that marked racial minorities, especially African Americans.

For example, George, a Korean American doctor, an ENT specialist, felt that the operation of affirmative action in medical school admissions stigmatized African American doctors in the eyes of the general public. In contrast, Asian Americans, who rather than receiving special preference had been judged more stringently, were seen by the public as competent:

> It's interesting that most people have the impression that Asian Americans are good at what they do. And I think they like the cultural background that sort of comes across in our demeanor, in our speech, and in the way we carry ourselves. [What do you mean by demeanor—can you be more specific?] We're polite to patients, and we're not overbearing, we listen to them, take our time with them. They also see the Asian American doctor as competent and well trained, particularly since it's been more difficult for Asians to get into medical school than other people.
>
> [Admissions standards have been stricter?] Well yeah, at least in the 1980s, when I went to medical school, there was talk of how there were just so many qualified Asian applicants that they were turning them down to make room for other groups. So I think that unlike, say, in the case of a black physician, where a patient might look at him and wonder if he got in with lower qualifications, the opposite is true for Asians. Mind you, I'm not saying it's true that black doctors are less qualified than Asian doctors. But I think there is that perception out there.

Mei Han, a Chinese American, also remarked that affirmative action could be potentially stigmatizing for Asian Americans. Mei Han was working as an attorney in a nonprofit service organization dedicated to providing legal services for Asian Americans. She was a strong and vocal supporter of affirmative action programs, yet at the same time, she was also somewhat ambivalent about their implications. There was, she felt, some truth to the idea that Chinese culture conflicted with affirmative action. Affirmative action was, furthermore, stigmatizing and detrimental to the self-esteem of those targeted by it:

A lot of Chinese I know are anti–affirmative action. It's partly a misunderstanding. I remember having a conversation with an uncle who insisted that it was like welfare, that it was giving jobs to undeserving people. I tried to explain that it wasn't like that. You know, in some sense women and the minority races have all benefited from affirmative action. But his position, and [that of] a lot of Chinese, including my husband, are that affirmative action is un-Chinese; the Chinese value is that you work and work, and you don't get special breaks. And that observation strikes me as having some truth to it. And I also think that knowing that you didn't get your job because of the color of your skin is important for self-esteem. I see it as one of the problems that African Americans face.

John, the Korean American who was attempting to break the glass ceiling in the corporate world, observed that affirmative action was more relevant in earlier times, when discrimination in hiring practices had been more explicit. The racial barriers of today were different, he said, and demanded other types of remedies. Like Mei Han, he also saw association with affirmative action as a potential liability for Asian Americans, leading them perhaps into self-doubt about their abilities:

I don't think affirmative action is really an Asian issue. I think in most places Asians don't have the official minority status—they're not an underrepresented minority. It's something that has more to do with blacks and Hispanics. [Do you think Asians should have minority status?] Minority status is almost like a double-edged sword. It used to be that law firms wouldn't hire any minorities one way or another. You needed affirmative action to break in. But that's not exactly the case now. Most Asians I know are wary of affirmative action. They always say, "I didn't get where I am because of any preference." I think that attitude is important. A minority person who knows that he was hired because of his skin color or whatever might start doubting his abilities. Asians don't really have that liability at this point.

Thus Asian Americans, according to my informants, were in a relationship to affirmative action that was different from that of other racial minorities, in particular blacks and Latinos. Unlike these other groups, Asian Americans, to put it simply, were not a central focus of affirmative action. They felt that Asian culture, with its emphasis on work and self-sufficiency, was an important part of the distance between Asian Americans and affirmative action.

■ *The Model Minority Stereotype and Asian American Identity*

The model minority stereotype is the ideology that undergirds what I have described as "a part yet apart," the double-edged position of Asian Americans today in straddling both integration into and marginalization from the dominant society. My informants experienced and understood the model minority stereotype in varied ways. Some used it as a yardstick of expectations for their own achievement, contributing at times to a powerful sense of failure, of not measuring up. As pervasive as it was even in my largely middle-class sample, this sense of inadequacy may be especially pronounced among working-class Asian Americans. But if some of my informants could internalize the expectations of high Asian achievement and use them to generate self-blame, others made them into a conscious focus of resistance and critique. My informants were acutely aware of the underbelly of the model minority stereotype: its negative aspects and connotations.

Other informants spoke of the model minority stereotype as a source of ideas about "Asianness," ones that informed their efforts to situate Asian Americans within the racial hierarchy of the United States. Their identification with the ethnic American model was apparent here. Asian Americans, these informants said, were distinguished, in particular by their culture, from other racial minorities, such as African Americans and Latinos. In contrast, they invoked the Jewish American experience as a positive point of comparison.

This tendency to draw parallels between Asian Americans and Jewish Americans is in many ways not surprising. While the term *model minority* specifically originated in relation to Asian Americans, there is no doubt that Jewish Americans have often been seen and described in similar terms. We see this similarity in the following description provided by Hochschild (1995) of a media report on Jewish Americans from the early part of the twentieth century: "the article goes on to describe in careful and admiring detail how these dirt-poor, ignorant, orthodoxly non-Christian immigrants work, save, cooperate, sacrifice for their children—and end up wealthy beyond anyone's wildest imaginings" (32). In important ways, then, popular ideas of Jewish culture and success echo model minority notions of Asian Americans.

By drawing analogies to Jewish Americans, as well as asserting difference from other racial minorities, my informants affirmed the *ethnic American* rather than the *racial minority American* identity of Asian Americans. Jewish Americans today are widely understood to have achieved a high level of integration and acceptance into American society, as evidenced by their economic, educational, and other accomplishments. The assertion that Asian Americans are like Jewish Americans affirms the possibility that for Asian Americans, too, such achievement is possible, if not likely.

There is, however, another aspect to the Jewish-Asian comparison that is important to note. If Jewish Americans are understood to be ethnic Americans, it is also the case that their experiences are seen to be somewhat unique ones in comparison to other European American groups. They encountered particularly sharp discrimination from the dominant society. Jewishness is also understood to be far more salient, powerful, and long-lasting for Jewish Americans than it is for other assimilated European-origin groups, such as Irish Americans or Italian Americans. Jewish Americans are, then, ethnic Americans, but with a twist, with some special characteristics.

If the Jewish-Asian comparison highlights my informants' identification with the ethnic American model, it also hints at their awareness of the complexity of the Asian American experience. Even as they identified with the notion of being ethnic American, they also grappled with the significance of race, attempting to make sense of the racial "otherness" of Asian Americans in U.S. society.

My informants used model minority notions of Asian culture to distance themselves from *American*. A homogenized American society/culture provided the contrastive backdrop here for their assertion of an ethnic American identity: Asian Americans were *not* the unhyphenated Americans, lacking a strong or clear sense of ethnic roots. As scholars such as Alba (1990) and Waters (1990) have noted, many white Americans today assert an ethnic American or hyphenated American identity as a way to assert distinctiveness as well as connection to the heroism and honor of an immigrant past. It was these connotations—of distinction, vigor, and morality—that were prominent in my informants' affirmations that Asian Americans were not simply Americans, but ethnic Americans.

CHAPTER SIX

Ethnic Futures: Children and Intermarriage

> While more and more Asian Americans have come to represent the best
> of what those who promulgate "Americanization" would like to create
> . . . they are not and will not be fully assimilated, at least, not in the
> foreseeable future. . . . No matter how adaptive in values and aspira-
> tions, no matter how similar to whites in mannerisms and actions, Asian
> Americans cannot be members of the majority.   (Rose 1985, 212)

ASSIMILATION into the dominant society is an important theme, and a point of debate and speculation, in many writings on Asian Americans. Pointing to the generally favorable socioeconomic profile as well as other features of the Asian American situation today, some writers consider the prospects for their assimilation to be quite favorable.[1] Others, by contrast, dismiss the whole idea of Asian American assimilation, noting the significance of race in their experience and seeing it as an insurmountable obstacle. In this chapter I look at how some Asian Americans themselves see their ethnic futures and their prospects for assimilation. More specifically, I explore their understandings about the emerging course of ethnic identity in their own lives and in those of their descendants. These understandings, I believe, offer a sharp window into the dynamics of ethnic identity for second-generation Chinese and Korean Americans, as well as some clues to the future of ethnicity in their lives.

I found two particular issues to be important points of discussion, lightning rods for my informants' musings on their ethnic futures. The first was the question of how, in their role as parents, they might transmit and cultivate ethnic identity in the lives of the next generation. The question of parenting turned out to be especially revealing of the *ethnic aspirations* of my informants—their

---

1. Most analysts are, however, cautious in these projections, noting that it is too early to tell, since the majority of Asian Americans today are either first- or second-generation immigrants (see Alba 1999).

wishes and desires about the developing form and character of ethnic identity in their lives. The second issue was intermarriage and its consequences for ethnic identity. For my informants, the topic of intermarriage was a powerful forum for reflecting on the meaning and significance of assimilation, both for themselves and for Asian Americans in general. Conceptually speaking, intermarriage implies the crossing of group boundaries (marrying outside), an act that brings those boundaries into sharp relief.

■ Raising Children with Ethnicity

The topic of children and parenting figured prominently in my informants' musings about the emerging shape of their ethnicity, even though most of them were not yet parents themselves.[2] In general, their thoughts on the "ethnic raising" of children were marked by three notions of ethnicity, which I will discuss in turn.

Distilled Ethnicity

The first of these notions of ethnicity was that of *distilled ethnicity*, in which ethnic culture and identity are pared of nonessential components down to their core essence. Thus my informants would affirm that there were some "basic things" about being Korean or being Chinese that they wished to pass on to their children, most notably "the values," which were defined broadly as an emphasis on family, work, and education. They also considered important a certain self-consciousness and pride in one's Chinese or Korean origins; they wished for their children to self-identify, at least in some measure, as Chinese or Korean.

This emphasis on distilled ethnicity reflected my informants' generally high level of acculturation to dominant, middle-class American cultural norms and beliefs. Many felt that they could not pass on anything much besides distilled ethnicity, because of their own limited knowledge of specific Chinese or Korean traditions and practices, such as the language. But they did have the "basics"—the values and the self-identification—to teach their children. Because these basics did not require commitment to a visible ethnic lifestyle, they were quite

---

2. A small number (14) of my informants identified themselves as parents, mostly of young children. Thus even among those who already had children, issues of parenting tended to be discussed in the future tense, with reference to what was expected to come up in the future.

compatible with a high degree of integration into the groups and institutions of the dominant society.

Relatedly, distilled ethnicity meshed easily with the idea of giving children cultural choices, of not forcing them to learn or practice Chinese or Korean customs. Brenda, who was married to a fellow Chinese American and was expecting her first child at the time of the interview, said that these considerations were likely to shape how she would raise her children with ethnicity:

> I think they should be made aware of their own heritage, but I think because I was not given much of a choice, myself I would be sensitive to them choosing, you know, how they would want to view it, or what they want to do with it. You know, I wouldn't force them to take Chinese and to learn how to read and write if they didn't really want to — but I would explain whatever customs I understood to them. I don't think the real cultural practices are going to get passed on very heavily, just because we kind of [laughter] argue about them ourselves, but there are certain things that I think stick with us, that work for us, and one of them is the view of the importance of education and hard work, you know, being a good employee, and so on and so forth.

Cliff, who had two children from a previous marriage to a Korean woman, also spoke of passing down a distilled ethnicity to his children. Here his "number-one priority," as he put it, was to instill in them a sense of ethnic pride. This would ensure a willingness and ability on their part to acknowledge their Korean ancestry:

> My kids are very Americanized, in fact very like Boston types. You know, "Pahk the cah in Hahvahd Squeah" [park the car in Harvard Square]. But I like to think they have some of the Korean culture in them, like being respectful to older people. My number-one priority has been to make sure that they're proud to be Korean. They know they're Korean on some level, and they aren't afraid of it, they're not ashamed of it.

Ken took a relatively selective approach, at times quite self-consciously so, to the definition of what is basic to the ethnic culture. Ken, like a number of other informants (especially of Korean origin), explicitly mentioned that he wished to discard the male dominance of Korean culture, to separate it out from a "big picture" emphasis on family. In this way the distillation of ethnicity could accommodate middle-class American sensibilities:

As far as particular Korean customs are concerned, they weren't particularly important to me, so I can't see them being important for my children. I think they're cute, and I think it would be nice if they know them, but if you ask me what Korean culture is really about, that's not it. [What is it about?] Values, like family. Of course, do I want to preach male dominance, which is also part of family values in Korean culture? Well no, but I want them to get the big picture.

Distilled ethnicity, then, suggests a passed-down ethnicity that meshes easily with established notions of a mainstream middle-class American lifestyle and sensibility. Like the symbolic ethnicity of white ethnics, as described by scholars such as Alba (1990), distilled ethnicity, for my informants, was only loosely, if at all, related to specific behavioral commitments. But it also differed from the symbolic ethnicity of white ethnics in the way that it intersected with some other notions of ethnicity.

Racialized Ethnicity

My informants' thoughts on raising children with ethnicity were also marked by a conception of ethnicity as a racialized matter—as deeply shaped by and intertwined with racial conditions and dynamics. They desired to convey to their children, they said, an understanding of the realities of this *racialized ethnicity*. It was important to them, for example, that their children understand that their ethnic choices were somewhat limited because of their racial identity as Asian. Ethnicity, for their children, would not be an entirely voluntary matter; they would be compulsory ethnics.[3] Some said that precisely for this reason, it was important to teach children more than the "basics" of Korean culture. In effect, these informants considered distilled ethnicity to be inadequate to address the demands of racialized ethnicity.

For Tae Bong, racialized ethnicity meant that it would be unacceptable if his children were not familiar with the Korean language—although as he himself noted, his own fluency in Korean was limited:

I've already decided that it would be unacceptable for me if my children didn't speak Korean or didn't understand Korean. That's going to be challenging for me because I'm not very versed in the language. But I'll do what it takes so that they

---

3. The assumption here was of the monoracial Asian identity of children.

can at least partially understand Korean, partially speak Korean. Because they will always be Korean, no matter what—they'll never be accepted as 100 percent American. I see the Japanese people as an example. There are Japanese Americans whose families have been here for many generations, and they cannot speak Japanese. They're American in every sense of the word except that people don't see them as American. I don't know what it is, I just can't accept the fact that they don't speak Japanese. It doesn't sit well with me.

Jeff, a Korean American, also envisioned educating his children about the realities of racialized ethnicity. He would make sure that his children did not think they were *Mayflower* descendants, he said, indicating the importance, from his point of view, that they not delude themselves into thinking that they were white Americans:

No matter how American you think you are, by the fact that your hair is black and your skin is yellow, you are different. I don't want my children to forget where they came from, I don't think they can afford to. It's important they know where they came from. If they think we all came from the *Mayflower,* and we're all Pilgrims, and we're all just kind of plain old white Americans, that's wrong. Their grandparents came on a plane to Los Angeles, to LAX [Los Angeles airport]. They need to know that.

Passing down an understanding of racialized ethnicity, these informants believed, would also involve educating their children about racism in the United States and how to cope with it. The messages of race that my informants spoke of conveying clearly bore the stamp of those with which they themselves had grown up. As their parents had counseled them, they too would tell their children to "work twice as hard as the next person" in order to overcome racial disadvantage. They would also tell them to maintain a sense of ethnic pride and consciousness in the face of racial denigration.

But in other ways their anticipated counsel would be somewhat different from that with which they had grown up. For one thing, as Dave put it, they would teach their children to "make waves" if it was necessary to do so. At times it would be important for their children to openly and vocally protest racist and unjust treatment and to take organized action against it. In general, my informants asserted that they would place greater emphasis than their parents had on the value of making political responses to racism.

As one might expect, this idea was especially prominent and clear among those with a history of involvement and exposure to official pan-Asianism (see Chapter 3) and the forums and activities that are a part of it:

> For my mom and dad it was always about working hard, about being so good that no one would dare to screw around with you, even though you were Chinese. I would want to be a little more direct with my children and say, "There are people out there who will look at you and say that you don't belong. Sure you have to be good at what you do, but it's also about making waves. If there's unjust treatment, don't pretend it's not there. Get together with others in the same boat, whether it's Chinese or other minorities, and work against it. Don't let the bastards get away with it. Why should you?"

Analysts have noted the importance of the 1992 Los Angeles rebellion in fostering political consciousness and activism among second-generation Korean Americans (Abelman and Lie 1995; Min 1995b; Park 1999). Confirming this observation, my Korean American informants made the L.A. riots into an important theme in their discussions of a need for political activism.

We see this in the words of David, a Korean American whose parents operated a small convenience store in a suburban part of New York. He said that the events in Los Angeles had had a profound psychological impact on his family, even though they had not been directly affected by them. "What the riots showed to us," he remarked, "and even people like my parents, who are kind of very old-fashioned type of people, was how important it was to have a political voice. It wasn't just about working day and night, and scrimping and saving, and staying out of trouble, keeping a low profile."

Earlier I noted that a sense of pride in one's ethnic origins was an element of the distilled ethnicity that my informants wished to convey to their children. But they also understood that the passing on of a sense of ethnic pride had strategic value, as a way of coping with racism. As their parents had taught them, they would teach their children to maintain a sense of ethnic pride in the face of racial assaults. But this anticipated counsel, too, was subtly different from the counsel of their parents. If their parents had emphasized pride in being Chinese or being Korean, my informants also emphasized pride in *being Asian*.

During my interview with Hea Ran, she slipped back and forth between the idea of pride in being Korean and pride in being Asian. When I explicitly questioned her about the slippage, she affirmed the importance of both. "With kids," she said, "the most important thing, as far as I'm concerned, is to be proud of who you are, your Korean ancestry. People will make fun of you, because you're different, you look different. But always walk tall, be proud of your Asian roots. [What do you mean by *Asian*? Are you talking of something more than Korean?] Both of those things are important, being Korean, being Asian, they're both a part of who you are."

Several informants spoke of teaching their children Asian American history, as a way of giving them a sense of pride in being Asian. Once again, this response was especially prominent, if by no means exclusively so, among those who had been involved in Asian American political organizations and activities. This was certainly the case for Sam, a Korean American who had been quite active in Asian American groups during his college years. Sam was married to a fellow Korean American, and they had two children:

> I want them to be proud of who they are, their roots. [And how would you do that? Are there specific ways that you try to do that?] There is a certain history that I want them to know, and I don't necessarily mean like Korean history, although I'm by no means against that. They're still young now, but as they get older, I want to talk to them about history: Asian American history, starting from the earliest Koreans who came to Hawaii, then the Chinese Exclusion Act. Their ancestors struggled hard to get to the point where we are today.

We see then that the second generation considered the raising of children with ethnicity to be intertwined with the task of raising children who held racial minority status in the United States, with all its attendant dilemmas. Some wished to give the ethnicity that they passed along to their children a political dimension, cultivating it as a self-consciously political response and strategy, a way of asserting a political place in the United States. If some expressed distilled ethnicity for the most part in private ways, in personal lifestyle choices and sensibilities, here it was expressed in collective organization and, relatedly, in a sense of collective Asian history *within the United States*. They also understood the significance of a pan-Asian collective and affiliation and wished to convey to the next generation an acceptance of the identity of Asian American. As we have seen in Chapter 2, informants remembered that their own parents had advised them to cope with racial assaults by keeping in mind that they were "Chinese/Korean, *not Asian*." But in their envisioned role as parents, my second-generation Chinese and Korean American informants were less inclined to recommend to their children this course of action, of self-consciously disidentifying from the identity of Asian.

Globalism Ethnicity

Last but not least, my informants expressed a *globalism ethnicity,* a conception of ethnicity that draws attention to the impact of globalization on the significance of ethnicity. I use the term *globalism* here to refer to a particular perspective on globalization, or the intensification of worldwide social relations and linkages between societies. From the vantage point of globalism, globalization is a more or less favorable development, working to make the world a smaller place, connecting societies to each other in ways that promote mutual self-understanding. Globalism also endows globalization with a certain aura of glamour, as exemplified by the image of the jet-hopping entrepreneur who moves between the privileged sectors of multiple societies with great ease and aplomb. Many of my informants held this largely favorable perspective on globalization, I believe, because of their class position (largely middle-class) as well as their affiliation with societies — China and Korea — that are often perceived today as, at least potentially if not already, important and powerful players in the world economy.

Globalism ethnicity contributed to my informants' understanding that Chinese or Korean ethnic membership was strategically valuable, endowing them with a sort of ethnic identity capital that was of great value in the globalizing world economy. This value was increased when a Chinese or Korean identity was coupled with an American one, which connoted power and privilege. My informants spoke of wanting to convey to their children a sense of the significance of these conditions and, relatedly, to give them some concrete or actual knowledge of Chinese or Korean culture. In the context of the global economy, such knowledge could be a valuable identity cue, effectively signaling to others a genuine membership and belonging in the Chinese or Korean collectivity.

But my informants also expressed doubts about whether they would be able to convey this knowledge, despite its value. Sung, a Korean American, was adamant about the value of exposing his (future) children to Korea. But he also expressed a preference for letting them make their own choices, and an aversion toward forcing them to be interested in their heritage:

I would want them to know some Korean. In the next century, the people who are going to be the most successful are the ones who can move freely in different environments. I would tell them to be American, be Korean, speak as many languages as possible. [How are you going to teach them Korean?] I don't know, it really depends on them. I don't think it's fair to force kids—they have to choose to be interested in their Korean heritage.

For a number of informants, trips to China or Korea had shown them how economically significant their homeland societies were becoming or had become already. They came away from these trips, they said, with a keen sense of the economic dynamism of Chinese and Korean societies and of their own pride in these achievements.

Jane, a Chinese American, had toured Hong Kong and mainland China with a study group. The trip, she said, had lifted from her a certain sense of inferiority that she had associated with being Chinese while growing up. The trip had made her regret her own lack of ability in the Chinese language and other Chinese cultural knowledge, and afterward she had resolved to look for ways to forge connections to China in the future:

It changed my feelings or my understandings of China. I got a sense of the economic potential of the country, and how people thrived and worked under all kinds of conditions. I guess I realized I was proud to be Chinese. It's such a rich culture. Now I've started to think about business connections, if there's some way to get into that. I'm at a disadvantage since I don't speak much Chinese. When I have children, I definitely want them to learn Chinese, to be able to take advantage of all this.

Robert, a Chinese American, echoed Jane's desire to see the next generation speaking Chinese. This would, he felt, give his children an advantage, an edge in a world that was rapidly getting smaller:

They say it skips a generation, the interest in your heritage. I don't know. I really want to give them the language. I lack that, and I really feel the disadvantage sometimes. Especially now that the Asian Pacific Rim is really active in the world. I want to make sure that they can read and write. Of course they will be American. But you've got to have a global perspective, know how to feel comfortable in all kinds of places. The world is getting smaller every day, and I would want to give my children an edge in that.

My informants' thoughts on childrearing, then, were informed by an understanding of the strategic value of Chinese or Korean ethnicity. This understanding was clearly related not only to globalization but to a variety of other conditions (such as the multiculturalist movement) that have worked to affirm the values of ethnic pluralism in contemporary American society. Believing that cultivating a Chinese or Korean identity was strategically valuable as ethnic identity capital, my informants wished to give their children the necessary tools (especially language) with which to enhance and to fully exploit it. But this desire was coupled with and often overshadowed by others, such as the need to accommodate the cultural demands of the dominant society.

The overall picture that emerged from my informants' reflections on childrearing was of a future in which ethnic identity remained decidedly salient, though not necessarily in the ways that it had been in the past. I turn next to their reflections on intermarriage and identity, which also offered important insights into the emerging character of ethnic identity in the lives of second-generation Chinese and Korean Americans.

■ Asian American Intermarriage Trends

Intermarriage for Asian Americans has historically been quite rare, limited by a multitude of conditions, including antimiscegenation laws and institutionalized structures of racial segregation (Chow 2000; Fong 1998) In the period after the Second World War, some U. S. armed services personnel married "Asian war brides," or women from the Asian countries in which they were stationed, such as Japan, Korea, and the Philippines. But for the most part, intermarriage remained quite rare for Asian Americans until the 1970s.

As we see in Table 6.1, Lee and Fernandez's analysis (1998) of 1980 census data reveals an intermarriage rate of 25.4 percent for Asian Americans, far higher than that among blacks (2.2 percent) and Hispanics (12.7 percent). But over the 1980–1990 period, rates of intermarriage appear to have declined for Asian Americans, dropping to 14.5 percent. For blacks and Hispanics, in contrast, intermarriage rates rose, to 5.8 percent and 18.6 percent, respectively.

But this 1980–1990 decline in rates of Asian American intermarriage does not hold up when we consider only U. S-born Asians. In fact, as shown in Table 6.2, among U.S.-born Asians the rates of exogamy or outmarriage did not decline but rose during the 1980s. Thus the overall recent decline in Asian American

TABLE 6.1

Rates of Exogamy for Asians, Blacks, and Hispanics, 1980 and 1990 (%)

	1980	1990
Asian	25.4%	14.5%
Black	2.2	5.8
Hispanic	12.7	18.6

SOURCE: Lee and Fernandez (1998)

TABLE 6.2

Rates of Exogamy for Native-Born Asians, Chinese, and Koreans,
1980 and 1990 (%)

	1980	1990
Asians	34.7%	40.1%
Chinese	37.2	46.4
Koreans	68.0	71.7

SOURCE: Lee and Fernandez (1998)

intermarriage is due to marriage patterns among foreign-born Asians and, relatedly, the recent growth of the foreign-born as a segment of the Asian American population. Table 6.2 also shows important differences among U.S.-born Asians by ethnonational group. Korean Americans have a higher rate of outmarriage (71.7 percent) than Chinese Americans (46.4 percent).[4]

The popular media have given some attention to the fact that Asian American exogamy has a gender differential: women marry non-Asians more frequently that men do (see Fong 1998, 226). In 1990, 27.1 percent of Asian American women had outmarried, compared with 14.1 percent of men. The direction of this gender differential contrasts to that prevalent among African Americans, where men are more likely to outmarry than women. It is of note, however, that the Asian gender differential, while still present, is far less pronounced among U.S.-born Asians. As shown in Table 6.3, in 1990, 44.5 percent of U.S.-born Chinese men married exogamously, compared with 48.2 percent of U.S.-born Chinese women. Similarly, 69.7 percent of U.S.-born Korean men married exogamously, compared with 73.3 percent of U.S.-born Korean women.

Among the most provocative findings to emerge from recent analyses of Asian American marriage patterns is the rise in intra-Asian marriages, or marriages

4. As noted by Jacobs and Labov (1995), the particularly high rate of outmarriage for Korean American women may be a reflection of a significant number of "war bride" marriages in the Korean American population.

TABLE 6.3

Rates of Exogamy, by Ethnicity, Gender, Native/Foreign-Born Status, 1990 (%)

	Asian	Chinese	Koreans
Native born			
Men	37.7%	44.5%	69.7%
Women	42.5	48.2	73.3
Foreign born			
Men	9.0	6.7	3.5
Women	24.3	11.3	33.0

SOURCE: Lee and Fernandez (1998)

TABLE 6.4

Rates of Exogamy, Intraethnic and Interracial, 1980 and 1990
(in percents)

	Asians	Chinese	Koreans
1980			
All	25.4	15.7	31.8
Intraethnic	10.7	22.2	8.7
Interracial	89.3	77.8	91.3
1990			
All	14.5	12.1	6.5
Intraethnic	21.0	32.7	23.1
Interracial	78.8	67.3	76.9

SOURCE: Lee and Fernandez (1998)

between persons of different Asian ancestry (see Shinagawa and Pang 1996). Referring to these relationships as *interethnic marriages,* Lee and Fernandez (1998) report that over the 1980–1990 period they grew from 22.2 to 32.7 percent of all intermarriages among Chinese Americans, and from 8.7 percent to 23.1 percent of those among Korean Americans (see Table 6.4).

All in all, these analyses show that intermarriage is clearly an important aspect of contemporary Asian American life, albeit uneven in its significance across the Asian American population. It is especially important for U.S.-born Asians, including second-generation Korean and Chinese Americans like those in my study.

Given these trends, most of my informants—despite their differences in age, dating histories, and marital choices—greeted the opportunity to talk about intermarriage with great enthusiasm. My sample included 26 married persons, of whom 14 were married to persons of the same ethnic background (Chinese or Korean) as themselves. Eight were married to whites, 3 to other Asians, and

1 to an African American. It is of note then that in comparison to the national trends for U.S.-born Chinese and Koreans, my sample included a somewhat higher proportion of persons who had married endogamously or within their own ethnonational group.[5] Of the unmarried informants, 2 were divorced, and 14 indicated that they were single-partnered—that is, they were in serious and committed relationships that might lead to marriage. In comparison to those who were married, a larger proportion of the single-partnered informants were involved in interracial and interethnic relationships. While 3 had partnerships with persons of the same ethnic background, 7 were involved with other Asians, 3 with whites, and 1 with a Latina.

■ *Parents and the Hierarchy of Preference*

For my informants, the subject of their parents' feelings about the prospect of their intermarrying seemed to offer a topical springboard, a place from which to step into more general discussions of intermarriage. Virtually all of my informants said that their parents wanted them ideally to marry a fellow Chinese or Korean American, but the strength and rigidity of this preference seemed to vary. Eugene was among those who saw it to be a very serious and unyielding preference on the part of his parents, pointing out that, in contrast, what was important to him was not the person's color but what was "inside." Still, because of his parents' wishes, he intended to marry someone Korean and perhaps even someone they chose for him. His parents had clearly worked to emphasize to him the dangers that marrying non-Korean would pose to his relationship with them and more generally to his Korean identity:

> They're trying to set me up with somebody. Even though I don't agree with them,
> I understand the importance for my parents to do it that way. They would not
> accept anything else. My parents are very traditional, and my wife would have
> a lot of responsibility to take care of them. In college, you know, there were no

5. This may be a reflection of the high levels of education in the sample. In his analysis of intermarriage patterns, Qian (1997) finds a higher prevalence of endogamy (intraethnic marriage) among Asian Americans with college degrees. He notes that in 1990, 39.1 percent of Asian American men and 33.5 percent of women married endogamously. The rates were higher for those with college degrees: 52.1 percent for men and 42.1 percent for women.

Koreans, so I dated Hispanics, whites, everyone else. It's not the color that's important but what's inside. But realistically speaking in a Korean setting it's almost impossible for cultural reasons to have a relationship with your family if the person is not Korean. You and your children lose the Korean identity. And I'm not willing to lose my relationship with my family.

Greg, a Chinese American, also felt strong pressures from his mother to marry a fellow ethnic, but he eventually rebelled against these pressures:

My sister married a white guy. I remember my mother crying during the wedding. Later on I found out that my mother had actually offered money to my sister's husband to go away and not marry her. My father didn't even come to the wedding. But after my sister had a son, everything was hunky-dory, and now they get along fine. My middle brother had become like a flower child; he was into free love and all that, so my parents just gave up on him. Then my older brother got married to an Irish Catholic woman, and that was too much for my mom to handle. It was my senior year in high school. I remember her pulling me aside and telling me that if I married outside, she didn't think her heart could handle it. She said this with a really grim face. After that, for quite a few years, I tried to date only Chinese girls. Then I had a kind of revelation. I thought, "I can't marry a person just to please someone else."

If some parents, like Greg's, expressed their preference quite directly, others did so in more indirect, but apparently no less powerful ways. For example, Terry, a Chinese American, could not recall her mother and father actually telling her to marry Chinese. But she had been deeply aware of their preference, so much so that she had not considered even dating a non-Chinese. "I've never dated anyone who was not Asian, in fact not Chinese," she told me. "I've just never considered it. Why? I guess my family. [So your parents talked to you about it?] No, they didn't. I guess I just assumed they wanted me to marry Chinese. I knew that if I came home wanting to marry someone who was not, it would be a big battle."

In contrast to these quite definite and seemingly inflexible preferences, Tom's parents had somewhat more casual and negotiable views. In a long series of family dinner table talks during his teenage years, Tom had vigorously argued against his parents' preference that he marry Korean. They had, as a result, eventually given up on the idea:

We would talk about it, and I have to admit that compared to what I've seen of the Korean community in general, my parents were pretty liberal, so we could actually discuss it openly. We would argue, and they really couldn't come up with a good reason that wasn't kind of racist. Now it's at the point where it's not even mentioned. It's just "Marry someone who loves you, who's a good person," that kind of thing.

Few informants understood the preferences of their parents to be quite as subject to debate and revision as did Tom. But conversely, few understood them as matters that were simple or set in stone. Even as my informants described in vivid detail the disapproval that they anticipated receiving (and in some cases actually experienced) from their parents to their marriage or dating partners, they also said that despite the initial objections, if all went well, their families would probably more or less "come around." In contemporary middle-class American society, most parents do not have the cultural and economic resources to exercise direct authority over their children's marital choices. Some informants noted that in the long run their parents had very little to gain and much to lose from continuing to disapprove of their children's marital choices after they had actually been made.

The complexity of parental attitudes toward intermarriage was made apparent to my informants in other ways as well. Even as the parents expressed a desire to see their children marry Chinese or Korean, they also urged other considerations; the preference for Chinese/Korean was actually not an absolute one. Some considerations could actually even negate, for the parents, the positive value of marrying Chinese or Korean. Ki Hong, for example, a Korean American, said that his parents had greeted his elder brother's marriage to a Korean American woman with great dismay. The wife was older, however, and had been divorced, which likely accounted for at least some of the parents' dismay.

More generally, parents widely recognized that a lower social class background could negate the positive aspects of a common ethnic background. Thus Lily's parents reacted with extreme disapproval to her Chinese American boyfriend, who was not only from a different Chinese region but from a more modest social class background:

When I was in high school, my parents talked to me about how it was best to date Chinese. When I asked them what their second and third choice would be, they said, "Chinese, Chinese, and Chinese." So when I started going out with a Chinese guy in high school, I thought they would be pleased, but no, they were not. He was a waiter in a Chinese restaurant, and his mom and dad were in those kinds of jobs too. They were Cantonese, and my parents are Mandarin-speaking. They were definitely in a different social class.

Even as parents expressed their preference for an intraethnic marriage, they had also tended to offer some alternatives, expressing a hierarchy of preferences that ranked groups according to their desirability as partners for their children. Among other things, the existence of these hierarchies of preference suggests that parents sensed that they did not have complete control over their children's choices; a strategy of providing some alternatives expanded the possibility that they could actually have some influence, even if not as much as they wished.

With few exceptions, the hierarchy of preference as recalled by my informants took the following shape. At the top, as the most preferred choice, was the family's own specific ethnonational group of origin (Chinese or Korean), while blacks were at the bottom as the least preferred. In the middle were Asians, followed by whites and then other racial minority groups such as Latinos. Jane, a Chinese American who had grown up in a central part of Los Angeles, described this ranking in her remarks about her parents' reactions to her dating partners in high school: "The Chinese they loved, of course. And the Asians they didn't mind. Our high school had a lot of Japanese Americans, and they didn't object to my dating them. The Hispanics they weren't crazy about, but it was okay. But they had a big problem with my dating any of the black boys at school. A big problem. I guess they were prejudiced."

If Asians were in general a second-ranked choice, not all Asians held this position. Greg recalled that his parents preferred that he date women of East Asian origin—Chinese, Japanese, and Korean. Greg's mother, as we have seen, had threatened at one point to have a heart attack if her son did not marry Chinese, but she also specified other acceptable partners for him as well:

> She ran off this list to me in the order of what was acceptable. If not Chinese, then Japanese or Korean. Whites were actually next, and I remember that Filipinos and Vietnamese were not so popular. [Why was that?] I guess because they look different from us, much more so than Japanese or Koreans. And they're also seen as not so successful. I know that the Vietnamese are recent immigrants. I'm sure that has something to do with it.

The extent to which my informants recalled parental preferences for Japanese Americans was quite striking to me, given the powerful histories of animosity and conflict that mark the relations of China and Korea with Japan. In fact, some informants did mention that their parents would find it difficult on some level to accept someone of Japanese origin, given the still-vivid historical memories of the brutal Japanese occupations of China and Korea during the first half of the twentieth century. Nonetheless, Japanese Americans appeared to be highly ranked partners. Other Asian-origin groups, such as Filipinos and Vietnamese, were far less preferred and at times, as we see in Greg's account, were quite explicitly ranked at a lower level of preference than whites (see Pang 1994). Greg's remarks also hint at the complex considerations, of perceived physical and socioeconomic affinity and difference, that went into his parents' differential ranking of Asians.

In summary, then, parental views underlined for my informants the gravity of intermarriage; it was a serious, consequential matter. They also affirmed that their children should ideally marry someone of the same ethnonationality. But at the same time, my informants understood that their parents' attitudes and responses to intermarriage were complicated matters—fluid, mediated, and gradational in character. These complications worked to raise the possibility of other, alternative definitions of intermarriage, opening up conceptual spaces for thinking about intermarriage along other lines besides ethnonationality. Especially prominent here was the parental preference for Asian-origin partners.

I turn next to look at "blood" and "culture"—two conceptual anchors of identity that were, for my informants, at the heart of the identity consequences of intermarriage. Much as their parents had, they exhibited a conceptual flux and a willingness to stretch ethnic boundaries, as well as a general preference for other Asian Americans as marriage partners.

■ *"Mixing Blood"*

For my informants, intermarriage would affect their identity, at least in part, because of the mixing of blood and the identity damages implied by such mixing. The basic definition operating here was of blood as a biological substance from which the identities of individuals derived in some essential or given fashion. Thus when blood is mixed (as in the case of the children of intermarriages), the identities marked by blood suffer damage or at the very least some serious complications. The mixing of blood was, then, at the heart of my informants' understandings of intermarriage and the ethnic losses implied by it.

Within this broad conceptual framework, my informants also held other ideas about "blood." Some understood it as a primordial marker, specifically a powerful and essential force behind the Chinese and Korean ethnonational collectivities. Immigrant parents, as one might expect, were deeply identified with this particular understanding of "blood," and they made it a fairly prominent part of their efforts to convince their children that "marrying Chinese" or "marrying Korean" was the wisest course of action. This was especially so among my Korean American informants, many of whom recalled vividly that their parents had urged them to marry Korean in order to "keep" their Korean blood; not doing so would damage the continuity of the family line. That is, the offspring of a non-Korean marriage would not be Korean, they said, and so their names would not appear in official family genealogy records.

While both men and women recalled hearing this warning, parents would give it particular emphasis with their sons. Thus Young Min observed that his parents had been more concerned that he, as a son, marry Korean, than that his sisters should. Like other parents, Young Min's did not make their arguments in favor of "keeping blood pure" in isolation from other considerations, such as that of cultural difference:

> My parents don't emphasize marrying Korean—they demand, they threaten. The reasons they give are to keep Korean tradition alive, to keep the blood pure. It's almost like a loyalty thing. I think a big reason is that the grandchildren would not be Korean. And there are the practical reasons too, that I can understand the cultural differences. I would have to say, though, that it's really important for the son. If, say, my sister married an American person, I don't think my father or mother would have that much of a fit. I mean, they drilled us all in the same ideologies. But I think there is a different perception about the role of the girl in the family, about her not carrying on the family name.

Parents thus implied that the children coming out of marriages to non-Koreans or non-Chinese would "lose blood," or have a weaker claim to a Korean or Chinese identity. More indirectly, they also implied that the individual who intermarried would herself suffer a loss of Korean or Chinese identity; quite apart from the question of her children, she too would represent a mixing of blood. As revealed by Young Min's reference to the "loyalty thing," the individual who intermarried was not "true" to her blood and, by extension, to family and nation; such disloyalty brought into question her "blood" or at least her ability to make identity claims based on it.

But another notion of blood as related to intermarriage was also at play here. If immigrant parents' notions of blood bore the stamp of ideologies of Chinese and Korean nationalism, this other notion bore the stamp of race as it is commonly understood in the United States. In both cases, "blood" is an essential and biological marker of identity, but in the latter it is also an explicitly *physical racial* marker. That is, "blood" expresses itself in visible physical characteristics that are considered to be signs of racial identity. Accordingly, the most crucial effects of intermarriage on blood and thus identity would be its consequences for the "racial looks" and thus identity of the children.

In fact, the question of "how the children would look" was a prominent theme in my informants' musings on the identity implications of intermarriage. For the most part, the offspring of Asian-white unions provided the most explicit point of reference here. While often observing that much depended on fate, the general feeling was that these children would have mixed racial looks and would indeed be identified by others as racially mixed. Reflecting popular and widespread conceptions of "race" as an essential and singular identity, American society would see these children as not quite Asian and not quite white: in effect, as not *really* either one.

According to my informants, others would recognize the "white blood" of the Asian-white child, but they would not see the child as white. Even a mere hint of "Asianness" in his features would be enough to bring his white identity into question. "Asian looks" were then quite powerful in their ability to raise doubts about a child's identity as white.

Hea Ran, a Korean American, expressed uncertainty about the ability of Asian-white children to fully enjoy the privileges that came with being white in the United States. She focused her remarks on Sue, the young daughter of a close Korean American friend who had married a white man:

> I look at Sue, and she's just a wonderful, beautiful, beautiful child. She has superb parents, so I know she'll be fine. But I do wonder about the special challenges she might have to face as a biracial. When we go shopping together, I notice people looking at her and you can see the wheels turning—"What is she?" You can definitely tell that she's not white. Even though as a society we've made a lot

of progress, I do think if you're white in this society, you feel like you have a right to be anywhere you want and do anything you want. For better or for worse, I don't think that's what it's going to be like for Sue. She's kind of in between, not white and not a minority.

If others would not see the offspring of Asian-white unions as fully white, my informants suspected, neither would they see them as fully Asian. Certainly persons of Asian origin were likely to have an especially discerning eye as to who looked and thus was "pure Asian." But more generally as well, these mixed children would not be seen as completely Asian.

The significance of this assessment becomes clearer when we contrast it to the identity outcomes that have generally been associated with the children of black-white unions. According to the "one-drop rule" (see Chapter 3), in persons with even one distant black ancestor, a black identity has been expected, at least in the eyes of others, not only to remain highly potent but to dominate, not just contaminating whiteness but overpowering it.

Connie, a Chinese American who was married to an African American and expected to have children with him in the near future, had given the matter of mixed children much thought. In her assessment, her own children would likely be seen by others as black and so would likely see themselves primarily as such. This was different, she felt, from what was faced by Asian-white children, whose mixture was more likely to be acknowledged by others. There were, she mused, both advantages and disadvantages to the situation of Asian-white children. Among the advantages was a certain flexibility in identity, an ability to successfully resist being pinned down and so forced to choose one identity over another one. On the other hand, this same ability had the disadvantages of identity confusion and marginality:

> My children will be half-black, and even though I will make sure they know and are proud of their Chinese heritage, I'm sure they will identify more as black, just because of the way they're likely to be seen by others. It's very different for Asian-white couples. I have Asian friends who are married to whites, and their kids are mixed. I mean, of course a lot of it depends on the looks of the child, who they take after, but generally, people look at them and know they're a mix, of something. That's good, and it's bad. On the good angle, they don't have to choose one side of their heritage or another, they're not so forced to do that. By the same token, they don't know who they are, where they really belong.

Some of my informants remarked that, since others would most likely not see or accept an Asian-white child as "fully Asian," the child would also not be presumed to have authentic ethnicity. In other words, the racialized assumption that often marked my informants' own experiences—that they had true and genuine ties to and knowledge of an ethnic collectivity—might not be present. This situation, in their assessment, had both pluses and minuses. It suggested a certain relief from the pressures, as I have described in earlier chapters, of having to meet the expectations of one's authentic ethnicity. But it also suggested vitiated prospects for deriving ethnic identity capital and, more generally, for enjoying the strategic benefits of Chinese or Korean membership. The mixed Asian-white child might be less able to position herself as genuinely Chinese or Korean and so ride the waves of the global economy.

Moreover, such a child was especially likely to become disconnected from her Chinese or Korean ethnic heritage. Thus Mei Han, who was married to a fellow Chinese American, speculated that an Asian-white child might be less pressured to cultivate her ethnicity, since in the eyes of others, she was not truly Asian:

A lot of my Chinese friends have married whites. I'm the exception. One of my friends kids me about going native. I do feel there's a benefit for my children in being a hundred percent Chinese. With these mixed marriages, the children come out, and some look more Asian, some look more white. But the bottom line is that they don't feel Chinese in the same way as my children. Sure you can send them to Chinese language school and church, but when they're out there in the world, the public won't say, "Oh, there goes a Chinese." They'll say, "There goes a biracial, an Asian and white individual." My children know they look Asian, other people see them as Asian, so they feel a pressure to deal with that. I don't think the same thing applies to the children of my friends in mixed marriages.

Children of intra-Asian unions, my informants said, did not have the same identity dilemmas as did children of Asian-white unions. When Wayne, a Chinese American, told his mother that he was dating a Korean American, his mother greeted the announcement with some relief, since Koreans and Chinese, at least in the eyes of others, "looked alike." From his perspective, too, the fact that the children of a Chinese-Korean union would look unambiguously Asian was an important plus. Besides not suffering identity confusion, the children would also, like their parents, be compulsory ethnics; that is, they would be unable, even if they so desired, to fade into the oblivion of the nonethnic ranks of the United States:

> Awhile back, my mother talked about how I was getting old and I should get married. I said, "I'm thinking I might marry someone who is not Chinese." She got really upset, and I was kind of surprised because we hadn't talked about this in a long time. But then I told her I was going out with a Korean woman pretty seriously, and she was really happy. She said, "Oh, Korean, Korean. They look like us, they look just like us. Sometimes you can't tell the difference. Americans can't tell the difference between Chinese and Korean."
>
> My girlfriend and I have talked about getting married and [having] children and all of that. Mixed children are known to have identity confusion. But our children won't be mixed. I mean, they will be on a certain level, they will be Korean and Chinese. But they will be Asian on the outside. It's important to me that they have that, it gives you that special edge. Even if they wanted to, they couldn't get away from the fact that they were part Chinese. [Why not? Can you explain?] Because when others look at them, they'll see an Asian face, and they'll go, "Hey, are you Chinese or Japanese or what?"

A similarly optimistic view was suggested by Meg, a Chinese American who was going out with a Japanese American. Marrying a person of Japanese origin, she acknowledged, would not have equivalent consequences for the children's ethnic identity as would marrying a Chinese-origin person. Nonetheless, marriage to a Japanese American would be far more favorable to the survival of her Chinese heritage than marriage to a white American:

> Now that my family has come around to him, even though he's not Chinese, I've started to think more about what it would be like to have Chinese-Japanese American kids. I do worry about losing the Chinese traditions. But they wouldn't be biracial children. They'd be Asian. Other Asians might know and understand that they're mixed. But for an American person, they would just see an Asian person. So really, it wouldn't really be that different for them. [Different from whom?] From me. They would have to acknowledge their Chinese roots. Also their Japanese ones I guess, although my mother definitely would prefer that we forget about that!

The discourse and imagery of the confused and alienated Asian-white child did not, it must be noted, go uncontested in my informants' accounts. While less pervasive, also present was a view of the mixed blood child as *not* incurring any identity losses by virtue of being mixed. "Blood," in these accounts, was conceptualized as a substance with additive qualities; it was not a zero-sum affair. It did not, with "mixing," become impure and lose potency as a marker of identity. Far from ethnic loss, the trademark of the mixed blood person was her ability to lay powerful and legitimate claims to multiple roots and identities.

As one might expect, this more optimistic perspective on "mixed blood" was especially prominent among those who were themselves in interracial marriages and had had, or expected to have, children. For example, Curt, a Korean American who was married to a white woman, said that he expected their two children to benefit from their mixed background. Besides the good looks that they enjoyed, they had the advantage of access to "two worlds" and the resources that were a part of them. Reflecting the notion of globalism ethnicity described earlier, Curt spoke of the emerging global economy and affirmed that mixed persons such as his children were excellently situated, given the multiplicity of their ethnic identity capital, to take advantage of it:

> I don't think they'll have any problems. They're good-looking kids. We get a lot of comments about how beautiful they are, a combination of the Asian and Caucasian features. I tell them, "You have the advantages of two worlds, but it's up to you to make the best use of that advantage. You're American, Scottish Irish American from your mother, so you have that connection. You're also Korean, and it's up to you to make sure you learn about that, or at least enough that you can go back to it whenever you want, if you need to. The world is changing, getting more connected." [Are there specific opportunities for going back to it that you're thinking of?] There's business opportunities. It's much easier to connect with Korea and Koreans if there's some of that Korean blood.

Jane, a Chinese American, also spoke of being mixed as an advantage, as expanding rather than contracting a person's identity resources. Like Curt, she emphasized that mixed blood persons needed to maintain a positive attitude in the face of the many negative ideas about them. She also hinted at a larger critique of the popular notions of blood and the loss of identity that results from its mixing. "It's important, I think, to have the right attitude about it," she told me. "If you say, 'Oh, I'm mixed, that's terrible, I don't belong,' that's likely to end up being true. I would like to think that it's a very positive thing, to have two very rich heritages. Why do they have to lose their Chinese identity? Is it something like a pair of shoes that you just lose, because your ancestry, your blood is mixed?"

Analysts note that today many multiracial persons of Asian descent are self-consciously embracing their multiple identities, refusing to be identified as monoracial. According to Spickard (1997), "Today multiracial people of Asian descent take a number of paths to ethnic identity. Very few are inclined or able to identify solely with one part of their inheritance" (50). This self-conscious embrace of multiple heritages is, I believe, an important challenge to popular notions of monoracial identity—the idea that racial categories and identities are inherently or naturally discrete and singular in nature. But my informants also suggested that embracing multiple heritages should be accompanied by larger critiques and challenges to the prevailing discourse on blood, race, and identity. Without a dismantling of this conventional logic, of what it means to have "mixed blood," multiracial persons of Asian descent may not be accepted as legitimate and authentic members of the communities that they embrace.

■ Culture Gaps

For my informants, the potential for ethnic loss in an intermarriage lay not only in the mixing of blood but also in the production of *culture gaps* or dissonances in cultural orientations and practices. These dissonances could occur not just between the marriage partners themselves but also between a partner and his or her in-laws. Through the unfolding and negotiation of these culture gaps, losses of ethnic identity and culture could and actually did occur.

The Advantages of Marrying a Fellow Ethnic

For some of my informants, culture gaps involved cultural differences with a spouse due to differing ethnonational origins. Among other things, these differences made it not so likely that Chinese or Korean cultural practices, such as language and food, would be part of the home environment. These practices would then not be cultivated and transmitted to the next generation; Chinese or Korean culture would, in effect, be lost. Certainly Chinese or Korean language and food could be present in an intermarriage, due to the influence and perhaps diligent efforts of the Chinese- or Korean-origin spouse. But my informants felt that their presence in an intermarriage would be less powerful than in an intra-Chinese or intra-Korean marriage, that they would have a superficial, surface-level, and thus ultimately less authentic quality. Relatedly, the passing down of Korean or Chinese culture to children in an intermarriage would likely be a self-conscious and contrived affair and so ultimately not very effective.

For Susan, Korean culture was embedded in her marriage to a fellow Korean American in ways that offered a point of contrast to the presumed deficiencies, in these respects, of intermarriage:

> My husband and I, there are certain things we say in Korean because there's no English word or phrase. It makes us feel close. Kind of like food, you know. I can say to him, "I really crave this particular food." I thought about this when I was going out with my white boyfriend [in college]; I thought about how we wouldn't be able to share those things. Even though my husband and I are pretty American-ized, we're still Korean in certain ways. My son picks up on those Korean things in a natural way; it's just a part of our family life. We don't have to teach him how to be Korean.

A few informants, notably men, asserted that the cultural losses of intermarriage were especially sharp for the Korean- or Chinese-origin man. The reason was that women play the critical role in shaping the cultural character of the home, in maintaining and organizing Chinese or Korean food, holidays, and so forth. Jae Wook, a Korean American man, spoke of the special role of women in retaining the ancestral culture. He had recently spent time in Korea, as part of his training in public health, and at the same time advancing his previously limited knowledge of Korean language and culture. He was sharply conscious that his hard-won "Koreanness" might be jeopardized by intermarrying:

> I want to marry a Korean woman for largely selfish reasons. I feel like I've worked so hard to get back in touch with Korea, the language and history. I don't want to jeopardize everything that I've gained by marrying a non-Korean. I see that with my sister—she married a white American. Although I think it's a little easier for women to keep the culture going, because women are more in control over what happens in the home, like what foods get cooked, the holidays that get celebrated. That's exactly why it's important for me, for especially guys who want to keep the Korean culture, to marry Korean.

Another advantage to intraethnic (Chinese-Chinese or Korean-Korean) marriage, my informants felt, was that conflicts over cultural matters would presumably be absent. That is, spouses of the same ethnic background would be less likely than spouses in an intermarriage to disagree about the presence of ethnic cultural practices within the home and the expenditures and efforts that were necessary for their cultivation. Tammy, a Korean American, was especially conscious of the possibilities for these kinds of conflicts within intermarriages:

> Part of the reason I want to marry Korean is for the sake of the children. They won't have that identity confusion. I mean, I don't expect them to be Korean Korean; they will be American kids. But we won't have to try too hard to pass along the Korean culture because it's just part of the way we are, the way we live. [Can you give me an example?] I'm talking of things ranging from eating kimchee and rice to respecting your grandparents, to going to church. If I want to send my son or daughter to Korean language school, that's what I'll do. What I mean is that I won't have to justify it to my husband. I sort of imagine that if I was, like, married to a white guy, we'd have to go through a discussion like "Why Korean classes? Why not classes in French or something?"

Culture gaps could arise, my informants felt, not only within the spousal relationship but in other family relationships as well, particularly relations between immigrant parents and the non-Chinese or non-Korean spouse. In these relations, they felt, culture gaps were likely to be sharply present and of some significance. They often spoke of Chinese or Korean immigrant parents as conduits of Chinese or Korean culture, critical channels in passing down the culture to the next generation—the grandchildren. Anything that might damage or introduce tensions into these relationships might also contribute to the loss of Chinese or Korean culture.

Glenn, a Chinese American, had a deep consciousness of these possibilities. For him, the role of immigrant parents as cultural emissaries went beyond the self-conscious teaching of the ancestral culture to their grandchildren. Parents were identified not just as transmitters in an active sense but also as emitters of Chinese/Korean culture, lending authenticity to the Korean or Chinese identity of those around them simply by their presence. Immigrant parents were, in effect, symbols of authentic Chinese or Korean culture. Thus Glenn was concerned that simply because of the absence of his parents, he would somehow be "less Chinese":

> Marrying someone of my own race always seemed like the right thing to do. There are all kinds of difficulties in having a non-Chinese be part of the family. There's

the cultural gap. My parents and my wife would speak different languages, have different customs. Just a whole different mindset. The children may not be close to their grandparents. And I do expect that my parents would have a major part in teaching the children about Chinese traditions. When you lose the connection to the family, you lose the connection to your heritage, your Chinese-ness. Without my parents, I would be less Chinese in some way. And who would teach my children about Chinese traditions?

Min, who was engaged to a fellow Korean American, also commented on the potential problems of culture gaps between partner and parents in an intermarriage, and the relationship tensions that could result. She, like many other informants, felt that her parents' role in passing down Korean culture was especially critical in light of her own limited knowledge of it:

I felt like if I really love that person, I don't think it would have mattered who they were or what they were—except my parents would have a huge fit about the fact that they're not Korean. My mom used to say, "I want a son-in-law who I can speak to and talk to. I don't want to be a deaf-mute person here." Now that I'm with him, I've slowly come to realize that it is important that he's Korean. He can communicate with my parents, and we have similar values and traditions. My mom and dad will be there to teach our kids about Korean culture. That's really important because I don't know that much, and I don't have much Korean culture to pass on. To me personally, race is not important. If I love someone, it doesn't matter. But it matters to my parents. And I do think about how I would prefer to be with someone who can understand and relate to my parents. I know it would affect my relationship with my parents a lot, if I married outside. I have to take care of my parents when they get old, and I don't think an American would understand that obligation.

Steve, a Chinese American, also mentioned the common language issue when speaking of his decision to marry a Chinese American woman. "Marrying someone Chinese was one of the values that my parents kept drilling into me as a child," he told me. "At one time I followed that path because they wanted me to do it, but as I became older and wiser, it seemed like the right thing for me— because of the common ground that you have. And the difficulty in having a non-Asian be part of our family is that my parents can't communicate that well in English." But at another point in the interview, Steve informed me that his wife spoke virtually no Cantonese, the language spoken by his parents. And in fact, his own knowledge of Cantonese was minimal. These issues suggest that the idea of a common language was at times offered by my informants in more than a literal sense, as a reference to a shared cultural vocabulary, of mannerisms, etiquette, customs, and outlook.

This discrepancy between presumed and actual common language is based on the assumption that in a Chinese-Chinese or Korean-Korean marriage, culture gaps are not present. But this was not always an easy assumption to maintain, especially in light of my informants' uneven and contested relationships to Chinese or Korean culture. In fact, even as my informants affirmed the idea that *not* marrying a fellow Chinese or Korean American would mean a culture gap, they also at times expressed uncertainty about the presumed counter-absence of culture gaps in an intraethnic marriage.

Another condition that might lead to a culture gap in an intraethnic marriage, my informants felt, was a disparity between the spouses in immigrant generation status. In a marriage between a second-generation Chinese and a first-generation Chinese, for example, they felt there was much scope for cultural dissonance, despite the fact that the marriage was intra-Chinese. But even in marriages that were generationally homogeneous, there was no guarantee that the partners and their families would all have a similar relationship to Korean/Chinese culture and identity.

Perhaps the most elaborate and forceful critiques of the cultural homogeneity assumption came from the ranks of those who had themselves married a fellow ethnic of the same immigrant generation. For Cynthia, cultural difference had emerged as a central dimension of her seemingly troubled marriage to a fellow second-generation Chinese American:

> My mother and father were always like, "Marry Chinese, marry Chinese, it's so much easier because you have the same culture." Maybe that's true for some marriages, but I feel like culturally, even though we're Chinese, we're so different. My husband and I are both ABC [American-born Chinese], but we are so different in how Chinese we are. I think it's because of the way he grew up — very traditional, with strict Chinese parents.
>
> He speaks more Chinese, Cantonese, than I do. And he feels very strongly about all the rituals and customs. Like at one point he wanted me to call his father by a certain Chinese name, which basically meant that I would be calling him

my master or lord. "No way," I said. We have fights about those kinds of things all the time. And I'm sure they're going to come up with our children, when we have them. He wants them to be very Chinese—he's already talked about that. I'm much more easy-going about it. I'm mainly interested in them getting the basics.

Sonia, who was married to a fellow Korean American, observed that cultural differences were also an important dimension of her marriage. These differences centered on her deep-seated commitments and involvements in a Korean church community, which were apparently not shared by her husband. Her sister had married a white man, which provided for her a point of contrast against which to muse on culture gaps, and how much they actually had to do with intermarriage:

My sister married a white guy, so I've thought a lot about intermarriage. I'm glad I married a Korean man, but I look at my sister, and she married a guy who is so supportive of her keeping up the Korean culture. He's learning Korean, and he wants to go with her to Korea to live after they have children. John [Sonia's husband] has had a hard time coming to terms with being Korean. And actually we have very different attitudes about that. We're working on it, and I think it will be okay, but I have to admit we've had some problems with that.

The good thing is that he's becoming more involved with the church. To me, being Korean and being a Christian are tied together, part of the same thing. I'm very involved in the Korean church community. We meet over the weekends and often once or twice during the week for fellowship and get-togethers. John is less into it; he would rather spend his time hanging out with buddies from college, his white buddies . . .

In general my informants understood culture gaps to be complex matters, centered on ethnonational boundaries but not in simple, linear ways. Both reflecting and contributing to this complexity was the presence of another conception of culture gaps, to which I turn next.

Culture Gaps as Value Gaps: Marrying Asian

Culture gaps between spouses in a marriage, my informants understood, could involve more than simply differences in language or knowledge of specific traditions and practices. They could also involve a dissonance in values.

The definition of *culture* loosely operating in such culture gaps was one that encompassed broad orientations of the self toward the world. By contrast, in the ethnonational conception of culture gaps, culture was viewed in relation to specific traditions and practices that required the participants' active and visible engagement.

Theoretically at least, a values-centered view of culture gaps offers an opportunity to critically analyze the significance of culture gaps generally in intermarriage. That is, if the partners do not share certain values, then the culture gap in their marriage may result from their individual characteristics and attitudes rather than their group membership. An invoking of "values" was in fact one of the ways in which some of my informants dismissed the arguments against intermarriage—what mattered, after all, were the two individuals and their basic approaches to the world, not their ethnicity. But they more often made the values-centered definition of culture gaps part of a redefinition rather than a dismissal of intermarriage, a shift in the boundaries that intermarriage affirmed. In effect, their assessments of culture gaps came to hinge on the question of which groups were more likely than others to have certain values. Because of differences in values, they felt, marriages to members of certain groups rather than others would be more likely to result in culture gaps.

My informants organized their assessments of the value gaps of intermarriage around the ideology of ethnic pan-Asianism (see Chapter 3). They began with the premise that what the Chinese- or Korean-origin person brought to a marriage were the core values of education, work, family, and so forth. These were, furthermore, not just Chinese or Korean but Asian values. Marriage to a fellow Asian thus meant minimizing culture gaps.

In effect, then, the focus on shared values worked to stretch the defined boundaries of intermarriage. It was even possible, in terms of this framework of values, to say that marriage to a fellow Asian American was not an intermarriage at all. Margaret, a Chinese American, said that "marrying out" meant something quite different when it involved another Asian:

> I think marrying out means something very different depending on what you're marrying into. I mean, okay, you're not marrying Chinese. But the next question is, are you marrying an Asian, or what? I've thought a lot about this. For us ABCs, it's usually not about making sure children speak Chinese. I mean, for God's sake, there are a lot of us who don't speak it ourselves. But we do want the values, the

stress on being close with your family, on respecting the elderly, on education. And in that way, you look for someone who was raised in a culture that's as close as possible to Chinese culture. And that's other Asian cultures.

Gordon also said that it was ultimately the values that mattered in choice of partner; he thus ultimately wanted to marry either a Chinese- or Asian-origin woman:

> I date all kinds of women—black, white, Middle Eastern, Latin. I enjoy that. But when it comes to marriage, it's different. When you get married, you want to approach your life in the ways that your parents taught you. And for the Chinese, that's education, hard work, and honesty. [So you would prefer to marry a Chinese woman?] Yeah, although I have to admit I have yet to date a Chinese woman! But yeah, I would want to marry either a Chinese or Asian woman because she would share my beliefs about how to live your life. It's about how you want to live your life, and what you want to pass on to your children. That little bit of Chinese in me, I don't want to lose. [And if you marry an Asian but not Chinese?] In my opinion, Asians have a lot in common, in their ideas about discipline, and education.

Like Gordon, other informants too often invoked Asians in general terms as preferred partners, but they also saw the various Asian-origin groups differently. These Korean and Chinese Americans, in a variation on the parental hierarchy of preference, designated other East Asians as being the "closest" to themselves and most clearly sharing the core values.

Thus Soo Jin, a Korean American, asserted that persons of Chinese, Japanese, and Korean origin, because of the common legacy of Confucianism, shared the values; but she was unsure about their presence in other Asian-origin groups. Because of this sharing, she expected that her upcoming marriage to a Chinese American would not be marked by serious culture gaps:

> As far as my relationship with Jim [her fiancé], I think it's important that Chinese have the same work ethic and the same sense of family as Koreans. I guess those are pretty much Asian things. [Do you think all the Asian groups share them?] Well, I think the Japanese do, and the Vietnamese and Filipinos to some extent, but not quite as strongly. It has to do with Confucianism—the countries that are more Confucian emphasize those things more.

If intra-Asian and especially intra–East Asian marriage signaled common values and minimal culture gaps, marriage to whites signaled the opposite: significant culture gaps, due to the relative absence in white culture of the core values. The notion of *white* at play here intersected with that of *American society/culture* as described in Chapter 2; it was culturally homogeneous and decidedly non-ethnic in character. Thus Katie spoke of wanting a partner who was ethnic and not simply Caucasian or white Anglo. The latter, she felt, tended to be not family oriented:

> My last two boyfriends have been Hispanic because of the culture. The family unit is very strong in a Hispanic family, and I'm looking for that same kind of strength. I find that Caucasians or white Anglos tend to be not as family oriented as the ethnic groups. So I've dated Chinese, Japanese, Hispanics, Armenians, Bulgarians—people that are more family oriented. The Caucasian men that I meet, they're very nice, but they're kind of self-centered and not close with their families. Like if I ask, "Oh, how's your mom?" They say, "Oh, I don't know." I go, "Doesn't she live close to you?" He says, "Yeah." I go, "Don't you go by and see her?" He says, "No." I find that amazing. I'm not used to that. That to me is disrespectful.

Culture Gaps and White Privilege: Asian-White Marriage

Many of my informants, then, felt that an Asian-white marriage would probably be plagued by culture gaps, not least because "whiteness" was a conceptual counterpoint, an "other" to the values of Asians. But they also felt that marriage to whites would have culture gaps because the white spouse's status as a member of the racial majority might translate into the exercising of greater power (than the Chinese or Korean spouse) in the negotiation of cultural matters in the marriage. That is, they felt that white dominance could widen the actual significance of culture gaps in a marriage.

With a focus on structures of gender, analysts have noted that a complex and wide range of conditions shapes the dynamics of power in marriages, including the relative economic and social resources of the partners, and their ideals and beliefs about gender roles in marriage (Hochschild 1989; Pyke and Coltrane 1996). The accounts of my informants bring our attention to race as another dimension of the dynamics of marital power. They spoke of the privileges of a white identity and the advantage that it confers to the white partner in an

Asian-white marriage. Several told me that the precise nature of these privileges was difficult to describe and name, because of their deeply entrenched and thus diffuse and taken-for-granted character. Kyung Sook, for one, recalled that the whites she dated had a sense of entitlement, a certain arrogance and expectation of control over the cultural terms of the relationship:

> It's the individual that matters, but I would say, given that this is a white world, it's better for a minority person to not marry white. I mean, I've gone out with whites, and I've always felt like it's a battle to not get overwhelmed by their culture, their way of life. They are the majority, they dictate. They also don't understand racism, they're like, "Oh, that's not racism." I'm being extreme of course, but it's part of their way of life to get what they want, they expect it.

Sung, a Korean American, also felt that intimate relationships with whites had a certain edge to them, because of the dynamics of white privilege. Sung was, at the time of the interview, going out with a Latina woman. He felt that intimate partnerships between members of different minority groups, while certainly involving culture gaps, were nonetheless quite different from those between minorities and whites. Like Kyung Sook, Sung punctuated his discussion of the significance of race in the dynamics of intimate partnerships with remarks that recognized the complexity of these relationships, and the importance of individual attitudes and temperament. I was repeatedly told that it was the individual who really mattered; people could not simply be reduced to their racial identities:

> I have no problem with Asians marrying whites, whatever. Marriage is not a political decision, it's a personal one. I find these Asian American types who argue otherwise to be a little insane. But at the same time, I do find that in relationships with whites, there tends to be a kind of edge to things. Especially if you're talking about, like, a WASP. They may not even realize it because it's so ingrained in them, but they think their culture is the best, most worthwhile. That other cultures are not worth anything except in a tourist way. It's different between minorities. It's kind of like a level playing field in the relationship. And if you were to marry a white person, then perhaps they cannot identify with the experience of racism, the stuff that a minority person has to face.

Renee, a Chinese American, also spoke of white privilege and its impact on the internal dynamics of intimate partnerships, especially as it bore on her own personal history of marriage to and divorce from a white American. The marriage had, as she recalled, been scarred by her husband's attitude of disrespect toward her family, especially her parents. Differences in cultural orientation had certainly been part of the problem, but the privileges of race and masculinity were also relevant, since they gave her ex-husband an attitude of superiority and entitled authority in the relationship:

> We were married for five years. Some of the problems we had were definitely cultural. Particularly the respect for the family, the respect for your elders. That became a huge factor in our marriage because my mother and he did not get along at all. He would argue with her and cut her down. And I had a real problem with that, that's not how I was brought up, how most Asians are brought up. This happened every time we walked into my parents' house.
>
> In our family, every Sunday, it's a ritualistic thing, but all the kids come home to see the folks and to have dinner. With Peter [the ex-husband], every time we'd go home on Sunday, on the drive back we'd get into a fight about it. And we started going less, till I realized, wait a minute, I'm not going to not see my family because of him. [So you think the problems were cultural?] It was cultural, and it was his personality, his race. I know I'm generalizing, but white men are so arrogant. They think their way is it. I'm the one who had to constantly justify what I was doing—he could just do it.

For Renee as for other female informants, the anticipated dynamics of power in relationships with white men were about both race and gender. They felt, to put it simply, that they could be at a disadvantage in such relationships, both as women and as nonwhite persons, perhaps especially in light of prevailing stereotypes of Asian women. In popular American culture, Asian women have been portrayed as exotic, hypersexual, and hyperfeminine, marked by their docility and desire to please men (Cheung 1990).[6] Elaine Kim (1994) has noted the enormous sex industry that has developed around this imagery.[7] For my female in-

6. Espiritu (1997) brings our attention to the dualistic quality of this popular imagery: "Asian women have been depicted as superfeminine, in the image of the 'China Doll,' but also as castrating, in the image of the 'Dragon Lady'" (88).

7. Elaine Kim (1994) notes the enormous demand in the United States for X-rated films and pornographic materials featuring Asian women in bondage. The booming Asian "correspondence club" (or mail-order bride) business offers men in the United States who are searching for Asian partners or wives, introductions to Asian women. A brochure from such a business, as presented in a 1994 *Asian Week* article, describes the Asian women with whom customers may correspond as follows: "They are sincere, faithful, devoted and

formants, the significance of this imagery was that it could foster demeaning expectations in others, especially in white men.

This view was highlighted by "the rice king phenomenon." The colloquial expressions "rice kings," also called OWLs (Oriental women lovers), AGWAs (Asian girl watchers), and "white men with yellow fever," all refer to white men who wish to go out with Asian women, in fact are obsessive about doing so. Underlying their strong special attraction to Asian women are the popular stereotypes, as I have described, of the exotic and subservient Asian woman. For Joan, a Chinese American, encounters with "rice kings" had made her a little cautious of relationships with white men:

> When I got to college, I found out that there were white men who only wanted to go out with Asians, and I didn't really know how I felt about it. A friend of mine, she was Korean, she called them rice kings, and she hated them. But I didn't know quite how I felt about it because on the one hand I thought it was flattering, a compliment. It was nice to be seen as so attractive. [She laughs.] I have to admit that I went out with a guy like that for about a month. But then I found out, if these guys are going out with you because you're Asian, not because of who you are, as a human being, that's kind of a sick thing.
>
> I've heard stories too about the rice kings that are kind of sick. Like wanting Asian girlfriends to engage in perverse sexual acts. And to do the geisha thing, serve them hand and foot. I'm kind of suspicious, I guess, and that's true of my other Asian women friends, even those who go out with white guys all the time. I mean, not all white guys are obviously like that, but you always need to make sure they don't have those ideas.

For my informants, then, intimate partnerships with whites were associated with marital power dynamics that advantaged the other (white) partner. Since many of my informants had been or were still in marriages or intimate partnerships with whites, I must emphasize, they viewed this association as a possibility rather than as a given or absolute matter. Nonetheless, the specter that such inequities might arise did seem to reinforce their prevailing sense that inter-

---

believe in a lasting marriage and happy home." The remarks of a manager of such a club make even clearer the ways in which these businesses are driven by the image of the traditional and subservient femininity of Asian women, in contrast to their "American" counterparts: "The men who use the service . . . sound like a broken record. They think American women are too career-minded, materialistic and competitive" (Cacas 1994).

marriage to whites did not in general bode well for the survival of ethnic distinctions in their own lives and those of their descendants. By contrast, they judged marriage to a fellow Asian American to be a situation that would favor the preservation of ethnic identity and culture as powerful and salient matters.

■ Assimilation and the Question of Intermarriage

In an often-cited work, the assimilation theorist Milton Gordon (1964) identifies marital assimilation, or intermarriage with members of the dominant group, as a stage of assimilation, one that follows acculturation and structural assimilation, or the entry of the minority group into the cliques, clubs, and institutions of the dominant society. With marital assimilation, the minority group begins to move into a stage of amalgamation into the larger society.

This vision of assimilation—as a melding into the dominant American landscape along with a loss of ethnic distinction—colored my informants' views on intermarriage, informing it in powerful ways. It marked a certain ambivalence about intermarriage and the ethnic loss that it implied. This ambivalence was at the heart of my informants' widespread engagement with the idea of "marrying Asian," as well as the general favor and optimism with which they viewed this marriage option. This preference for intra-Asian marriage over any other type of intermarriage emerged in part as a response to the specter of assimilation and the dangers to ethnicity that it signaled. "Marrying Asian" thus became a strategy of ethnic preservation, of creating life conditions favorable to the survival of ethnicity, but without having to limit oneself to partnerships with those only of the same ethnonational background.

It is important, I believe, to neither over- nor underestimate the significance of these attitudes for patterns of marital behavior among second-generation Chinese and Korean Americans. The general favor with which my informants viewed "marrying Asian" did not necessarily mean that they had taken or were going to take this particular course of action. Like Asian Americans in general, a significant number of them had married persons of the same ethnonational background as themselves, while others had married whites. Given prevailing conditions, these diverse marriage patterns, including that of marriage to whites, will continue, I believe, to be part of the Asian American future. But my informants' attitudes do also suggest the growing importance of intra-Asian marriage as a type of intermarriage among Asian Americans, especially among those who are U.S.-born, middle-class, and of East Asian origin. This observation is supported by the findings of statistical studies, as described earlier, that rates of marriage between members of different Asian-origin groups in the United States have increased (Lee and Fernandez 1998; Shinagawa and Pang 1996).

Besides offering some tentative clues to the future, the findings that I have reported here provide insight into attitudes toward intermarriage among some Asian Americans today. Analyses of intermarriage often assume that minority group members are driven by a desire to marry those of the majority group because of the attendant rewards of acceptance and status in the larger society. This assumption is quite starkly expressed by hypergamy theory, which proposes that people seek and gain marriage partners in a system of exchange—a "marriage market" (see Davis 1941). The marriage of a minority to a dominant group member is more likely to occur when the former has some valued resource, such as high socioeconomic status, that he can exchange in the "market" for a spouse who is a member of the majority group. My findings underscore the need to consider the complexity of minority group attitudes toward marriage to dominant group members, since my informants expressed considerable ambivalence about marriage to whites. Suspicious that the mixed Asian-white child might not be accepted as white, they were uncertain as to how and whether Asian-white marriage signaled the declining significance of *Asian* as a marginalizing racial marker in the dominant society. Another possible outcome that they foresaw was ethnic loss, which they did not view with much favor.

■ *Envisioning Ethnic Futures*

> I think the further out you get from the immigrant generation, the [more the] culture fades away. It drops off, the more you go on. Like what's happened to the Caucasians, and how they see their European backgrounds. It's all kind of fuzzy and blended in for them. The same thing is likely to happen to Asians. But probably in the long run they'll be more ethnic than the Caucasians. [Why in the long run will they be more ethnic?] Because we look different, we're not white. (Glenn, Chinese American)

As highlighted by what I have called *distilled ethnicity,* my informants envisioned a future in which ethnicity was likely to be more selective and less distinctive in its expression than it had been in the lives of their immigrant parents.

But if ethnic identity and culture would be different and in the final analysis less powerful than they had been before, my informants nonetheless expected them to remain salient matters, both in their own lives and in those of their descendants. At the heart of this expectation was that race would continue to be of significance. Even as they spoke of the future of ethnicity in a manner reminiscent of the symbolic ethnicity of white ethnics, they also noted that their ethnic experiences, unlike those of European Americans, would be shaped by race.

With notions of *racialized ethnicity,* my informants acknowledged the nonoptional character of ethnicity in their lives. Yet neither did they see themselves simply as passive victims of an unwanted ethnicity that had been thrust upon them. They valued their identity as ethnics and were actively engaged in the work of refashioning its meaning and character. Even as they chafed at the restrictions of the ethnic bind, they also viewed its unraveling with some regret. They generally felt much ambivalence about the prospects of ethnic loss, of the disintegration of ethnic claims and distinctions. The ethnic American model of identity is marked by a fundamental tension of balance between *ethnic* and *American;* at some point the scale tips too far one way or another and so endangers an aspect of identity. If my informants felt marginalized from *American,* it was also the case that they viewed with some trepidation the prospect that the scale would tip too far toward *American* and away from *ethnic.*

As highlighted in particular by their reflections on intermarriage, my informants responded to the identity challenges posed by processes of assimilation in part by affirming the idea of Asian American ethnicity. The notion of *Asian American* seemed to offer another possible way, besides ethnonationality, to "be ethnic," to think about and define one's ethnicity. Ethnic pan-Asianism was the ideological glue, the means of making sense of *Asian American* as an aspect of identity. With its emphasis on values and worldview rather than specific behaviors, Asian American ethnicity as defined by ethnic pan-Asianism meshed easily with the demands posed by integration into the dominant society.

CHAPTER SEVEN

Becoming Asian American

Will members of the nation's fastest-growing racial group identify
themselves as Chinese-Americans or Filipino-Americans, the way Italian-
Americans or Irish-Americans often designate themselves? With a nod
to their ethnic roots but their feet planted in the mainstream? Or will
they end up defining themselves as Asian American, a term like black or
African-American, with its suggestion of a separate race?   (Onishi 1996)

THE TERM *assimilation* is widely understood today to refer to an
outcome, a point at which a minority group has successfully and completely
blended into the dominant society. More useful, I believe, is an understanding
of assimilation as a *process,* one of integration into the dominant society. It is a
process whose eventual outcome is fundamentally uncertain and that is influenced by the active efforts of the minority group to shape the terms of their own
integration (Alba and Nee 1997; Barkan 1995; Kazal 1995).

It is with this conception of assimilation in mind, as a contested and uncertain process, that I describe second-generation Chinese and Korean Americans
as *assimilating Asian Americans.* They are becoming part of the American mainstream, but not, I believe, in a manner and direction that is a simple duplication
of the European American experience.

As suggested by the *New York Times* article quoted in the epigraph above,
a variety of future scenarios has been proposed for Asian Americans. Among
them is their transformation into "whites," and the expansion of the "white"
category to include Asian Americans. Only time can tell for sure, but the findings that I report in this book raise doubts about the possibility of such a future.
Even as second-generation Chinese and Korean Americans are assimilating, becoming part of the mainstream, the concept of *Asian race* remains potent as
a marker of distinction and separation from the marker of "white." Assuming
that processes of assimilation will continue to occur for Asian Americans, the

dominant society may itself be redefined to reflect the presence of Asians as well as other racial minorities, such as Latinos, within it. In other words, the synonymity that now exists between *mainstream America* and *white* will come to be revised.[1]

In recognition of just how intractable the boundary between *white* and *Asian* has been in the United States, pan-Asian ethnogenesis has been proposed as a possible trajectory of assimilation for Asian Americans, an alternative to that of amalgamation into white society (Lopez and Espiritu 1990; Tuan 1998). Reflecting popular notions of ethnic identity as a singular, zero-sum matter, pan-Asian ethnogenesis is envisioned to involve replacing the specific ethnonational identities of Asian Americans with the identity of *Asian American*. I do not foresee this trajectory as possible, however. Rather, what I see is the emergence of a *dual Asian and ethnonational* identification pattern. For many of those who fall under its official rubric, *Asian American* is quite likely to grow in meaning and significance, becoming something more than an unwanted, externally imposed label. But ethnonational identities will also remain important. The emerging dynamic is not, as I see it, one in which pan-Asian identity overtakes and replaces the specific ethnonational identities of *Asian American*. Instead, the two will coexist, perhaps uneasily at times, but at other moments in comfortable and even seamless ways.

■ The Interplay of "Thick" and "Thin" Ethnicity

A powerful argument can be made for the idea that *Asian American* is itself an identity of assimilation, both reflecting and facilitating integration into the dominant culture and society. For second-generation Chinese and Korean Americans, "becoming Asian American" offers a means to fill the identity gaps left by their own weakening ties to the ethnic communities and cultures of their immigrant ancestors. *Asian American* is also a way of being ethnic that meshes quite easily with the social and cultural expectations of the dominant

---

1. The disintegration of the synonymous quality of *mainstream American* and *white* has given rise to several possible scenarios. As reviewed by Foner (2000), these include the possibility that "the current white-nonwhite division will give way to a new black-nonblack dichotomy. . . . A more optimistic forecast sees black-white relations evolving in a different way. In this scenario, increasing intermarriage and intermingling will reduce the salience of current racial and ethnic boundaries, including the black-white divide" (229–30).

society. It is, in this regard, perceived to be quite different from Chinese or Korean membership, with their more demanding and exclusionary qualities. Indeed, the participants of my study described their understanding and practice of Asian American culture in ways that were frequently reminiscent of the symbolic ethnicity of white ethnics, although they are ultimately quite different in their underlying racial dynamics (Alba 1990; Gans 1979; Waters 1990).[2] The behavioral expectations for both are loose and do not pose much conflict with those of the dominant society.

For these reasons then, "becoming Asian American" makes sense for the assimilating Asian. But what, then, is the fate of one's ethnonational identity, the affiliation of one's immigrant ancestors? The continued significance of ethnonational identification, simultaneous with the development of Asian American identification, is suggested, I believe, by their relationship to each other as "thick" and "thin" ethnicities. Cornell and Hartmann (1998) point out that ethnic collectivities may be either thick or thin depending on their comprehensiveness—the degree to which they organize social life and collective action for their members. They further point out that while ethnic collectivities may be generally characterized as thick or thin, the comprehensiveness of these designations will vary for individual members. Thus within an ethnic collectivity that is thick, there are at least some members who experience it as thin—something that organizes their existence in only sparse ways.

As an ethnic collectivity, Asian America today is relatively thin. In comparison, Chinese America and Korean America, as well as many other Asian-origin communities in the United States, are thick: institutionally and culturally dense, and shaping the lives of many members in deep and extensive ways. Thus the assimilating Asian experiences what I have described as a dual identity pattern. It is precisely the thinness of Asian American culture and community that makes it attractive to the assimilating Asian, but its very sparseness also makes appealing in contrast the thickness of the ethnonational-origin collectivity.

Even if the assimilating Asian is engaged with the ethnonational-origin collectivity in only loose and minimal ways, acknowledged membership holds some advantages. Paramount among them is the ever-present possibility of being part

---

2. While there certainly is a sense in which one's Asian American identity can be more or less salient across different times and situations, it is never completely absent. There is no option, as there is for the symbolic ethnic, to not be ethnic, but simply "American."

of a dense community with a rich and well-defined cultural tradition, in which members feel and experience a deep and extensive sense of belonging and support, as well as distinction and pride. For European Americans, similarly, as Halter (2000) notes, "Europe" is inadequate as a homeland reference: "Modern ethnic identity may be convenience ethnicity, but it still needs to provide some sort of significant primordial reference for the expressive self. Europe is too nebulous a construct to serve as a mythical homeland. It lacks a symbolic matrix and the cultural particularity needed to satisfy the yearnings for a sense of belonging and a more distinctive ethnic identity" (196).

The generally thick quality of Asian-origin ethnonational communities in the United States today may certainly lessen over time. But at present it is supported by a powerful configuration of structural circumstances, many of which are defining features of the new immigration. As highlighted by the Chinese and Korean American experiences, these circumstances include continuing immigration and the presence of intensive transnational networks of exchange and flow with the homeland societies. Such conditions work to revitalize and energize these communities, ensuring their continued thickness and thus their continued attraction for the assimilating Asian American.

There are, however, a number of issues that complicate the picture I have painted thus far and also underline the importance of variations across specific ethnonational groups. Among these issues is the question of how the assimilating ethnic is received in the ethnonational community of his immigrant ancestors. By definition, the assimilating Asian is somewhat detached from this community, but precisely for this reason, his or her connection to it requires at least some affirmation and support. In their work on Japanese American ethnicity, Fugita and O'Brien (1991) note that ethnic collectivities differ in their traditions of organizing membership and community life, and that these traditions have important implications for their ability to "keep" assimilating members, to ensure their continued integration into the community. For Japanese Americans, they argue, such community integration has been quite high, facilitated by an elaborate network of ethnic voluntary associations through which members remain connected to the community.

The question of whether and how the Chinese and Korean American communities will successfully integrate their later-generation members is best left to future studies. My study, however, offers some clues to the specific mechanisms that can play an important role in this integration. Among these mechanisms, as we have seen, is a powerful albeit contested ideology of "Chinese by blood" or "Korean by blood." Also important, as most notably suggested by the experiences of Korean American informants, are ethnic associations, especially churches and those specifically oriented toward bringing later-generation Korean Americans together (Alumkal 1999; Chong 1998). Given current trends toward intermarriage, such organizations will likely be increasingly faced with the identity questions posed by the mixed children of intermarriages about their place in the Korean American community.

Let me make one last point with respect to the interplay of thick and thin ethnicity. Ethnonational communities differ in their connotations of power and significance in the global economy. For the assimilating Asian, a situation that considers these connotations to be favorable can reinforce the attractions of the thick ethnicities of immigrant ancestors. For my informants, certainly, the attractions of Chinese or Korean membership were reinforced by an understanding that this membership was strategically valuable in the globalizing economy. One's Chinese or Korean roots were not, then, something to be shunned or dismissed but something to be deliberately cultivated. In the contemporary world, these roots, it was felt, were a valuable source of ethnic identity capital.

■ *Racial Labeling and Its Qualities*

As scholars have understood, the experience of a common imposed racial label is a driving force behind racial ethnogenesis, or the formation of an ethnic group around racialized boundaries. Less attention, however, has been paid to the various qualities of the racial labeling experience and their implications for identity formation. There is, first of all, the quality of consistency, or similarity of racial labeling experience, which can be further subdivided into two types: within-individual consistency and within-group consistency. By *within-individual consistency* I mean the degree of consistency with which individual members of the group find themselves identified by a particular racial label. For example, Asian American persons may or may not find themselves consistently labeled "Asian," across varied social settings, in different parts of their lives. By contrast, I use the term *within-group consistency* to refer to the extent to which members of a particular racialized group actually share the experience of a common racial label. For example, those falling under the label *Asian American* may experience that labeling to differing degrees.

Since the 1970s, as analysts of the Asian American movement have noted, the "within-group consistency" of racial labeling for Asian Americans has declined, due to immigration from a wider range of regions in Asia than in the past, as well as the official expansion of the Asian American umbrella to encompass this diversity (Dirlik 1996; Espiritu 1992). The inclusion of South Asian–origin persons in the category dramatically highlights this decline in within-group consistency, given that the experience of imposed racial labeling for South Asians is quite different from that of many other Asian-origin groups, certainly Chinese and Koreans (Fisher 1980; Kibria 1998). But even with these developments, I would argue that the overall consistency of racial labeling for Asian Americans is relatively high. The Asian American population contains a significant portion of persons who experience the imposed label of *Asian* quite consistently in their lives. To put it another way, even though within-group consistency is perhaps less for Asian Americans than it was in the past, the experience of within-individual consistency is high for a substantial segment of persons.

With respect to both types of consistency, racial labeling seems to be quite different for Asian Americans than it is for Latinos today. In her work on Latino identities, Rodriguez (2000, 4) notes a low degree of within-individual consistency: "many Latinos are assigned a multitude of 'racial' classifications," she remarks, "sometimes in one day." Within-group consistency also appears to be low, given the vast array of classifications (including *white* and *black*) by which Hispanics are racially identified in American life (Oboler 1995). This variability is perhaps both reflected in and reinforced by the absence, in the U.S. census, of *Hispanic/Latino* as a racial category. At least in this regard, then, the prospects for ethnogenesis appear more favorable for Asian Americans than they do for Latinos. A generally high consistency in racial labeling is among the conditions that underlie the emerging significance of *Asian American* as a meaningful basis of affiliation for many of those who fall under its rubric.

The situation looks a little different, however, when we turn to another quality of racial labeling. This is its degree of *overshadowing:* the extent to which the racial label works to block out other ethnic identities. In the United States, it is important to note, minority racial identities in general have the potential ability to overshadow, to trump all other ethnic identities. But the ability to successfully resist this potential, to assert to others the significance of one's ethnic identity, may be quite different across racial groups. Among immigrants from the Caribbean, for example, the racial label of *black* is high in its overshadowing qualities, often rendering other ethnic affiliations invisible (Waters 1999). In contrast, those labeled as *Asian* are more successfully able to persuade others that they are Chinese, Japanese, and so forth. For my second-generation Chinese and Korean American informants, the experience of being labeled as *Asian* was deeply intertwined with such efforts at persuasion, indeed often inseparable from them. In this dance of racialization and resistance, both the Asian and the ethnonational were present as aspects of identity, locked together in close if oppositional partnership.

Among Asian Americans, then, ethnonational identities appear to be an important vehicle for resistance to racialization or absorption into imposed racial identities. I see this resistance to be of a bypassing sort, rather than a direct challenge to established racial classification schemes. Once again, the comparative perspective offered by the Latino experience is instructive here. In general, traditions of race and identity in Latin America and the Spanish-speaking Caribbean speak relatively directly to established ways of thinking about race in the United States *and at the same time* bring them into question. Many of these societies have been concerned with the divisions and identities of *black* and *white*, seeing them not in dichotomous terms, as they are in the United States, but rather as marking a continuum of racial identity (Fernandez 1992; Rodriguez 2000). Furthermore, while "race" is popularly understood in the United States to be a biological given, racial identities are widely understood in Latin America and the Spanish-speaking Caribbean to be fluid and shaped by culture and class. Rodriguez (2000) has argued that these notions of race are expressed in the tendency of Hispanics to choose "other" when asked to place themselves in the U.S. racial classification scheme.[3] My point is that Latino resistance to imposed racial identities may involve not only an assertion of an alternative identity but a repudiation of the very basis and rationale for the imposed identity itself.

Among Asian Americans, by contrast, resistance has had a more limited scope, focused as it is less on denying an Asian racial identity per se than on asserting the greater significance of ethnonational identity. This absence of direct challenge to the established racial classification scheme is another condition that supports the development of a dual identity pattern, of *Asian* and ethnonational, among Asian Americans.

3. Rodriguez (2000) notes that in the 1990 census, 43.5 percent of Hispanics chose "other" for their racial identification.

■ *What 'Asian American' Means to Asian Americans*

As Espiritu noted in *Asian American Panethnicity* (1992), *Asian American* has, since the 1970s, emerged as a basis of political organization for Asian-origin groups in the United States. Asian Americans of varied backgrounds have chosen, at particular moments, to come together to protect their shared interests. My informants understood and appreciated the political dimensions and strategic uses of *Asian American,* but they also appreciated the shared culture and worldview of Asian Americans—ethnic pan-Asianism. Future studies may provide insight into the understandings of Asian American community among other segments of the Asian American population besides Chinese and Korean Americans. Quite clearly, the ideology of ethnic pan-Asianism described in this book does *not* tell us about the meaning of *Asian American* for all Asian Americans. But it does, I believe, offer clues to some thematic tensions that are likely to organize the nature and course of pan-Asian ethnogenesis in the years to come.

■ *The Boundaries of Community*

Among the notable characteristics of the ideology of ethnic pan-Asianism was its boundedness. In contrast to more inclusive notions of pan-Asianism, my informants spoke of feeling a sense of shared community with some Asian Americans rather than others. There were two points of distinction that they made quite often. The second-generation and more generally the later-generation Asian American experiences, they asserted, were unique. The shared culture and worldview of Asian Americans were fundamentally about the experience of *growing up in the United States as an Asian-origin person.* They expressed concerns about being mistaken for an Asian immigrant or national. Given the persistence of the foreigner stereotype of Asians in the United States, it seems likely that understandings of Asian American ethnic community will continue, in the foreseeable future, to be marked by this tension.

In their understandings of Asian American ethnic community, my informants also focused on persons of East Asian origin. It was with persons of Chinese, Japanese, and Korean origin that they felt a special bond, the tugs of common cultural roots and historical origins bringing them together. My findings then point to the possibility that pan-Asian ethnogenesis, as it evolves in the future, may actually emerge among subgroups of Asian Americans—East

Asians, South Asians, and so forth—rather than across the vast spectrum of what is now Asian America. Although my informants tried not to make explicit reference to it, their focus on community among East Asian Americans was nonetheless apparent. In other words, they at times spoke of what "Asian Americans" shared when they actually meant to discuss what East Asian Americans shared. This tendency toward an unconscious appropriation of the term *Asian American* reflects the historical centrality of Chinese and Japanese to the Asian-origin presence in the United States and the development of the Asian American movement. Other groups, of non–East Asian origin, may be less inclined toward such appropriation and may develop other terms, besides *Asian American,* to describe their sense of community.

■ *Racial Positioning and Questions of Class*

Ethnic pan-Asianism is an account not simply of what Asian Americans share in culture and worldview but also of their location within the racial ethnic landscape of the United States. For my informants, its construction was marked by efforts to position Asian Americans away from other racial minorities and toward European Americans. This effort clearly reflects their largely middle-class, upwardly mobile characteristics and their sense of identification with the European American experience promoted by these characteristics. The growing numbers of Asian Americans who are less economically privileged, however, may well be inclined to identify more with racial minorities than not. Further studies are clearly needed to shed light on the question of how working-class and low-income Asian Americans understand and construct notions of Asian American commonality and community.

There are, however, also some dynamics of convergence across class lines in the racial consciousness and stance of Asian Americans. For one, middle-class Asian Americans, in their quest for acceptance in the dominant society, experience ongoing tensions. In describing the complex confluence of inclusion and exclusion from the dominant society that marks the collective situation of Asian Americans today, I have used the phrase "a part yet apart." The middle-class and second-generation characteristics of my sample created a heightened experience and awareness of the contradictions of this position. Not only were my informants deeply involved with the institutions and groups of the dominant society, but they also expected to be accepted on equal terms in this engagement.

When these expectations were dashed, they felt much frustration. Thus even as they identified with the European American experience, they also felt that the parallels between them were limited. Moreover, constrained by the terms of a popular racial discourse that has centered on black and white experiences, they struggled to make sense of what it meant to be Asian within the racial order of the United States. Out of this struggle also emerged elements of positive identification with the experience of other racial minorities: their histories, predicaments, and worldviews. Here too pan-Asian organizations and forums (especially those associated with Asian American studies) could play an important role in shaping racial consciousness and cultivating such identification.

On the flip side, working-class Asian Americans may share the middle-class impulse, as described in this book, to disidentify from other racial minorities. In a repetition of a theme that has tragically been so constant in U.S. history, they may, in their struggles to realize the American dream, draw a sharp line of differentiation between themselves and the most stigmatized members of American society: blacks. Working-class Asian Americans may then have a particular investment in identifying with the European American experience, as a strategy of upward mobility. Relatedly, it is important to note that the label *Asian* does not, at the present time, carry the stigma of "underachievement" in the dominant society, as does *black* or *Latino*.[4] Instead, Asian Americans are considered a "model minority." Fueled by the very fact of their racialized marginality, Asian Americans may ironically affirm the stereotype of themselves as a model minority, in an effort to ease their own path of integration into American society.

4. The absence of the "underachieving" stigma may be part of the reason why middle-class Asian Americans seem to be more inclined to accept the *Asian American* designation than their Latino counterparts. Portes and Macleod (1999) report that middle-class Latinos are more likely than lower-socio-economic-status Latinos to reject the *Latino* label.

Abelman, Nancy, and John Lie. 1995. *Blue Dreams: Korean Americans and the Los Angeles Riots.* Cambridge: Harvard University Press.

Alba, Richard. 1990. *Ethnic Identity: The Transformation of White America.* New Haven: Yale University Press.

———. 1999. "Immigration and the American Realities of Assimilation and Multiculturalism." *Sociological Forum* 14:3–26.

Alba, Richard, and John Logan. 1993. "Minority Proximity to Whites in Suburbs: An Individual-Level Analysis of Segregation." *American Journal of Sociology* 98:1388–1427.

Alba, Richard, and Victor Nee. 1997. "Rethinking Assimilation for a New Era Immigration." *International Migration Review* 31:826–74.

Almaguer, Tomas. 1994. *Racial Fault Lines: The Historical Origins of White Supremacy in California.* Berkeley: University of California Press.

Alumkal, Antony. 1999. "Preserving Patriarchy: Assimilation, Gender Norms, and Second-Generation Korean American Evangelicals." *Qualitative Sociology* 22:127–40.

Applebome, Peter. 1995. "Nation's Campuses Confront an Expanding Racial Divide." *New York Times.* October 25.

AsianWeek. 1996. "APA Agenda: Asian Americans on the Issues." August 23–29.

Barkan, Elliot. 1995. "Race, Religion and Nationality in American Society: A Model of Ethnicity—From Contact to Assimilation." *Journal of American Ethnic History* 14:38–101.

Billingsley, Andrew. 1992. *Climbing Jacob's Ladder: The Enduring Legacy of African American Families.* New York: Simon and Schuster.

Blauner, Robert. 1972. *Racial Oppression in America.* New York: Harper and Row.

Cabezas, Amado, and George Kawaguchi. 1988. "Empirical Evidence for Continuing Asian American Income Inequality: The Human Capital Model and Labor Market Segmentation." In *Reflections on Shattered Windows: Problems and Prospects for Asian American Studies,* edited by G. Y. Okihiro, S. Hune, A. A. Hansen, and J. M. Liu, 144–64. Pullman: Washington State University Press.

Cacas, Samuel R. 1994. "The Booming Business of Modern Day 'Mail Order Bride' Services." *AsianWeek.* January 14.

Chen, Nina. 1995. "Love Boat: Scamfest or Cultural Exchange?" *AsianWeek.* March 17.

Cheung King-Kok. 1990. "The Woman Warrior Versus the Chinaman Pacific: Must a Chinese American Critic Choose Between Feminism and Heroism?" In *Conflicts in Feminism,* edited by Marianne Hirsch and Evelyn Fox Keller, 234–51. New York: Routledge, Chapman, and Hall.

Child, Irving L. 1943. *Italian or American? The Second Generation in Conflict.* New Haven: Yale University Press.

Chong, Kelly H. 1998. "What It Means to Be Christian: The Role of Religion in the Construction of Ethnic Identity Among Second Generation Korean Americans." *Sociology of Religion* 59:259–86.

Chow, Sue. 2000. "The Significance of Race in the Private Sphere: Asian Americans and Intermarriage." *Sociological Inquiry* 70:1–29.

Coleman, James. 1988. "Social Capital in the Creation of Human Capital." *American Journal of Sociology* 94:95–120.

Cornell, Stephen, and Douglas Hartmann. 1998. *Ethnicity and Race: Making Identities in a Changing World.* Thousand Oaks, CA: Pine Forge Press.

Cose, Ellis. 1993. *The Rage of a Privileged Class.* New York: HarperCollins.

Curry, George E. 1996. "Introduction." In *The Affirmative Action Debate,* edited by George Curry, xiii–xv. New York: Addison-Wesley.

Davis, James F. 1991. *Who Is Black? One Nation's Definition.* University Park: Pennsylvania State University Press.

Davis, Kingsley. 1941. "Intermarriage in Caste Society." *American Anthropology* 43:376–95.

Der, Henry. 1993. "Affirmative Action Policy." In *The State of Asian Pacific America: Policy Issues to the Year 2020.* Los Angeles: LEAP Asian Pacific American Public Policy Institute and UCLA Asian American Studies Center.

Dikötter, Frank. 1992. *The Discourse of Race in Modern China.* Palo Alto, CA: Stanford University Press.

Dirlik, Arif. 1996. "Asians on the Rim: Transnational Capital and Local Community in the Making of Contemporary Asian America." *Amerasia Journal* 22:1–24.

Espiritu, Yen L. 1992. *Asian American Panethnicity: Bridging Institutional Identities.* Philadelphia: Temple University Press.

———. 1994. "The Intersection of Race, Ethnicity and Class: The Multiple Identities of Second-Generation Filipinos." *Identities* 1:249–73.

———. 1997. *Asian American Women and Men.* Thousand Oaks, CA: Sage Publications.

Espiritu, Yen L., and Paul Ong. 1994. "Class Constraints on Racial Solidarity Among Asian Americans." In *The New Asian American Immigration in Los Angeles and Global Restructuring,* edited by Paul Ong, Edna Bonacich, and Lucie Cheng, 295–321. Philadelphia: University of Pennsylvania Press.

Fernandez, Carlos. 1992. "La Raza and the Melting Pot: A Comparative Look at Multiethnicity." In *Racially Mixed People in America,* edited by Maria Root, 126–43. Newbury Park, CA: Sage Publications.

Fernandez-Kelly, Patricia, and Richard Schauffler. 1994. "Divided Fates: Immigrant Children in a Restructured U.S. Economy." *International Migration Review* 28:662–89.

Fisher, Maxine. 1980. *The Indians of New York City.* New Delhi, India: Heritage Publishers.

Foner, Nancy. 1997. "What's New About Transnationalism: New York Immigrants Today and at the Turn of the Century." *Diaspora* 6:355–76.

———. 2000. *From Ellis Island to JFK: New York's Two Great Waves of Immigration.* New Haven: Yale University Press.

Fong, Timothy. 1998. *The Contemporary Asian American Experience: Beyond the Model Minority.* Englewood Cliffs, NJ: Prentice Hall.

Fugita, Stephen S., and David J. O'Brien. 1991. *Japanese American Ethnicity: The Persistence of Community.* Seattle: University of Washington Press.

Gans, Herbert J. 1979. "Symbolic Ethnicity: The Future of Ethnic Groups and Cultures in America." *Ethnic and Racial Studies* 2:1–20.

———. 1992. "Second Generation Decline: Scenarios for the Economic and Ethnic Futures for the Post 1965 American Immigrants." *Ethnic and Racial Studies* 15:173–92.

Glazer, Nathan, and Daniel P. Moynihan. 1963. *Beyond the Melting Pot.* Cambridge: MIT Press and Harvard University Press.

Glick-Schiller, Nina, Linda Basch, and Cristina Blanc-Szanton. 1992. "Towards a Definition of Transnationalism." *Annals of the New York Academy of Sciences* 46:1–24.

Goffman, Erving. 1963. *Stigma: Notes on the Management of Spoiled Identity.* Englewood Cliffs, NJ: Prentice Hall.

Gordon, Milton. 1964. *Assimilation in American Life.* New York: Oxford University.

Greeley, Andrew M. 1974. *Ethnicity in the United States.* New York: John Wiley.

Gutierrez, David G. 1995. *Walls and Mirrors: Mexican Americans, Mexican Immigrants and the Politics of Ethnicity.* Berkeley: University of California Press.

Hall, Stuart. 1996. "Introduction: Who Needs Identity?" In *Questions of Cultural Identity,* edited by Stuart Hall and Paul DuGay. Thousand Oaks, CA: Sage Press.

Halter, Marilyn. 2000. *Shopping for Identity: The Marketing of Ethnicity.* New York: Schocken Books.

Hayano, David. 1981. "Ethnic Identification and Disidentification: Japanese Americans Views of Chinese-Americans." *Ethnic Groups* 3:157–71.

Herberg, Will. 1960. *Protestant-Catholic-Jew.* New York: Doubleday.

Hill, Shirley A. 1999. *African American Children: Socialization and Development in Families.* Thousand Oaks, CA: Sage Publications.

Hing, Bill O. 1993. *Making and Remaking Asian America Through Immigration Policy, 1850–1990.* Palo Alto, CA: Stanford University Press.

Hochschild, Arlie. 1989. *The Second Shift: Working Parents and the Revolution at Home.* New York: Viking Press.

Hochschild, Jennifer. 1995. *Facing Up to the American Dream: Race, Class, and the Soul of the Nation.* Princeton: Princeton University Press.

Hollinger, David. 1995. *Postethnic America: Beyond Multiculturalism.* New York: Basic Books.

Hsu, Ruth Y. 1996. "Will the Model Minority Please Identify Itself? American Ethnic Identity and its Discontents" *Diaspora* 5:37–64.

Humes, Karen, and Jesse McKinnon. 2000. "The Asian and Pacific Islanders Population in the United States: March 1999." U.S. Census Bureau, Current Population Report. Washington: GPO, 20–529.

Hune, Shirley, and Kenyon S. Chan. 1997. "Special Focus: Asian Pacific American Demographic and Educational Trends." In *Minorities in Higher Education,* edited by D. Carter and R. Wilson. Washington: American Council on Higher Education.

Hurh, Won Moo, and Kwang Chung Kim. 1989. "The 'Success' Image of Asian Americans:

Its Validity and Its Practical and Theoretical Implications." *Ethnic and Racial Studies* 4:512–38.

Hwang, David Henry. 1990. *FOB and Other Plays.* New York: Plume Books.

Ignatiev, Noel. 1995. *How the Irish Became White.* New York: Routledge.

Jacobs, Jerry A., and Teresa Labov. 1995. "Sex Differences in Asian American Intermarriage: Asian Exceptionalism Reconsidered." Unpublished paper presented at the Annual Meetings of the American Sociological Association, Washington, D.C., August.

Kang, Connie. 1993. "Separate, Distinct—and Equal." *Los Angeles Times.* January 20.

Kazal, Robert. 1995. "Revisiting Assimilation: The Rise, Fall, and Reappraisal of a Concept in American Ethnic History." *American Historical Review* 100:437–72.

Kibria, Nazli. 1998. "The Contested Meaning of Asian American: Racial Dilemmas in the Contemporary United States." *Ethnic and Racial Studies* 21:939–58.

Kim, Elaine. 1993. "Home Is Where the Han Is: A Korean American Perspective on the Los Angeles Riots. In *Reading Rodney King/Reading Urban Uprising,* edited by Robert Gooding-Williams, 215–35. New York: Routledge.

———. 1994. Preface. In *Charlie Chan Is Dead: An Anthology of Contemporary Asian American Fiction,* edited by Jessica Hagedorn, vii–xiv. New York: Penguin.

Kim Jae-Un. 1991. *The Koreans: Their Mind and Behavior.* Trans. Kim Kyong-Dong, Kyobo Book Central, Korea Research Foundation.

LEAP (Leadership Education for Asian Pacifics). 1996. *The California Civil Rights Initiative. Special Report on Proposition 209.* Los Angeles: LEAP Asian Pacific American Public Policy Institute and UCLA Asian American Studies Center.

Lee, Sharon, and Marilyn Fernandez. 1998. "Trends in Asian American Racial/Ethnic Intermarriage: A Comparison of 1980 and 1990 Census Data." *Sociological Perspectives* 41:2.

Levine, Arthur. 2000. "The Campus Divided, and Divided Again." *New York Times.* June 11.

Lieberson, Stanley. 1980. *A Piece of the Pie: Black and White Immigrants Since 1880.* Berkeley: University of California Press.

Liu, John. 1992. "The Contours of Asian Professional, Technical and Kindred Work Immigration, 1965–88." *Sociological Perspectives* 35:673–704.

Loeb, Paul R. 1994. *Generation at the Crossroads: Apathy and Action on the American Campus.* New Brunswick, NJ: Rutgers University Press.

Lopez, David, and Yen Espiritu. 1990. "Panethnicity in the United States: A Theoretical Framework." *Ethnic and Racial Studies* 13:198–224.

Lowe, Lisa. 1996. *Immigrant Acts: On Asian American Cultural Politics.* Durham, NC: Duke University Press.

Mar, Don, and Marlene Kim. 1994. "Historical Trends." In *The State of Asian Pacific America: Economic Diversity, Issues, and Policies,* edited by Paul Ong, 13–30. Los Angeles: LEAP Asian Pacific American Public Policy Institute and UCLA Asian American Studies Center.

Massey, D. S., and N. Denton. 1987. "Trends in the Residential Segregation of Blacks, Hispanics and Asians." In *American Sociological Review* 1:802–25.

Min, Pyong Gap. 1995a. "Introduction." In *Asian Americans: Contemporary Trends and Issues,* edited by Pyong Gap Min, 10–37. Thousand Oaks, CA: Sage Publications.

———. 1995b. "Korean Americans." In *Asian Americans: Contemporary Trends and Issues,* edited by Pyong Gap Min, 199–231. Thousand Oaks, CA: Sage Publications.

Nee, Victor, and J. Sanders. 1985. "The Road to Parity: Determinants of the Socioeconomic Achievements of Asian Americans." In *Ethnic and Racial Studies* 8:75–93.

Newsweek. 1982. "Asian-Americans: A 'Model Minority.'" December 6.

Nagel, Joanne. 1994. "Constructing Ethnicity: Creating and Recreating Ethnicity and Culture." In *Social Problems* 41: 152–76.

Oboler, Suzanne. 1995. *Ethnic Labels, Latino Lives.* Minneapolis: University of Minnesota Press.

Ogbu, John, and Margaret Gibson. 1991. *Minority Status and Schooling: A Comparative Study of Immigrant and Involuntary Minorities.* New York: Garland.

Okihiro, Gary. 1994. *Margins and Mainstreams: Asians in American History and Culture.* Seattle: University of Washington Press.

Omi, Michael, and Howard Winant. 1986. *Racial Formation in the U.S.* New York: Routledge.

Ong, Paul M. 2000. "The Affirmative Action Divide." In *Transforming Race Relations: The State of Asian Pacific America,* edited by Paul Ong, 313–62. Los Angeles: LEAP Asian Pacific American Public Policy Institute and UCLA Asian American Studies Center.

Ong, Paul, and Evelyn Blumenberg. 1994. "Scientists and Engineers." *The State of Asian Pacific America, a Public Policy Report: Policy Issues to the Year 2020,* 165–92. Los Angeles: LEAP Asian Pacific American Public Policy Institute and UCLA Asian American Studies Center.

Ong, Paul, and Suzanne Hee. 1994. "Economic Diversity." In *The State of Asian Pacific America: Economic Diversity,* 31–56. Los Angeles: LEAP Asian Pacific American Public Policy Institute and UCLA Asian American Studies Center.

Onishi, Norimitsu. 1996. "New Sense of Race Arises Among Asian Americans." *New York Times.* May 30.

Osajima, Keith. 1988. "Asian Americans as the Model Minority: An Analysis of Popular Press Images in the 1960's and 1980's." In *Reflections on Shattered Windows,* edited by Gary Okihiro, Shirley Hune, Art Hansen, and John Liu, 165–74. Pullman: Washington State University Press.

Pan, Lyn. 1994. *Sons of the Yellow Emperor: A History of the Chinese Diaspora.* New York: Kodansha International.

Pang, Gin Y. 1994. "Attitudes Towards Interracial and Interethnic Relationships, and Intermarriage Among Korean Americans: The Intersections of Race, Gender and Class Inequality." In *New Visions in Asian American Studies: Diversity, Community, Power,* edited by Franklin Ng, Judy Yung, Stephen Fugita, and Elaine Kim, 112–19. Pullman: Washington State University Press.

Park, Edward. 1999. "Friends or Enemies? Generational Politics in the Korean American Community in Los Angeles." *Qualitative Sociology* 22:161–75.

Perlmann, Joel, and Roger Waldinger. 1997. "Second Generation Decline? Children of Immigrants, Past and Present—A Reconsideration." *International Migration Review* 31:893–922.

Portes, Alejandro, and Dag MacLeod. 1999. "What Shall I Call Myself? Hispanic Identity Formation in the Second Generation." *Ethnic and Racial Studies* 19:523–47.

Portes, Alejandro, and Richard Schauffler. 1994. "Language and the Second Generation: Bilingualism Yesterday and Today." *International Migration Review* 28:640–61.

Portes, Alejandro, and Min Zhou. 1993. "The New Second Generation: Segmented Assimilation and Its Variants." *Annals of the American Academy of Politics and Social Science* 530:74–96.

Pyke, Karen. 2000. "The Normal American Family as an Interpretive Structure of Family Life among Grown Children of Korean and Vietnamese Immigrants." *Journal of Marriage and the Family* 62:240–55.

Pyke, Karen, and Scott Coltrane. 1996. "Entitlement, Obligation and Gratitude in Family Work." *Journal of Family Issues* 17:60–82.

Qian, Zhenchao. 1997. "Breaking the Racial Barriers." *Demography* 34:263–76.

Rodriguez, Clara E. 2000. *Changing Race: Latinos, the Census, and the History of Ethnicity in the U.S.* New York: New York University Press.

Roediger, David R. 1991. *The Wages of Whiteness: Race and the Making of the American Working Class.* London: Verso.

Rose, Peter. 1985. "Asian Americans: From Pariahs to Paragons." In *Clamor at the Gates: The New American Immigration,* edited by Nathan Glazer, 181–212. San Francisco, CA: ICS Press.

Sengupta, Somini. 1999. "Asian-American Programs are Flourishing at Colleges." *New York Times.* June 9.

Shankar, Lavina, and Rajini Srikanth, eds. 1998. *A Part Yet Apart: South Asians in Asian America.* Philadelphia: Temple University Press.

Shinagawa, Larry, and Gin Pang. 1996. "Asian American Panethnicity and Intermarriage." *Amerasia Journal* 22:127–52.

Shrage, Laurie. 1996. "Ethnic Transgressions." In *Color, Class, Identity: The New Politics of Race,* edited by John Arthur and Amy Shapiro, 191–98. Boulder, CO: Westview Press.

Sidel, Ruth. 1994. *Battling Bias: The Struggle for Identity and Community on College Campuses.* New York: Penguin Books.

Spickard, Paul. 1997. "What Must I Be? Asian Americans and the Question of Multiethnic Identity." *Amerasia Journal* 23:17–28.

Spitzberg, Irving, and Virginia Thorndike. 1992. *Creating Community on College Campuses.* Albany: State University of New York Press, 1992.

Takagi, Dana Y. 1992. *The Retreat from Race.* New Brunswick, NJ: Rutgers University Press.

———. 1994. "Post–Civil Rights Politics and Asian American Identity: Admissions and Higher Education." In *Race,* edited by Steven Gregory and Roger Sanjek, 229–42. New Brunswick, NJ: Rutgers University Press.

Takaki, Ronald. 1979. *Iron Cages: Race and Culture in Nineteenth Century America.* New York: Alfred Knopf.

Tan, Amy. 1989. *The Joy Luck Club.* New York: Ivy Books.

Tang, Joyce. 1993. "The Career Attainment of Caucasian and Asian Engineers." *Sociological Quarterly* 34:467–96.

Taylor, Robert J., et al. 1990. "Developments in Research on Black Families: A Decade Review." *Journal of Marriage and the Family* 52:993–1014.

Thorne, Barrie. 1993. *Gender Play: Girls and Boys at School.* New Brunswick, NJ: Rutgers University Press.

Tuan, Mia. 1998. *Forever Foreigners or Honorary Whites? The Asian Ethnic Experience Today.* New Brunswick, NJ: Rutgers University Press.

U.S. Department of Commerce. 1993. "We The American . . . Asians." Economy and Statistics Administration, Bureau of the Census.

Vo, Linda Trinh. 2000. "Performing Ethnography in Asian American Communities: Beyond the Insider-versus-Outsider Perspective." In *Ethnographic Explorations of Asian America,* edited by Martin Manalansan, 17–37. Philadelphia: Temple University Press.

Watanabe, Paul, and Carol Hardy-Fanta. 1998. *Conflict and Convergence: Race, Public Opinion and Political Behavior in Massachusetts.* Boston: Institute for Asian American Studies, University of Massachusetts.

Waters, Mary. 1990. *Ethnic Options: Choosing Identities in America.* Berkeley: University of California Press.

———. 1994. "Ethnic and Racial Identities of Second-Generation Black Immigrants in New York City." *International Migration Review* 28: 795–820.

———. 1999. *Black Identities: West Indian Immigrant Dreams and American Realities.* New York: Russell Sage Foundation and Cambridge: Harvard University Press.

Weston, Kath. 1995. "Forever Is a Long Time: Romancing the Real in Gay Kin Ideologies." In *Naturalizing Power: Essays in Feminist Cultural Analysis,* edited by Sylvia Yanagisako and Carol Delaney, 87–110. New York: Routledge.

Wong, Morrison. 1995. "Chinese Americans." In *Asian Americans: Contemporary Trends and Issues,* edited by Pyong Gap Min, 58–94. Thousand Oaks, CA: Sage Publications.

Woo, Deborah. 2000. *Glass Ceilings and Asian Americans: The New Face of Workplace Barriers.* Walnut Creek, CA: Altamira Press.

Wu, Diana Ting Liu. 1997. *Asian Pacific Americans in the Workplace.* Walnut Creek, CA: Altamira Press.

Yanagisako, Sylvia. 1995. "Transforming Orientalism: Gender, Nationality and Class in Asian American Studies." In *Naturalizing Power: Essays in Feminist Cultural Analysis,* edited by Sylvia Yanagisako and Carol Delaney, 275–98. New York: Routledge.

Yip, Alethea. 1996. "The Asian American Mosaic." *AsianWeek.* August 15.

———. 1997. "Careers on The Fast Track." *AsianWeek.* March 7.

Zhou, Min. 1999. "Coming of Age: The Situation of Asian American Children." *Amerasia Journal* 25:1–28.